IN SEARCH OF COMMON GROUND ON ABORTION

Gender in Law, Culture, and Society

Series Editor
Martha Albertson Fineman, Emory University School of Law, USA

Gender in Law, Culture, and Society will address key issues and theoretical debates related to gender, culture, and the law. Its titles will advance understanding of the ways in which a society's cultural and legal approaches to gender intersect, clash, and are reconciled or remain in tension. The series will further examine connections between gender and economic and political systems, as well as various other cultural and societal influences on gender construction and presentation, including social and legal consequences that men and women uniquely or differently encounter. Intended for a scholarly readership as well as for courses, its titles will be a mix of single-authored volumes and collections of original essays that will be both pragmatic and theoretical. It will draw from the perspectives of critical and feminist legal theory, as well as other schools of jurisprudence. Interdisciplinary, and international in scope, the series will offer a range of voices speaking to significant questions arising from the study of law in relation to gender, including the very nature of law itself.

Other titles in the series

Sister Wives, Surrogates and Sex Workers: Outlaws by Choice?
Angela Campbell
ISBN 9781409435211

Vulnerability: Reflections on a New Ethical Foundation for Law and Politics
Edited by Martha Albertson Fineman and Anna Grear
ISBN 9781472421623

Exploring Masculinities: Feminist Legal Theory Reflections
Edited by Martha Albertson Fineman and Michael Thomson
ISBN 9781472415110

Feminism, Law, and Religion
Edited by Marie A. Failinger, Elizabeth R. Schiltz and Susan J. Stabile
ISBN 9781409444190

In Search of Common Ground on Abortion

From Culture War to Reproductive Justice

Edited by

ROBIN WEST
Georgetown University Law Center, USA

JUSTIN MURRAY
Public Defender Service for the District of Columbia, USA

MEREDITH ESSER
Arnold & Porter LLP, USA

ASHGATE

Published by
Ashgate Publishing Limited
Wey Court East
Union Road
Farnham
Surrey, GU9 7PT
England

Ashgate Publishing Company
110 Cherry Street
Suite 3-1
Burlington
VT 05401-3818
USA

www.ashgate.com

British Library Cataloguing in Publication Data
A catalogue record for this book is available from the British Library

The Library of Congress has cataloged the printed edition as follows:
In search of common ground on abortion : from culture war to reproductive justice / by Robin West, Justin Murray and Meredith Esser.
pages cm. -- (Gender in law, culture, and society)
Includes bibliographical references and index.
ISBN 978-1-4724-2045-9 (hardback) -- ISBN 978-1-4724-2046-6 (pbk.) -- ISBN 978-1-4724-2047-3 (ebook) -- ISBN 978-1-4724-2048-0 (epub) 1. Abortion--Law and legislation--United States. 2. Abortion--Social aspects--United States. 3. Abortion--Government policy--United States. I. Murray, Justin (Lawyer) editor of compilation. II. Esser, Meredith B., editor of compilation. III. West, Robin, 1954- editor of compilation.

KF3771.I5 2014
362.1988'80973--dc23

2013033242

ISBN 9781472420459 (hbk)
ISBN 9781472420466 (pbk)
ISBN 9781472420473 (ebk – PDF)
ISBN 9781472420480 (ebk – ePUB)

Transferred to Digital Printing in 2014

MIX
Paper from responsible sources
FSC
www.fsc.org
FSC® C013483

Printed and bound in the USA by Thomson-Shore, Inc.

Contents

Notes on Contributors

Editors

Meredith Esser is a litigation associate at Arnold & Porter LLP. She received her J.D. degree from the Georgetown University Law Center, where she served as president of Law Students for Reproductive Justice and represented indigent clients in the District of Columbia as part of the Law Students in Court Legal Clinic. Upon graduation, she clerked on the US Court of Appeals for the Eleventh Circuit and the Superior Court of the District of Columbia.

Justin Murray is an appellate attorney at the Public Defender Service for the District of Columbia. After receiving his J.D. degree from the Georgetown University Law Center, where he served as president of the pro-life student group Progressive Alliance for Life, he worked as a law clerk on the US Court of Appeals for the Fourth Circuit and the US District Court of Maryland. He has written articles on the constitutional status of the right to abortion, the intersection of legal ethics and racial justice, and criminal procedure.

Robin West is Frederick Haas Professor of Law and Philosophy at the Georgetown University Law Center, where she has taught since 1986. She previously taught at the University of Maryland School of Law from 1986 to 1991 and the Cleveland-Marshall College of Law from 1982 to 1985, and served as Visiting Professor at Stanford Law School and Chicago Law School. She has written extensively on gender issues and feminist legal theory, constitutional law and theory, jurisprudence, legal philosophy, and law and humanities.

Authors

Kristen Day is the Executive Director of Democrats For Life of America and oversees all operations of the Washington, DC office. She served 10 years on Capitol Hill, including two years as Chief of Staff to Congressman Jim Barcia (D-MI). Day is the author of *Democrats For Life: Pro-Life Politics and the Silenced Majority*, published by New Leaf Press in July, 2006. The book outlines the history of the pro-life Democrat movement. Day resides in Virginia with her husband and three children.

Shari Motro teaches tax, mindfulness, and related courses at the University of Richmond School of Law. She is the author of *West's Income Tax Map: A Bird's-Eye View of Federal Income Taxation for Law Students*. Her scholarship—which has appeared in the *Stanford Law Review*, *Northwestern Law Review*, and *Iowa Law Review*—focuses on intimate relationships and money. Professor Motro is also a commenter in the popular press, and has published editorials in the *New York Times*, *Wall Street Journal*, and *Boston Globe*, among other venues.

Shauna R. Prewitt is an associate at Skadden, Arps, Slate, Meagher & Flom LLP. Her *pro bono* and academic work are focused largely on the legal rights of women who mother through rape. In this area, Ms. Prewitt is the nationwide expert.

Dorothy Roberts is the fourteenth Penn Integrates Knowledge Professor, George A. Weiss University Professor, and the inaugural Raymond Pace and Sadie Tanner Mossell Alexander Professor of Civil Rights at University of Pennsylvania, where she holds appointments in the Law School and Departments of Africana Studies and Sociology. She is the author of the award-winning books *Killing the Black Body: Race, Reproduction, and the Meaning of Liberty* (Random House/Pantheon, 1997) and *Shattered Bonds: The Color of Child Welfare* (Basic Books/Civitas, 2002), as well as co-editor of six books on constitutional law and gender. She has also published more than 80 articles and essays in books and scholarly journals, including *Harvard Law Review*, *Yale Law Journal*, and *Stanford Law Review*. Her latest book, *Fatal Invention: How Science, Politics, and Big Business Re-create Race in the Twenty-First Century*, was published by the New Press in July 2011.

Elizabeth R. Schiltz is a Professor of Law at the University of St. Thomas School of Law in Minneapolis, Minnesota, where she serves as the Thomas J. Abood Research Scholar and Co-Director of the Terrence J. Murphy Institute for Catholic Thought, Law and Public Policy. Her scholarship addresses the relationship of federal and state law in regulating consumer credit, disability and consumer law theory, and feminist legal theory. She is co-editor (along with Marie Failinger and Susan Stabile) of *Feminism, Law, and Religion*, published by Ashgate in 2013.

Susan J. Stabile is the Robert and Marion Short Distinguished Chair in Law at the University of St. Thomas School of Law (Minneapolis). She is a fellow of the Holloran Center for Ethical Leadership, Affiliate Senior Fellow of the St. John's University Vincentian Center for Church and Society, and Research Fellow of the New York University School of Law Center for Labor and Employment Law. A spiritual director and retreat leader, Professor Stabile is also the author of *Growing in Love and Wisdom: Tibetan Buddhist Sources for Christian Meditation* (Oxford University Press, 2013). She is co-editor (along with Marie Failinger and Elizabeth R. Schiltz) of *Feminism, Law, and Religion*, published by Ashgate in 2013.

Introduction

Justin Murray, Meredith Esser and Robin West

This collection of chapters stems from a symposium that was held at the Georgetown University Law Center in the fall of 2009. Originally titled "A New Abortion Debate," the goal of the symposium was to bring together pro-choice and pro-life scholars in an effort to explore the common philosophical, moral, or political ground that might be shared by these groups who so rarely come together, and more generally to support new and emerging scholarship that is self-reflective on the issue of abortion. The symposium included scholars working on common ground policy or philosophical scholarship, as well as other voices seeking to broaden the scope of the abortion debate to non-legal and non-constitutional themes. This collection includes work from some of the scholars who participated in the symposium, as well as new work from others, but the themes remain the same. Taken collectively, the chapters explore the possibilities for cultural, philosophical, moral, and political common ground on the subjects of abortion and reproductive justice more generally.

The position of the three editors is that any common ground project such as this one in this contentious area must emerge from joint reflection and genuine collaboration among persons who harbor diverse perspectives concerning the subjects that divide us. In this spirit, rather than attempting to sum up the quest for commonality in a unitary voice, each of the three editors has individually composed some brief reflections on central concepts that recur throughout the chapters of this book. Those individual editors' introductions appear immediately below; first Justin Murray's, then Meredith Esser's, then Robin West's. Following that set of comments, we then briefly summarize the chapters.

Editors' Introductions

Comments from Justin Murray

Since the middle of the twentieth century, many Americans have begun to dramatically rethink traditional views about women's place in society, the appropriate link between sex and reproduction, and the moral stature of unborn human life. As a result, many social practices that were once unthinkable are now familiar features of American life. Women work side-by-side with men in virtually every sector of the economy. The vast majority of sexually active Americans use some form of contraception at least some of the time. Unmarried couples routinely live together in preparation for, or even as a permanent substitute for, marriage. And every year, approximately one million pregnancies are terminated by abortion.

These momentous social developments are not, however, backed by a settled moral consensus. Far from it. Indeed, a prominent social movement—the Moral Majority—came into being for the expressed purpose of turning back the clock on the sexual revolution. Ever since these battle lines were drawn, presidents have been elected, Supreme Court Justices appointed, and wealthy businesses imperiled, based largely on their views about sex and abortion. Public dialogue between representatives of the opposing viewpoints has been largely acrimonious and uncomprehending, leading many observers to characterize it as a *culture war*.

Whether we like it or not, countless politicians, religious leaders, and influential media figures ceaselessly seek to re-enlist us as participants in a culture war against our fellow citizens. The 2012 presidential election, which was in full swing when I first composed this introduction, offered no reprieve from this drumbeat. The leading Republican presidential aspirants accused President Obama of orchestrating a "war on the Catholic Church" (Rick Santorum) and even a full-blown "war on religion" (Mitt Romney). Not to be outdone, a chorus of liberal columnists denounced the GOP's purported "war on women," and Vice President Biden added his voice to their accusation. These bipartisan invocations of warfare as a metaphorical description of our social predicament are nothing new; they are simply the most recent iterations of a long-standing pattern that has endured for the better part of the last century.

Some might be tempted to dismiss these exchanges as empty posturing or politics-as-usual, but that response would be a mistake. In a heterogeneous society such as ours, disagreement among citizens is par for the course, and most of these disagreements can be addressed more or less effectively through the conventional problem-solving mechanisms of democratic politics: tolerance for opposing viewpoints, mutual efforts at persuasion, coalition politics, and (when necessary) compromise. None of these tools for achieving political consensus are available, however, when opinion leaders on both sides of a dispute habitually characterize their disagreements as though they were episodes in a protracted military struggle. Language drives our perception of reality and, by extension, our conduct. A dispute that has been framed as a war will be handled through the typical instruments of warfare: propaganda, exaggeration or outright distortion of relevant facts, vilification of outsiders, zero-sum decision-making, and the single-minded pursuit of victory at any price. Each and every one of these warlike dynamics is on full display in our contemporary culture war.

The divisiveness of current conversations about abortion derives, in large measure, from the narrow range of problems and proposals that have come to dominate the discussion. Public debate has revolved almost entirely around the two issues that most sharply pit the pro-life and pro-choice camps against one another: legal restrictions designed to impede access to abortion, on the one hand, and public funding to facilitate access to abortion, on the other. On these subjects, policymaking has an unavoidably zero-sum character: the law can *either* enhance the freedom of women to opt for abortion (through minimal restrictions and maximal funding), *or* protect fetal life against abortion (through the opposite mix of restrictions and funding), but never both. Because one of these objectives must be sacrificed for the other to prevail, principled compromise is difficult—perhaps impossible—to achieve. Thus, a national discourse fixated primarily on these themes will almost inevitably be a combative and unaccommodating one.

Nevertheless, it is possible to imagine, and work to achieve, a different kind of conversation about abortion that extends beyond the issues of legal prohibition and public funding. For culture war veterans of all stripes, this possibility might initially seem dangerous or fanciful. Understandably so: all too often, partisans on both sides who call for common ground on abortion insist that their adversaries dilute their central moral convictions and political goals as a precondition for dialogue.

That is not the kind of conversation we have in mind. Rather than urging either of the contenders to abandon its core ideals, we envision a discussion that calls upon both sides to reflect more deeply and broadly on the meaning of their respective ideals. We are confident that sustained exploration of the fundamental principles that underlie the pro-life and pro-choice positions on sex, pregnancy, and abortion will uncover promising opportunities for common ground—opportunities that have been obscured by the deafening background noise of culture-war politics.

Beginning with my own philosophical orientation, I believe that the foundational ethical norms that animate the pro-life movement—at least in its finer moments—are the profound dignity of human life and a commitment to care for those who are most vulnerable and dependent on others. Taking these principles seriously certainly means taking meaningful steps to diminish the rate of abortion—including, in my view, legal restrictions on abortion—because few human lives are more vulnerable, dependent, and in need of care than developing children within the womb. But the very same principles the pro-life movement invokes to restrict abortion should lead it to support progressive measures to counteract the many social and economic obstacles that imperil the vulnerability of many pregnant women, parents, and their children—especially when those obstacles generate pressure upon women to consider abortion.

Similarly, the central concerns that motivate the pro-choice movement—enhancing women's health, autonomy, and life opportunities—cannot be set right merely by preserving the formal right to end a pregnancy. As my co-editors and several contributors to this book eloquently explain, a sound agenda for promoting reproductive justice must focus more broadly on expanding the safety net for pregnant women and mothers, thus ensuring that abortion is truly a choice and not a default dictated by economic necessity. Within these expanded parameters for discussion, we believe that it is possible for former enemies in the abortion debate to form mutually advantageous coalitions on highly significant social and political issues, even as they continue to struggle over the more intractable—and, of course, important—topics of abortion prohibition and funding.

Recent years have brought several positive signs of a shift in tone and priorities, but much more remains to be done. Many pro-life organizations have become ardent advocates for, and direct providers of, social support and healthcare to pregnant women and young mothers. Legislators from both parties have begun to explore authentic common ground measures, such as the Pregnant Women Support Act spearheaded by Democrats for Life of America. And during the early months of his presidency, President Obama struck a conciliatory note in his commencement address at the University of Notre Dame, laying groundwork for national reflection on how pro-choice and pro-life groups might work together to reduce abortion and honor the dignity of pregnant women and their children.

Nevertheless, old habits die hard, and it remains to be seen whether these developments prove to be durable or successful. Pro-life healthcare organizations have been widely criticized by pro-choice activists and health providers for allegedly deceiving their patients about the nature of their services and delivering incomplete, inadequate medical care. Media discussions and legislative agendas relating to abortion continue, by and large, to operate within the traditional restrict-or-fund paradigm, overlooking the broader socioeconomic context in which men and women make decisions about sex, pregnancy, and parenting. And, as I noted toward the beginning of these remarks, the lofty appeals to tolerance, collaboration, and common ground with which President Obama began his term have largely given way to mutual recriminations and culture-war rhetoric on both sides of the partisan divide.

All things considered, the future outlook of the half-century-long culture war is anyone's guess. The upshot is that the future lies in our hands. We hope that this book will supply ideas and energy to those who are working to transform the breadth, content, and civility of this important national dialogue.

Comments from Meredith Esser

Over the past decade, the pro-choice movement has undergone an important rhetorical shift from talking about reproductive "rights" to using the more expansive term, reproductive "justice" to describe the movement's central goal. The concept of reproductive justice aims to describe women's reproductive health as connected to and affected by conditions that are much broader than just the decision to terminate a pregnancy. Women's lives are shaped by their socioeconomic status, religious views, race, sexuality, nationality, family life, geography, level of education, and other factors that—until recently—the reproductive rights movement had failed to fully conceptualize when developing a political agenda.

Legal scholars have been slow in adopting this framework, preferring to stick to the rights-based language that is so central to the legal field in general. At first blush, this rhetorical distinction—between "rights" and "justice"—may seem indicative of merely a semantic trend rather than a true ideological change. However, I would argue that this shift within the reproductive rights field is actually a reaction to the polarization that a younger generation of women (and men) involved in these issues has grown up with, and that the adoption of the phrase "reproductive justice" is an attempt to describe a viewpoint that is often buried by the polarized rhetoric of the abortion debate in general: the way that these issues affect real people, every day. Indeed, as we are beginning to understand, "rights" don't always make sense in this context. At the same time, the "justice" in the phrase "reproductive justice" means something very different from the court-centric notions of justice. It encompasses a wide range of issues and values such as access to health services, racial justice, socioeconomic justice, and all of the potential barriers to obtaining not just abortion and reproductive services, but education, contraception, and the basic tools that women should have at their disposal for controlling not just their reproductive lives, but their entire lives.

In my view, the reproductive justice movement should also embrace a "common ground" approach to understanding women's experiences of and surrounding abortion—if not always to the fundamental rights and prohibitions that each political stance embraces. To that end, part of my personal motivation in embarking on this project was to give a voice to the stifled middle ground—if not undertake the daunting task of finding a common ground—on the issue of reproduction and abortion. For example, many women who self-identify as "pro-life" still believe that women should be allowed to abort in the case of rape. On the other side, many individuals who call themselves "pro-choice" agree that late-term abortion is a morally grey area.

So much of the way that political activists talk about abortion and reproduction is divorced from the stories of real individuals; the rhetoric is couched in absolute terms with neither side wanting to cede any "ground" to the other. For example, on the pro-life side, moral arguments against abortion are reduced to abstractions that are difficult for ordinary, non-scientists to grasp, but which nonetheless form the foundation of the fundamental objections to abortion: life begins at conception; human life is sacred; ergo the "morning-after pill" is abortion. On the pro-choice side, the autonomy of woman is paramount, bodily integrity and boundless reproductive freedom must be maintained, ergo late-term abortions should be approached with the same detached attitude as taking the pill or going in for a routine checkup.

In reality, however, neither one of these extremes describes the vast middle ground in which most Americans exist on the spectrum of this debate. Similarly, neither of these arguments captures the moral balancing that women undergo when actually facing the prospect of taking the morning-after pill, or obtaining abortion services. In conversations with friends and colleagues about this project, I have heard a wide range of views on abortion, but very few people actually identify with the extreme pro-choice or the extreme pro-life positions. However, such middle-ground views are—more often than not—eclipsed by the extreme positions that have become the white noise of politics.

At the same time, however, each side employs certain stories—myths—to advance their political agendas. Indeed, while women's real experiences are suppressed, imagined experiences of women have become rhetorical weapons.

For example the mythical woman who aborts and then "comes to regret her choice," was a central figure in the Supreme Court decision, *Gonzales v. Carhart*,[1] and served as a primary justification in that opinion for restricting access to certain kinds of abortion procedures. In justifying its decision, the dissent wrote, "the Court invokes an antiabortion shibboleth for which it concededly has no reliable evidence: Women who have abortions come to regret their choices, and consequently suffer from '[s]evere depression and loss of esteem.'"[2] As the dissent in that case pointed out, rather than implement policies that educate or inform women regarding the controversial partial-birth abortion procedure, the court took a paternalistic and protective stance, choosing instead to justify its decision on the ground that women were incapable of making that decision with sound mind, and equally incapable of dealing with the consequences.[3]

The uncomfortable implication of this story is that women are unable to fully appreciate the emotional impact of such a decision.[4] But the pro-choice reaction to this story may also be overly-simplistic: the pro-choice camp can equally stifle the voices of women for whom regret, remorse, and true sorrow is an inevitable part of abortion.

For example, post-abortion counseling service providers are caught in the middle of this debate, and though they provide a valued and necessary service, are vilified by both movements. Aspen Baker, one of the participants in our symposium and the founder of Exhale, a post-abortion counseling hotline based in Oakland, California, explained that "[s]ome people have characterized us as pro-choice; some people have characterized us as pro-life; some people have characterized us as confusing, or as wishy-washy … [i]n a pro-choice/pro-life world — in a black-and-white world — we're trying to say there's something else."[5] Thus the woman "who regrets her choice" is at once turned into a tool of pro-life paternalism, and is simultaneously silenced by pro-choice extremism, but has few places to turn for support.

In so many ways, the gorilla in the room (or standing on the steps of the Supreme Court)—with the pro-life protesters on one side and pro-choice protesters on the other—is sex. Sex is an integral part of this debate, but is rarely discussed in legal and academic discourses on abortion. And attitudes about sex come with its own set of stereotypes and myths. On the one hand, pro-choice activists are viewed as advancing a culture in which unbounded sexual freedom—with no consequences—is the norm. Pro-life activists, on the other hand, are viewed as

1 *Gonzales v. Carhart*, 127 S. Ct. 1610, 1634 (2007).

2 *Id.*

3 *Id.* at 1649 (Ginsberg, J., dissenting).

4 *See generally*, Reva B. Segal, *The Right's Reasons: Constitutional Conflict and the Spread of Woman-Protective Antiabortion Argument*, 57 DUKE L.J. 1641 (2008).

5 Shoshanna Walker, *Post-Abortion Counseling Group Finds Itself on the Firing Line*, N.Y. TIMES, January 14, 2011, http://www.nytimes.com/2011/01/14/us/14bcexhale.html?pagewanted=all&_r=0.

advancing a worldview in which sex should be restricted and the consequences of sex—wanted or unwanted—should be borne by the women and girls, men and boys who engage in it.

Few exchanges so poignantly highlight this division as the recent controversy involving one of our Georgetown Law colleagues, Sandra Fluke, and a prominent talk radio personality, Rush Limbaugh. The actual transcript of Limbaugh's words illustrate the polarized nature of political rhetoric around sex:

> What does it say about the college co-ed Susan Fluke [*sic*], who goes before a congressional committee and essentially says that she must be paid to have sex, what does that make her? It makes her a slut, right?
>
> It makes her a prostitute. She wants to be paid to have sex. She's having so much sex she can't afford the contraception. She wants you and me and the taxpayers to pay her to have sex. What does that make us? We're the pimps … So, Ms. Fluke and the rest of you feminazis, here's the deal. If we are going to pay for your contraceptives, and thus pay for you to have sex, we want something for it, and I'll tell you what it is. We want you to post the videos online so we can all watch.[6]

There are so many tragedies that this transcript illustrates. The first is that, for women, there is no sexual middle ground—either you are not having sex at all, or you are a prostitute. In this political climate, an accomplished and highly educated law student—who publicly admits that she is sexually active—is "a woman who is happily presenting herself as an immoral, baseless, no-purpose-to-her life woman." Another is that this public figure—followed by so many Americans—is actually completely ignorant of the pure-and-simple biology of birth control pills ("Ms. Fluke, have you ever heard of not having sex? Have you ever heard of not having sex so often? … did you ever think about maybe backing off the amount of sex that you have?"). Finally, it is tragic that the base and divisive language used to describe Ms. Fluke dehumanizes, demonizes, and "archetypizes" women (and men) who do not fit into one of two very polarized political groups—so much so that the space between the two "camps" becomes a "no-woman's land."

The link between sexual extremism and political extremism thus leads to another source of potential "common ground" regarding abortion: reforming the political rhetoric around sex. Is there room for a common ground conversation about how we talk about sex in the political arena? Surely—with sex an integral

---

6 *See*, Jack Mirkinson, *Rush Limbaugh: Sandra Fluke, Woman Denied Right To Speak At Contraception Hearing, A "Slut"*, The Huffington Post, February 20, 2012, http://www.huffingtonpost.com/2012/02/29/rush-limbaugh-sandra-fluke-slut_n_1311640.html; J. Bryan Lowder, *Has Rush Limbaugh Finally Gone Too Far in Slut-Shaming Sandra Fluke?*, Slate.com, March 2, 2012, http://www.slate.com/blogs/xx_factor/2012/03/02/has_rush_limbaugh_finally_gone_too_far_in_slut_shaming_sandra_fluke_.html.

part of personhood, and an essential prerequisite to abortion—there is a way to talk about the consequences of sex, the pure-and-simple biology of sex—without resorting to base and unhelpful stereotypes that only further serve to stifle the helpful conversations that we could be having.

Just as the polarization of the abortion debate serves to cut women out of the political conversation about approaches to abortion, adoption and birth control, the repressive nature of the political rhetoric surrounding sex has caused an equally problematic gap. Just as the middle-ground voices and perspectives on the debate are being shut out, there is also an entire piece of the abortion story that is entirely missing from the political conversation. How did this woman become unintentionally pregnant? Was it lack of education about her reproductive cycle? Was it lack of family support? Was there sex-based violence or coercion involved? Was there social pressure to engage in sex or become pregnant? Or was it something less concrete—just an inability or unwillingness to say "no"?

All of this leads back to the idea of reproductive justice. What does this term mean in relation to attitudes toward sex in particular? As I mentioned above, many women feel conflicted about the decision to undergo an abortion. Many women feel conflicted about talking about sex. "Reproductive justice" may thus be best served not by silencing these perspectives, but by supporting the organizations and individuals who seek to bring these conversations to the forefront of the national debate.

Comments from Robin West

What is meant by "common ground," and is there any, in the recently intensified abortion wars?

The questions are related: whether there is any common ground might depend on what we mean by the phrase. The self-labeled search for "common ground" between "pro-life" and "pro-choice" advocates in the abortion debates goes back at least to the mid-1980s, when activists on both sides began to worry about the corrosive effects of this issue on both politics generally, and politics surrounding reproductive justice more particularly.[7] Since that time, for some activists, and for some purposes, the search for common ground denotes the attempt to find those areas of agreement on the morality or legality of abortion, and the morality, wisdom, and constitutionality of anti-abortion laws. From that common ground, the hope holds, we might reason our way together toward the best resolution of these difficult moral and legal problems. For example, most activists and scholars on both sides of these debates might agree that performing or procuring an abortion to save the life of the mother is generally morally justified, and all or most might agree that multiple abortions sought by a woman who has access to birth control

7 For a history of common ground efforts during the decade following *Roe v. Wade*, see Mary Ziegler, *The Possibility of Compromise: Antiabortion Moderates After* Roe v Wade, 87 Chi.-Kent L. Rev. 571 (2012).

but finds it inconvenient to use, raise serious moral questions. All or most might agree on the immorality of late-term abortions for anything other than a very few reasons, and likewise agree that a law that criminalizes the use of at least some birth control methods, whatever the morality of the practice, violates constitutional norms of privacy and liberty. Likewise, all or most might agree on the wrongness of infanticide, and that the inclusion of intentional killings of newborns in a state's homicide statutes bear no constitutional infirmities.

From these shared premises, it is not unreasonable to think, it might be possible to reason one's way, either in law or morality, toward conclusions that are not shared but should be and would be, were the lines of argumentation made clear: if we all agree that abortion to save the life of the mother is generally morally justified, then perhaps all or most might agree on the morality of abortions to prevent grave bodily harm. If we all agree that abortions procured because of a too casual failure to prevent conception are immoral, perhaps all might agree that abortions procured so as to forestall or prevent other inconveniences likewise are immoral (whether or not they should be criminalized, and whether or not it would be unconstitutional to try to do so). If all agree that the criminalization of some forms of birth control is a fool's errand, and unconstitutional to boot, perhaps all would likewise agree that the same is true of other forms of birth control.

"Common ground" in this understanding refers to initial common premises which might be shared by both sides of the abortion wars. The "common ground project," then, refers to the hope that both sides might reason together toward common conclusions on more contentious issues regarding the morality of abortion, and the wisdom or constitutionality of criminalizing it, rather than resolve them through methods more suited for irreconcilable differences, such as the blunt political tool of the ballot box, or self-segregation into separate and gated communities.

Understood in this way, the "common ground" project has a prestigious and important lineage; it is basically the same method, with the same hope, behind the academic disciplines of applied ethics, moral philosophy, and normative political theory. Practitioners in those fields likewise begin with what they hope are shared premises, and then argue on that basis toward surprising conclusions on contentious issues, all on the heroic assumption that if the argumentation is sound, listeners who accept the premises will accept the conclusions, even if those conclusions are at odds with what their beliefs had been before encountering the argument. Unsurprisingly, then, moral and political philosophers have responded to the abortion debates in just this way. Perhaps most famously, Judith Thomson argued in an important article in the early 1970s[8] for the moral permissibility of some abortions by analogizing the predicament of a woman who has been impregnated against her will, to that of a hypothetical individual, kidnapped and strapped to a hospital bed for nine months, so that his body and its organs might service those of a stranger, threatened by some fatal disease for which the kidnapped victim's

8 Judith Jarvis Thomson, *A Defense of Abortion*, 1 PHIL. & PUB. AFF. 47 (1971).

organs might provide an antidote, with no harm done the latter save the nine-month confinement. Perhaps, Thomson apparently believed, if we all agreed that the kidnapped victim would be morally justified in severing the lines between them and attempting an escape, even if it meant the death of the sick beneficiary, then we all might agree likewise on the moral permissibility of abortion, at least where the pregnancy is a result of rape or otherwise involuntary. She then went on to discuss the harder case of the woman impregnated against her will, or at least against her desire, not because of rape but because of the failure of birth control. Twenty-five years later, Professor Eileen McDonagh argued that the pregnant woman's dilemma, at least where her life is endangered by a pregnancy, is best analogized to someone undergoing a life-threatening assault by an incompetent but powerful born individual, even if that individual was consensually conceived and raised by the victim him or herself, and as we should all agree that such a person would have a right to defend himself even with lethal force against the latter, we should agree that the woman whose life is threatened by a pregnancy would likewise be entitled to defend herself against the fetus by procuring an abortion—even if the pregnancy and conception were consensual.[9] She then goes on to discuss the harder case of the woman who is pregnant and whose wellbeing rather than life are threatened by the pregnancy. On the other side, numerous theorists from a range of disciplines have argued that as we all agree that no parent is entitled to commit infanticide, no matter what the reason, we should agree that late-term abortions are likewise morally forbidden, and ought to be legally forbidden as well. Constitutional arguments both inside and outside the courts have the same structure. The first premise states the common ground—a statutory or constitutional text, or a controlling precedent—on which we all stand. The advocate then argues toward a contentious conclusion which, the lawyer believes, the other side will be forced to accept if the argument is sound.

If this is what is meant by common ground, it's fair to say that common ground projects in the abortion wars have not been demonstrably successful. Thomson's argument most strongly justifies abortion in the case of rape, and McDonagh's in the case of life-threatening pregnancies, yet the Republican Party Platform, as it has for the past 20 years, makes no exceptions in its proposed ban on all abortions, for women pregnant as a result of rape, or for women whose lives are endangered by their pregnancies. More generally, the "common premises" are losing their commonality: it is now clearer than it might have been 20 years ago that politically powerful actors within the larger American society, such as the organized Catholic Church, do not share a belief in the moral permissibility of any form of artificial birth control, or that any publicly backed healthcare plan should facilitate its use, whether or not a state could constitutionally criminalize the practice. It is equally clear that large numbers of Americans do not believe that late-term abortions, particularly when indicated by fatal birth defects or maternal

9 Eileen McDonagh, Breaking the Abortion Deadlock: From Choice to Consent 7 (1996).

health, raise insurmountable moral issues. And, although there may be wide agreement that infanticide is and should be criminalized comparably to homicide, except in cases of severely mitigating circumstances, there is no movement within pro-choice activism toward making similar concessions for late-term abortion, whatever the reason for the abortion. While pro-choice activists may individually find some abortions immoral, such as abortions of pregnancies brought on by the reckless failure to use available birth control, there is also no movement toward any compromise view that would permit or advise the criminality of some abortions, but not others, on the basis of the motives of the woman seeking to obtain it.

What might be concluded from this history of failure, in a quest toward common ground? One possibility of course is that the arguments that will eventually successfully convince skeptical listeners simply have not yet been uncovered: perhaps with just a bit more litigation, scholarship, study, or argument, we can still yet societally uncover the truth of the matter regarding the constitutionality or wisdom of anti-abortion laws, or the morality of various abortions in various circumstances. It may be that the best, and yet undiscovered, argument will convince those otherwise not inclined to agree that the Constitution, properly read, really does prohibit bans on abortions like the ones contained in the Republican Party Platform, or that, properly read, the Constitution protects the right to life of the fetus, thereby mandating fetal protection laws, or that the Constitution in fact is silent on the issue, as Robert Bork argued some years ago, leaving the issue to be resolved in the political realm. Likewise it may be that the best and yet undiscovered argument will convince the currently unconvinced that abortions in all or most circumstances are inexcusably and nonjustifiably homicidal, other than those obtained in genuine defense of the mother's life, or perhaps the best and yet undiscovered argument will convince those not inclined to agree that most or all abortions, particularly early term, are in fact morally unproblematic. The existence of these live possibilities is what keeps research, litigation, and argument over the wisdom, morality, criminality, and constitutionality of abortion and abortion laws something other than a massive waste of social and material capital.

On the other hand, it may be that the failure to achieve any progress, on this understanding of the "common ground" argument, follows from a deeper cause, and that is the foundational incompatibility of values and worldviews of antagonists on either side, making "shared ground" illusory and the shared ground project a fool's errand. As Kristin Luker demonstrated 30 years ago,[10] the differences between pro-choice activists and pro-life activists even at that relatively early stage of this evolution are so profound, it's not at all clear that shared premises and sound logic will ever bring them together. The differing views on abortion have little to do with unsound argument, and much to do with foundational understandings of the role of choice, rather than God's will, in women's lives, the importance of "planning" to a well lived life, and the meaning of responsibility, intimacy, and care, in the context of parental and marital relationships: thus, to take just two

10 Kristin Luker, Abortion & The Politics of Motherhood (1984).

examples, pro-life activists, particularly the leadership, view the exalted role of "choice" in not just pro-choice but all liberal worldviews as an arrogant usurpation of authority over profoundly religious questions regarding the nature of the good life, while liberals and choice activists view the failure to plan one's parenthood as tantamount to grotesque irresponsibility; pro-life activists and leaders view the openness to the creation of new life in the context of a marital relationship as the quintessence of the meaning of sexuality, while liberals view the meaning of sexuality as only contingently related to procreation in any guise. In the last 30 years, these quite fundamental commitments on both sides seem to have deepened, rather than weakened, in the face of the political wars over abortion. The search for common ground as a consequence looks more and more like a mirage.

There is, however, a different possible understanding of "common ground" and "common ground" projects, that might be more in keeping with President Obama's invocation of the phrase in his famous Notre Dame speech from the beginning of his first term several years ago,[11] and more in keeping with the spirit of most of the contributions to this volume. "Common ground" might refer not to shared *premises*, from which agreement might or might not follow on the more divisive points, but rather, shared political or intellectual *projects*, grounded in values that might be shared or congruent, but then again might not be, and with no aim of moving from that shared ground toward agreement on either the morality or criminality of abortions, or the constitutionality of anti-abortion bans. This understanding of "common ground" is more closely connected to ordinary coalition building in ordinary politics, than to forms of argument in academic philosophy or even law: the point of "common ground projects" on this understanding is not to compel agreement to conclusions from the logical force of an argument based on shared premises, but rather, to encourage cooperation on projects that may be grounded in differing worldviews, and with no aim of reconciling those views, or forging a convergence between them. On this understanding of "common ground," there is no need to identify starting premises that are agreed upon, but rather, there is a need to identify projects that might be viewed as imperative, or desirable, by both sides. Therefore, the possibility, quite real in the context of abortion debates, that pro-life and pro-choice advocates operate on the basis of radically conflicting values and worldviews, is not fatal to the possibility of common ground. Those with radically different worldviews might nevertheless have overlapping goals. Working toward them, whatever the starting points of advocates, might then create common ground of the more conventional sort: it might reveal shared values, and forge more commonality than had been previously perceived.

In his contribution to this joint introduction, my co-editor Justin Murray suggests one possible shared project that might create common ground in this way: both pro-life and pro-choice forces, he argues, should have an interest in reducing

11 President Barack Obama, Remarks by the President of the United States in Commencement Address at the University of Notre Dame (May 17, 2009), *available at* http://www.whitehouse.gov/the-press-office/remarks-president-notre-dame-commencement.

the incidence of *unwanted abortions*, or at least, those unwanted abortions which are sought because of the cost of mothering. Both sides then should have an interest in reducing maternal costs, including the costs of pregnancy, childbirth, and parenting. Many abortions in this country are sought for economic reasons: a family or a mother cannot afford another child, and despairs of the prospect of bringing a child into the world in poverty, and which she cannot support. A stronger safety net for new mothers or new parents, and particularly publicly available and high quality childcare for toddlers and pre-schoolers, would go a long way toward reducing the demand for abortion. This result should be not only acceptable but worth fighting for, for both pro-life and pro-choice activists: on the pro-life side, because it brings the abortion rate down, and on the pro-choice (or loosely feminist groups) side, because it would enhance the life prospects of poor women who want to be or are mothers, as well as the quality of their parenting. The goal of reducing such pregnancies should be a common goal of both sides, and pursuing it could quite conceivably broaden the common ground beneath them: it would strengthen the commitment of both to the work of improving the lives of poor people, and align their joint interests with a vulnerable people.

Let me add another example. Pro-life and Pro-choice activists might also have a shared commitment to the goal of reducing the incidence of unwanted *pregnancies*, whether caused by rape, by unwanted but consensual intercourse, or by desired intercourse and a failure of birth control. Some of these unwanted pregnancies, of course, are then ended by abortions. From the pro-life perspective, the abortion that is chosen to end an unwanted pregnancy has many of the same harms and costs regardless of the reason for the pregnancy: the abortion that terminates a pregnancy may cause fetal pain, end a human life or a potential human life, and degrade and coarsen our cultural commitment to the value of life regardless of whether the pregnancy is the result of failed birth control, unwanted sex, or rape. It would be better, surely, to have the conception not occur, than to have it occur and the resulting pregnancy aborted. Presumably, then, pro-life activists (or at least some) should be committed to bringing down the number of such unwanted pregnancies, whether caused by rape, unwanted sex, or the unavailability or failure of reliable birth control. From a pro-choice perspective, an unwanted pregnancy is an infringement on a woman's autonomy and physical integrity: it is the use of her body by the fetus and, if caused by rape, by a man against her desires and against her will. If we could reduce the number of unwanted pregnancies, we would not only bring down the abortion rate, we might also boost women's autonomy, sense of self-sovereignty, and physical integrity.

But not only the unwanted pregnancy, but also the causes of those pregnancy might be independent harms. The unwanted pregnancy might be the result of rape, in which case it is and represents an assault on her physical sovereignty over her own body. Less remarked upon, though, unwanted pregnancies might also be the result of unwanted, albeit *consensual*, sex. Unwanted, but consensual, sex does not carry the harms of rape, but it does carry its own harms: it represents a degradation of a woman's (or girl's) sense of self-possession, autonomy, and physical sovereignty. A woman who is engaging in sex that she does not physically desire is alienating herself from her body and its pleasures: she is putting her body to the use of another, for his pleasures rather than hers, and on the basis of his desires rather than her own. If she becomes pregnant in the process, then she will eventually alienate her body likewise to the needs of the fetus growing inside her. Pro-choice activists, and feminists generally, and I would urge all the rest of us as well, should have an interest in preventing the unwanted sex, even if it is short of rape, that might in turn lead to unwanted pregnancies. That unwanted sex has costs and harms of its own that go to the core of female autonomy, agency, and pleasure: the sex can be painful, it is an alienation of one's body and one's power over one's body and pleasures, and it renders one's own hedonic life subservient to that of another. Sex, even if consensual, that is contrary to one's own desires, creates a gap between one's decisions and actions on the one hand, and the teaching of one's own body on the other.

Both sides, then, should be committed for different although likely overlapping reasons to empowering women and girls to definitively resist sex that they do not themselves physically desire. Doing so would bring down the numbers of unwanted pregnancies and hence the abortion rate. Doing so would also, though, bring down a form of invasion of women's bodies—the sex, as well as the pregnancy—that carries real harms of its own: it infringes women's autonomy, self-respect, physical self-possession, and hedonic awareness.

Lastly, some unwanted pregnancies are the result of birth control, but perhaps a greater number are the result of the failure to use birth control responsibly. It would seem, then, that anyone committed to the project of bringing down the numbers of abortion might be interested in an attempt to articulate, and then instill, a moral duty incumbent upon sexual partners to use birth control, wherever unprotected sex carries the risk of pregnancy: from both perspectives, it brings down the role of unwanted pregnancies, which are properly regarded by both as harmful. It is odd, then, that there has been so little movement on either side toward the articulation of a duty, incumbent upon sexual partners whose unprotected sex might lead to an unwanted pregnancy, to use birth control responsibly. Yet, this hasn't occurred: some, although certainly not all, pro-life activists are opposed on moral grounds to the use of birth control, and pro-choice activists have been absorbed by the recurrent and recurrently difficult and consuming work of defending the right to use birth control rather than the duty to do so.

Nevertheless, and as I will argue in my contribution to this volume, it seems to me that this is fertile territory for common ground and for a common ground project. Although some pro-life activists oppose the use of birth control, not all do by any means: many pro-life activists, particularly among the rank and file rather than the leadership, are opposed to abortion because of the pain caused the fetus, the humanity of fetal life, and the degradation to the culture by virtue of the easy availability of the abortion procedure. They do not necessarily share the antipathy to birth control. And, while pro-choice activists have been absorbed in the work of defending the right to use birth control, there is no incongruity between insisting upon that right, and at the same time insisting upon the existence of a duty to do so. Yes, women and girls as well as men should have a right to the birth control that allows them control over their destiny, at least as that destiny involves the decisions whether and when to parent. They should also be able to choose to enjoy a full and active sexual life, regardless of their decision regarding parenting, and they should have access to the birth control that will permit them to do so. But it should also be incumbent upon them, should they so choose, to do so in a responsible manner that does not risk an unwanted pregnancy.

I would suggest that pro-choice and pro-life activists could embark upon not only a common project of preventing unwanted abortions, as Justin argues, but also a common project of bringing down the incidence of unwanted pregnancies, or perhaps for the sake of clarity, unwanted *conception*, not only by resisting rape and rape culture, but also by encouraging girls and women to resist unwanted sex, and by articulating the grounds of a duty shared by sexual partners, when engaging in wanted sex, to use birth control so as to prevent the unwanted pregnancies that might ensue.

There are of course other possible common ground projects, some of which are elucidated by contributors to this volume. I argue in my contribution that one of the costs of constitutionalizing these issues, beginning with *Roe v. Wade* through to the present, is that it makes these projects harder: it hardens conceptions of identity, aligning one with the peculiar and peculiarly non-political voice of national identity, articulated by the undemocratic Supreme Court, and that is an unfortunate side effect (among others) of the institution of judicial review. Adjudication has the effect of articulating contrasting worldviews, and pronouncing one of them consistent with a deep American constitutional identity—not conducive to the project of coalition politics. But we've lived with this reality now for 40 years. Perhaps within the next decade we will discover a way to re-engage in ordinary political work in spite of it. Pro-life and pro-choice leaders could from time to time drop their identification with a political movement based on a view of life's meaning that is inconsistent with that of so many of their co-citizens, and could again become ordinary citizens in a common project of nation-building through the ordinary means of persuasion and politics, all with an eye toward improving the quality of the lives, and the quality of parenting, of men and women, whatever might be their understanding of the morality of abortion, and the constitutionality of laws that regulate it. By engaging in common projects, they would undoubtedly find much common ground between them as well.

The Chapters

One of the primary questions that emerged during our collaboration was whether the predominantly constitutional and legal focus of the current debate about abortion has narrowed and constricted the rhetoric and aspirations of both the pro-life and pro-choice movements. That question is the focus of Robin West's chapter, which argues that the right to abortion as constitutionalized in *Roe v. Wade* is fundamentally a negative right that strives to keep the state out of the domain of family life. By equating reproductive justice with a right to terminate a pregnancy, the decision legitimates a minimalist state response to the challenges faced by pregnant women who carry their pregnancies to term and low-income parents who might need greater public support. West's chapter also explores some of the gains that might come from returning the struggles over abortion to ordinary democratic politics, including: facilitating common ground efforts, achieving more durable political compromises, and strengthening the role of moral restraints in bringing down the need for and rate of abortion.

The central conviction that animates most of the chapters in this book is that there are plenty of fruitful areas for political and cultural collaboration on abortion and reproductive justice, many of which have escaped notice because they do not conform to the adversarial parameters of the traditional abortion dialogue. Shari Motro's chapter addresses a set of problems that fits this description. She explains that laws relating to pregnancy among unmarried lovers presume that nonmarital sex happens between strangers and comes with no strings attached. These laws therefore treat unmarried women as the sole decision-makers regarding whether to abort or proceed with a pregnancy, and also as the appropriate party to bear the extensive costs associated with pregnancy and childbirth. Motro criticizes the foundational assumption and inequitable results of this legal regime and proposes a system in which men would be more involved not only in the *choice* of whether to proceed with an out-of-wedlock pregnancy, but also in bearing the *costs* of that choice.

In a similar vein, Shauna Prewitt's chapter aims to resolve a problem that ought to be of common concern to proponents of choice as well as opponents of abortion. She explains that women who conceive through rape and opt to give birth are treated as imposters, not genuine rape victims, because entrenched social and legal norms—particularly those reflected in current abortion laws—expect that true rape victims will inevitably abort those pregnancies. Due to this misimpression, current laws fail to protect women who bear rape-related pregnancies to term when the rapists attempt to gain custody or visitation rights for the children. Prewitt cogently argues that all sides in the abortion debate have a common interest in reforming these laws to ensure that women impregnated by rape have a genuine choice whether to give birth or terminate the pregnancy.

Many promising avenues for common ground seek to further the principles of human dignity and equality, principles shared by many participants in the abortion dialogue. To that end, Dorothy Roberts's chapter documents various ways in which "[r]eproductive health policies have been shaped by … a striking race and class hierarchy that values the childbearing of white and middle-class women more highly than that of poor women and women of color." In particular, she criticizes eugenically inspired family-planning policies and demeaning cultural messages—paired with criminal laws—targeting low-income black women who use drugs during pregnancy. Likewise, Elizabeth Schiltz's chapter problematizes the widely shared belief that an abortion of a disabled fetus is less morally troubling than an abortion of a healthy one. In so doing, she explains how disability-selective abortions perpetuate negative stereotypes about, and unequal treatment of, individuals with disabilities. Both Roberts and Schiltz argue that whatever one thinks about the proper legal status of abortion, our shared commitment to equality warrants caution about reproductive practices and policies that reflect or foster entrenched hierarchies and prejudices.

Because the opposing sides of the abortion debate are not internally homogeneous but instead embrace a variety of groups, interests, and perspectives, common ground depends in large measure on the depth and adaptability of these diverse constituencies. The last two chapters in the collection discuss ways in which two key players on the abortion issue—the Democrat Party and the Catholic Church—might meaningfully further common ground efforts. Kristen Day, the executive director of Democrats for Life, a Democrat-affiliated pro-life organization, summarizes the progress her organization has made—and the challenges it has faced—in promoting common ground within her party and within the US Congress. Finally, Susan Stabile's chapter proposes criteria to guide committed Catholics in deciding what kinds of common ground to embrace: in her view, a Catholic should consider not only whether an abortion-related policy is consistent with Church teaching, but also whether it is politically viable and has a realistic chance of reducing abortion rates. Applying these criteria, she argues that Catholics may prioritize abortion-reduction strategies that involve expanding the safety net for pregnant women over more traditional approaches that emphasize legal restriction.

Together, these chapter merely scratch the surface of a burgeoning and exciting area of scholarship, activism, and advocacy. We hope that this book helps foster a more expansive and reflective dialogue about how to address abortion that builds upon our shared convictions and commitments.

Chapter 1
From Choice to Reproductive Justice: De-Constitutionalizing Abortion Rights

Robin West

Introduction

The preferred moral foundations of the abortion right created in *Roe v. Wade*[1] and its progeny continue to shift, from marital and medical privacy,[2] to women's equality,[3] to individual liberty or dignity,[4] and back, in the minds of both the Supreme Court Justices and the pro-choice advocates and legal scholars that have argued or celebrated these famous cases. What has not shifted is the commitment of the pro-choice community to the right itself, and to the propriety of its judicial origin. Legal abortion, according to this near-universal pro-choice consensus, is and should be an individual, constitutional right protected against political winds, rather than simply good policy reflected in a state's laws, and it is therefore entirely fitting that we look to the courts, and to the Supreme Court in particular, for its articulation and enforcement. It is the work of the courts and their actors—judges, lawyers, litigants, amici, judicial clerks, and academic commentators—to orate the basis of this important individual right, to develop its contours, and to expand or contract it when appropriate—to subject it in effect to the ordinary and extraordinary processes of constitutional adjudication.

This chapter tabulates some of the costs to feminist and democratic ideals that are produced by our reliance on the creation of an individual right as the conceptual vehicle for legal abortion, and our reliance on adjudication as the strategic vehicle for the right's development and justification. I will argue that while the court-

1 410 U.S. 113 (1973).

2 *Id.* at 152–53.

3 *See*, e.g., Ruth Bader Ginsburg, *Some Thoughts on Autonomy and Equality in Relation to* Roe v. Wade, 63 N.C. L. Rev. 375 (1985) (arguing that Roe should have been decided on narrow Equal Protection Clause grounds); Sylvia A. Law, *Rethinking Sex and the Constitution*, 132 U. Pa. L. Rev. 955 (1984) (same); Reva Siegel, *Reasoning from the Body: A Historical Perspective on Abortion Regulation and Questions of Equal Protection*, 44 Stan. L. Rev. 261, 349–77 (1992) (same).

4 See Reva B. Siegel, *Dignity and the Politics of Protection: Abortion Restrictions Under Casey/Carhart*, 117 Yale L.J. 1694 (2008) (arguing that dignity is a universal value that can structure disagreements between subcommunities on abortion).

focused methods and the various "choice-based" arguments put forward by the pro-choice advocacy community have jointly secured for individuals a fairly robust constitutional right to legal abortion, those same arguments have ill served not only progressive politics broadly conceived, but also have ill served women, both narrowly, in terms of our reproductive lives and needs, and more generally. I ultimately will urge a broader political argument for reproductive justice in women's lives that embraces, but does not center upon, rights-based claims, and for a reorientation of legal resources to secure those claims away from the judicial realm and to state and federal legislative arenas.

The chapter is organized as follows. The first part asks a (somewhat) rhetorical question: why has there not been more feminist and pro-choice criticism of both *Roe v. Wade* specifically and our reproductive rights jurisprudence more generally? To be clear, there is of course plenty of criticism of *Roe* from those who abhor legal abortion on moral grounds,[5] as well as from legal scholars and Court watchers who object to the Court's perceived freewheeling activism in this field.[6] There is also a fair amount of critique of *Roe* from progressive scholars worried about *Roe*'s demonstrated propensity to create backlash against the Democratic Party and progressivism more generally.[7] What is missing from the massive amounts of critical commentary on *Roe* is an examination by pro-choice scholars of both the abortion right itself and the Court's central role in its creation for the possible harms done to the broader cause of reproductive justice. There is, bluntly, almost none of this scholarship.[8] I will argue that while there are quite understandable reasons for the reluctance of this community to offer constructive critiques, those reasons are not in the end persuasive.

5 See, e.g., Michael Stokes Paulsen, *Paulsen, J., Dissenting*, *in* WHAT ROE V. WADE SHOULD HAVE SAID: THE NATION'S TOP LEGAL EXPERTS RELATE AMERICA'S MOST CONTROVERSIAL DECISION 196, 211–14 (Jack M. Balkin ed., 2005) (equating support for legal abortion with support for state-sponsored genocide).

6 See, e.g., ROBERT H. BORK, THE TEMPTING OF AMERICA 120–26 (1990) (arguing that *Roe v. Wade* was an illegal exercise of judicial power); John Hart Ely, *The Wages of Crying Wolf: A Comment on* Roe v. Wade, 82 YALE L.J. 920, 935–36 (1973) (arguing that *Roe v. Wade* creates a right to privacy with less constitutional support than any other decision in the previous 20 years).

7 *See*, e.g., GERALD N. ROSENBERG, THE HOLLOW HOPE: CAN COURTS BRING ABOUT SOCIAL CHANGE? (1991) (arguing generally that courts were ineffectual in bringing about progressive social change in the middle and late twentieth century, using Roe as an example).

8 Exceptions include works such as Ginsburg, *supra* note 3, at 385–86, which expresses the concern that *Roe* had undercut a grassroots legalization movement, inviting backlash; Catharine MacKinnon, Roe v. Wade*: A Study in Male Ideology*, *in* ABORTION: MORAL AND LEGAL PERSPECTIVES 45, 51 (Jay L. Garfield & Patricia Hennessey eds., 1984), which argues that the privacy rationale of *Roe* legitimates the sexual aggression that often leads to unwanted pregnancy; and Mark Tushnet, *An Essay on Rights*, 62 TEX. L. REV. 1363, 1364–70 (1984), which uses the abortion right as exemplary of unstable features of constitutional rights.

The second part argues that there are unreckoned moral and political costs of the judicially created, individualist, and negative right to an abortion—costs that ought to be troubling for all, but particularly for feminist legal scholars.

Briefly, I look at three such costs of the abortion right, which I refer to as (1) legitimation costs, (2) democratic costs, and (3) aspirational costs. All three of these general types of costs of rights have been well developed in the various "rights critiques" produced by critical legal scholars during the 1970s and 1980s.[9] None, however, has been applied to the particular case of abortion rights. Individual, negative, constitutional rights, according to their critics, keep the state off our backs and out of our lives, but they also run the risk of legitimating the injustices we sustain in the insulated privacy so created; they denigrate the democratic processes that might generate positive law that could better respond to our vulnerabilities and meet our needs; and they truncate our collective visions of law's moral possibilities. All three costs, I will argue, attend to the abortion right created by *Roe v. Wade*. The second and major part of the chapter specifies how this is so.

The third part of the chapter looks at opportunities for promoting reproductive justice—including legal, moral, political, and rhetorical—that the pro-choice community might have lost because of its focus on rights and Supreme Court authority in the abortion debates. The conclusion briefly points toward a reproductive justice agenda that incorporates, without centralizing, a strong political case for access to legal abortion as central to women's equal citizenship, without compromising or undercutting other progressive and feminist aims.

I. A Missing Critical Jurisprudence

Why is there not more pro-choice criticism of *Roe*, and of its varying and various rationales? The lack of such commentary is odder than it might first seem. The liberal adjudicated victories of the Warren and Burger Courts, with the one exception of *Roe*, generated massive amounts of critical commentary

9 See Peter Gabel, *The Phenomenology of Rights-Consciousness and the Pact of the Withdrawn Selves*, 62 Tex. L. Rev. 1563, 1580–81 (arguing that rights function as an impoverished connection among people that replaces genuine connection); Morton J. Horwitz, *Rights*, 23 Harv. C.R.-C.L. L. Rev. 393, 399–404 (1988) (arguing that rights require an individualistic perspective on social relations, at a cost to both democracy and redistribution, and that rights shift the focus away from the question of whether the right is socially desirable, an aspirational cost); Duncan Kennedy, *The Critique of Rights in Critical Legal Studies*, *in* Left Legalism/Left Critique 178, 216 (Wendy Brown & Janet Halley eds., 2002) (acknowledging Marxist critique that rights serve as a fantasy resolution of conflict between collective altruism and selfish individualism, legitimizing capital exploitation); Tushnet, *supra* note 8, at 1363–64 (arguing that we ought to value rights in and of themselves, and that because of their negativity, rights impede advances by progressive social forces).

from theorists purporting to speak for the interests of the victorious parties in those cases and the communities they roughly represented. *Brown v. Board of Education*,[10] to take the most iconic example, has generated a burgeoning cottage industry of critique, eventually coalescing in the creation of an entire scholarly movement—critical race theory—that was rigorously critical, on left-wing and racial-justice grounds, of that decision's liberal, rights-expansive, and integrationist ideals.[11] Thus, according to its progressive critics, *Brown* hid the massive problems of underfunded public education under the false covering of a legally reformed and racially fair integrationist ideal,[12] and articulated an account of *de jure* segregation as the evil to be addressed by civil rights law that left an insidious pattern of *de facto* segregation both intact and legitimated.[13] It birthed an entire ideology of "color blindness" that did little but undercut serious attempts at redistributive racial justice, including affirmative action programs in employment and education both.[14] *Brown* lent a veneer of fairness to purportedly meritocratic hierarchic orderings that result from individual and state decision-making and that continue to subordinate poor people.[15] It relied on a cramped and ungenerous vision of "rights" and "integration" that both truncated rather than generated political progress on these and other progressive causes.[16] All of this criticism, again, came from the champions of racial justice, not antagonists. Other less revered but nevertheless substantial Warren, Burger, and Rehnquist

10 347 U.S. 483 (1954).

11 See generally Critical Race Theory: The Key Writings That Formed the Movement 5, 20, 127–91 (Kimberlé Crenshaw et al. eds., 1995) (identifying two of Derrick Bell's articles on *Brown v. Board of Education* as the intellectual precursors to Critical Race Theory and presenting "Progressive Alternatives to Mainstream Civil Rights Ideology").

12 See Derrick A. Bell, *Bell, J., Dissenting, in* What Brown v. Board of Education Should Have Said 185, 186–87 (Jack M. Balkin ed., 2001) (arguing that *Brown v. Board*'s abolition of segregation in education does not address harm caused by unequal educational opportunity).

13 See Alan David Freeman, *Legitimizing Racial Discrimination Through Antidiscrimination Law: A Critical Review of Supreme Court Doctrine*, 62 Minn. L. Rev. 1049 (1978) (arguing that race discrimination law since Brown has served to legitimate racial subordination).

14 See Derrick Bell, Silent Covenants: Brown v. Board of Education and the Unfulfilled Hopes for Racial Reform 151–59 (2004); Derrick A. Bell, Jr., *The Unintended Lessons in Brown v. Board of Education*, 49 N.Y.L. Sch. L. Rev. 1053 (2005).

15 See Louis Michael Seidman, *Brown and Miranda*, 80 Cal. L. Rev. 673, 717 (1992).

16 *Id.*; Alan D. Freeman, *Antidiscrimination Law: A Critical Review, in* The Politics of Law: A Progressive Critique 96, 114 (David Kairys ed., 1st ed. 1982) [hereinafter Politics of Law] (concluding, in this condensed version of Freeman, *supra* note 13, that "race as a historical problem of oppression … cannot be remedied alone unless one is willing to accept nothing more than token bourgeoisification within the structure of a presupposed system of equality of opportunity—in short, one must become part of the legitimation process. To challenge that limited view is to tackle the pretense of equality of opportunity directly, to see it for what it is in relation to class structure").

Court progressive victories also have prompted scathing critiques by progressive legal scholars. *Miranda v. Arizona*[17] prompted worry as well as celebration among advocates for the interests of criminal defendants: the right the Court created might constitute a triumph for nothing but a formalistic and legitimating conception of interrogatory justice, setting back, rather than advancing, the cause of respectful and non-coercive treatment of criminal defendants.[18] Likewise, the more recent *Lawrence v. Texas*[19] decision prompted plenty of accolades but also its share of criticism from equality-minded legal scholars. In elevating sex into the realm of those aspects of life and identity so highly regarded as to be worthy of constitutional protection, some argued, it might further burden the work of protecting vulnerable people against sexual harassment and assault.[20]

Whatever the merits of the criticisms of these famously progressive cases, my point here is comparative: unlike *Brown*, *Miranda*, or *Lawrence*, *Roe v. Wade* remains largely insulated from friendly critique. Why is that? I think there are three reasons for the critical reticence. None, however, is a particularly compelling justification.

Part of the story—maybe the major part—is a widespread belief among the pro-choice community in the opinion's relative vulnerability. This alone deters criticism of the decision by those who politically support legal abortion. *Roe*, by contrast to *Brown*, *Miranda*, and even *Lawrence*, seems to be in perpetual and great danger of being overturned.[21] *Roe* is a perennial—permanent?—presidential campaign issue, and has been since it was decided. Its "hanging by a thread" status, furthermore, is perhaps the one thing that was not changed by Barack Obama's world-altering victories in 2008 and 2012. President Obama may replace retiring liberal Justices with younger liberal Justices, but that will still leave the opinion with only five-to-four support. A Republican presidential victory in 2016 might result in a fifth vote on the Court for overturning *Roe*. Even assuming Democratic administrations far into the future, however, it does not follow that a newly constituted Court dominated by Democratic Party nominees will be committed to *Roe*. The pro-life wing of the Democratic Party will likely grow, not shrink, with Democratic dominance, as will the risk that a Justice appointed by a Democratic president will see his or her way to reverse *Roe*. There is, in short, no end in sight to the compulsive vote counting with respect to *Roe v. Wade*. We are seemingly today, just as we were on November 3, 2008, one judicial appointment away from the decision's reversal.

---

17 384 U.S. 436 (1966).

18 Seidman, *supra* note 15, at 745–47.

19 539 U.S. 558 (2003).

20 See Marc Spindelman, *Surviving Lawrence v. Texas*, 102 MICH. L. REV. 1615, 1655–67 (2004) (arguing that Lawrence might prove overprotective of coercive sexuality).

21 See, e.g., Dawn Johnsen, *Why the 2008 Election Matters for Reproductive Rights*, BALKINIZATION, September 24, 2008, http:// balkin.blogspot.com/2008/09/why-2008-election-matters-for.html.

The second reason has to do with a belief in *Roe*'s efficacy. The gains secured by *Roe* seem more tangible than the gains secured by *Brown* and *Lawrence*, so the potential cost of reckless critique seems higher. *Brown* ended *de jure* segregation of the schools—but not *de facto* segregation, and much less real racial subordination: schools as well as neighborhoods remain segregated and unequal in much of the country. *Lawrence* struck from the books criminal statutes that had not been directly enforced anyway, and left untouched the unequal treatment of gay and lesbian citizens on any number of fronts, from marriage to military service, employment, and tenancy rights. There is much to criticize, if one keeps the focus on the paltry consequences of these decisions, compared with what they promised. *Roe*, by contrast, was by no means an empty victory, much less a Trojan horse. Rather, *Roe* sent a clear material and rhetorical signal to women, girls, and the larger society: women's reproductive lives should be, and henceforth would be, governed by a regime of choice—whose choice is not so clear—and not by fate, nature, accident, biology, or men.

The gains of this one decision, in terms of the autonomy and broadened options for women and girls, were felt to be enormous. With the advent of birth control and safe and legal abortion, women can avoid life- and health-threatening pregnancies, can limit the number of children they will mother, and can plan the major sequence of their lives—pregnancies, education, marriage, job, and career—so as to increase hugely their chances of succeeding at all. Without that control, women's and girls' control of these life-changing events is severely compromised. Dangerous, injurious, or simply too many pregnancies in one's teens, twenties, thirties, and forties make completion of high school, college, professional school, graduate school, or vocational training for skilled crafts much harder even to imagine, much less to accomplish. The burdens of unwanted, dangerous, or just too many pregnancies are harder to measure but just as real in private and intimate life. Dangerous pregnancies shorten lives. Too many pregnancies make for difficult and unrewarding mothering. All of it leaves the woman feeling, justifiably, hostage to fate. If she cannot control her reproductivity, she cannot control her life. Without self-sovereignty over her body, all that remains of her life—her work, her sociability, her education, her mothering, and her impact on the world—is miniaturized. She lives a smaller life.

Lastly, there may be no pro-choice criticism of *Roe* because *Roe* got so much exactly right, and it is both understood and appreciated by the pro-choice community for doing so. Criticism, then, might just seem churlish. Thus, it may simply be true that women must have a right to legal abortion if women are to be equal citizens, and it may also be true that equal citizenship is what the Constitution requires. As the political philosopher Eileen McDonagh has argued at length, where abortion is criminal, women, but not men, are required to donate body parts for a substantial part of their adult lives and at substantial risk to their own health and life, to the cause of nurturing and preserving the life of another, and they are required to do this regardless of whether they consent to this appropriation.[22] Women's ownership of the use of their own bodies is therefore contingent, or conditional, in a way which men's is not: another human life (the fetus) has a primary right to their bodies, and they have no right to ward off what would be a criminal assault were it a born child making these demands. This contingent self-sovereignty is not conducive to equal citizenship. If equal citizenship is the goal of the Constitution's declarations of equality and liberty, then women seemingly must have a right to legal abortion in order to achieve it. And equal citizenship does seem to be what our Constitution contemplates, at least as we now understand it. Whatever the problems with *Roe*'s rhetoric or rationale, that conclusion seems both important and right.

None of this, however—*Roe*'s perceived vulnerability, its consequences, or the truth it partially expresses—justifies the relative dearth of critical inquiry by pro-choice scholars into the costs of either *Roe*'s genesis in the Court or its various stated rationales. First, with respect to both the decision's vulnerability and its efficacy, the goal of the pro-choice movement should be women's access to legal and safe abortion, not preservation of a right that may be increasingly hollow. Of course, there is a danger that *Roe* could be overturned (although perhaps smaller than the pro-choice community claims[23]), but there is also a danger with the road we are on: we preserve the right, while growing numbers of women across large swaths of the country lose access to the service. With *Roe* on the books, we are nevertheless witnessing a gradual diminution in the availability of abortion for poor, teenaged, and rural women, as state legislatures pass, and the Court upholds, first funding restrictions,[24] then parental notification requirements,[25] and then waiting periods.[26] The threat to legal, safe, affordable abortion is not so much that the Court may overturn *Roe*, but that abortion will become less and less available, because of the impact of legislative and political decisions made far from the Supreme Court's doors. Either way, the challenge to legal and safe abortion comes primarily from state politics and only secondarily from court action. Fixation on the Court and the narrowing constitutional right it has created as a way to secure legal abortion is just counterproductive.

More important, even if it is true that legal abortion is necessary to women's equal citizenship, it by no means follows that a judicially created individualized constitutional right, rather than political persuasion, is the best way to achieve it, for two reasons. First, it bears emphasizing that what the Court created

---

22 Eileen L. McDonagh, Breaking the Abortion Deadlock: From Choice to Consent (1996).

23 See Neal Devins, *How Planned Parenthood v. Casey (Pretty Much) Settled the Abortion Wars*, 118 Yale L.J. 1318 (2009).

24 Harris v. McRae, 448 U.S. 297 (1980).

25 Planned Parenthood of Se. Pa. v. Casey, 505 U.S. 833, 899 (1992) (joint opinion of O'Connor, Kennedy, Souter, JJ.).

26 *Id.* at 886–87.

in *Roe v. Wade* is not a right to legal abortion; it is a negative right against the criminalization of abortion in some circumstances. That no more creates a genuine right to a legal abortion than *Brown* created a right to an integrated school. To be a meaningful support for women's equality or liberty, a right to legal abortion must mean much more than a right to be free of moralistic legislation that interferes with a contractual right to purchase one. It must guarantee access to one. And, for a right to legal abortion to guarantee that a woman who needs an abortion will have access to one, whether or not she can pay for it, the state must be required to provide considerable support. But the Court has consistently read the Constitution as not including positive rights to much of anything from the state,[27] and certainly not to abortion procedures.[28] It is so unlikely as to be a certainty that neither this Court nor likely any Court will commence a jurisprudence of positive constitutional rights, by beginning in the contested terrain of mandating public funds for abortions. By comparison, the state legislative arena is not so constrained: it is very much the business of state legislatures to create legislative programs to meet the positive needs of citizens. Whatever obstacles there might be to a legislative initiative to publicly fund abortions, a refusal to see "positive rights" in the Constitution is not among them.

But second, and aside from the growing doctrine that cuts against funding, even a purely negative right, assuming it exists, might be better secured through what is now sometimes called political,[29] popular,[30] or legislative constitutionalism,[31] rather than through the adjudicated Constitution as interpreted by courts. That is, a right to abortion might be better understood to be a part of our constitutional self-understanding that is achieved through political and legislative victories, rather than adjudicative pronouncement. It would not be the first time a right would be better secured politically rather than judicially—think of the "right" to social security, or the "right" to be free of a military draft, or for that matter women's right to equality itself. No Supreme Court decision ever secured any of these in

27 *See*, e.g., DeShaney v. Winnebago County Dep't of Soc. Servs., 489 U.S. 189, 196 (1989) (stating in dicta that there is no right to government aid); San Antonio Indep. Sch. Dist. v. Rodriguez, 411 U.S. 1, 29-39 (1973) (holding that there is no right to a public education).

28 Harris, 448 U.S. at 316–18.

29 See Mark Tushnet, Taking the Constitution Away from the Courts 154 (1999) (arguing broadly against judicial exclusivity and supremacy in constitutional interpretation).

30 Neal Devins & Louis Fisher, The Democratic Constitution 235–39 (2004) (arguing for the Court to play a dialogic, rather than exclusive or final role in the interpretation of the Constitution); Larry D. Kramer, The People Themselves: Popular Constitutionalism and Judicial Review 247–48 (2004) (arguing for popular engagement in the search for constitutional meaning); cf. Robert Post & Reva Siegel, *Popular Constitutionalism, Departmentalism, and Judicial Supremacy*, 92 Cal. L. Rev. 1027, 1043 (2004) (affirming that constitutional law can endanger political participation and self-governance).

31 See generally Robin West, *The Missing Jurisprudence of the Legislated Constitution, in* The Constitution in 2020, at 79 (Jack M. Balkin & Reva B. Siegel eds., 2009) (arguing for a larger legislative role in determining constitutional meaning).

constitutional doctrine, yet they seem at least as secure against political change as the various unenumerated rights the Court has discovered or created. A woman's right to legal abortion likewise might be better inferred from contemporary understandings of equality and citizenship than from any constitutional language or configuration of past cases that a court is likely to recognize as authoritative. This is, at least, a possibility we ought to consider. The academic-feminist attachment not only to *Roe*, but to its origination in the courts, and our resistance to even the suggestion that we have become overly reliant upon courts, precludes our ability to do so.

Neither the vulnerability nor efficacy of *Roe*, nor the partial truth it expresses, is a good reason not to engage in critique. There are also, however, costs to the reticence. The lack of such a critique, I will argue, has dulled us to the degree to which the rhetoric of adjudicated abortion rights might have weakened reproductive justice more broadly conceived. But it is also worth noting that even if feminism's or progressivism's or the Democratic Party's sole goal were to strengthen this embattled right, there is a strong pragmatic case for pro-choice feminist critiques of the way that right is now constructed: by its steadfast loyalty to *Roe* the pro-choice community is in danger of losing this war by fighting—even if winning—yesterday's battle. Pro-life movement activists increasingly look to reduce abortions not by reversing *Roe* and criminalizing abortion, but rather through a three-pronged strategy, no part of which is dependent upon *Roe*'s reversal: first, by passing restrictions the Court will uphold even with Roe on the books;[32] second, by reducing abortion supply and demand by intimidating clinics and clinicians and shaming the women who use them;[33] and third, by reducing the long-range cost of pregnancy by urging more political and communitarian support for motherhood, particularly for poor women.[34] For pro-life constituencies, the grounds of contestation of legal abortion have shifted to the local, political, and moral, and away from the constitutional-adjudicative. The pro-choice community's fixation on the apparently never-ending project of finding adequate grounds for adjudicated abortion rights blinds it to this development.

The pro-choice community, for purely pragmatic reasons, might be well advised to take up a challenge made a few years ago by Janet Halley and Wendy Brown in a different context[35]—to wit, that we subject liberal constitutional victories to criticism in an unfettered way, as though we were not in fear of the wolf at the door. It is past time to apply this simple enough prescription to abortion rights. Not only is critique valuable for its own sake, but here, we thereby might push the wolf further back. The *Roe* to *Casey* line of decisions stands in need of progressive,

---

32 See Siegel, *supra* note 4, at 1704.

33 Johnsen, *supra* note 21.

34 See Jacqueline L. Salmon, *Some Abortion Foes Shifting Focus from Ban to Reduction*, Washington Post, November 18, 2008, at A1.

35 Wendy Brown & Janet Halley, *Introduction* to Left Legalism/Left Critique, *supra* note 9, at 1, 25–33.

feminist, and pro-choice critique and transformation. The first without the second may well be irresponsibly reckless, but the second without the first is impossible. And both are necessary.

II. Critique

There are at least three major costs of the right created in *Roe* that seem to be underappreciated by the pro-choice community. All three are suggested by the various critiques of negative rights, of the Left's reliance on courts to create and protect them, and of the liberal-legal political commitments that underlie them, which were pioneered by the critical legal scholarship of the 1970s and 1980s. They are as follows: (1) choice-based arguments for abortion rights legitimate considerable injustice, both in women's reproductive lives and elsewhere; (2) the Court's active role in creating this jurisprudence exacerbates anti-democratic features of US constitutionalism, to women's detriment; and (3) the arguments do not do justice to the aspirational goals of the women's movement's early arguments for reproductive rights.

A. Legitimation

"Legitimation" has come to mean many things in critical legal scholarship, but two particular meanings are of relevance to the right to abortion; the first concerns the legitimating consequences of legal change, and the second concerns the legitimating consequences of individual choice. In the case of the right to abortion, of course, these are deeply intertwined: the legal change effected by this right is an expansion of individual choice. It is nevertheless helpful to treat them separately.

By the first meaning, apparent gains in justice wrought through legal change are sometimes offset by what might be called the "legitimation costs" of the same legal breakthrough. The idea here is that a concededly just legal change will sometimes legitimate a deeper or broader injustice with the legal institution so improved, thus further insulating the underlying or broader legal institution from critique. This ought to be understood, then, as a cost of the reform—one that, in some circumstances, might be quite high. For example, although *Brown* ended *de jure* racial segregation of the public schools, it might have thereby legitimated an entire host of evils, including *de facto* segregation, unequally funded urban schools, private sphere rather than state-sponsored subordination of African Americans, and the purportedly meritocratic classifications and hierarchies of market economies themselves. All of these are left not just untouched by *Brown*, but legitimated by it. The decision's equation of injustice with state-sponsored racism carries the implicit suggestion that so long as those segregated or underfunded schools, or market-generated hierarchies of class and race privilege, are not polluted by the pernicious impact of state-sponsored racial classifications, then they are not only constitutional, but also morally and politically untroubling.[36] The legitimation cost of Brown is the possibly increased insularity against criticism and political reform of these greater injustices. The critics' claim is not that the goal of the legal breakthrough—ending *de jure* segregation—is undesirable. Rather, the worry is that the goal comes at the cost of legitimating deeper racial injustices. At some point, the critics worry, these legitimation costs might outweigh the benefit of the breakthrough itself.

The second meaning of "legitimation," developed in critical scholarship of the late twentieth century, concerns the nature and role of consent and the specific impact of an individual's consent to the perceived justice of either particular transactions or entire institutions to which consent is given. In liberal market economies and the legal orders that govern them, the act of consent generally insulates the object of consent even from criticism, much less legal challenge. Consent to the terms of a contract, for example, almost always insulates the fairness of the terms of that contract from both public scrutiny and legal attack, regardless of how harmful or injurious that contract turns out to be to any of the parties that consented to it. If the contract was consensual, it cannot possibly be unfair to execute it against a later regretful party, no matter how harmful its terms might appear to be. Widely shared norms against paternalistic legislation,[37] an ideological and seemingly bottomless belief in the ability of individuals to understand and act on their own welfare,[38] skepticism regarding the motivation of regulatory bodies or meddling individuals who would seek to upset consensual individual transactions, and at least for some, a definitional commitment to consent as that which maximizes value,[39] all burden attempts to intervene in or even question contract terms. They may do so through "unconscionability" or "duress" limits in the common law of contract, or through more explicitly regulatory means, such as consumer protection legislation or workers' rights laws. I have argued elsewhere that the same dynamic increasingly limits critique of intimate sexual relations: consensual sex is viewed not only as not rape, but also as not subjected appropriately to moral or political criticism. To subject consensual sex to criticism is puritanical, moralistic, or worse.[40] Lastly,

36 See sources cited *supra* notes 11–14.

37 The surrogacy debates of the late 1980s and early 1990s present a stark example of the application of this principle in policy debates. *See*, e.g., Richard A. Epstein, *Surrogacy: The Case for Full Contractual Enforcement*, 81 Va. L. Rev. 2305 (1995); Richard A. Posner, *The Ethics and Economics of Enforcing Contracts of Surrogate Motherhood*, 5 J. Contemp. Health L. & Pol'y 21 (1989).

38 *See*, e.g., Epstein, *supra* note 37, at 2313 (arguing for a presumption favoring the validity of market exchanges because individuals know their own interests best).

39 *See*, e.g., Richard A. Posner, *The Ethical and Political Basis of the Efficiency Norm in Common Law Adjudication*, 8 Hofstra L. Rev. 487, 488–89 (1980) (arguing that consensual trades increase value by definition).

40 Robin West, *The Harms of Consensual Sex*, *in* The Philosophy of Sex: Contemporary Readings 317 (Alan Soble & Nicholas Power eds., 5th ed. 2008) (arguing that according to prevailing cultural and liberal norms, consensual sex is morally unproblematic).

in the public sphere, "consent" operates similarly: the consent of the governed legitimates whatever governance follows. We can generalize from these three examples of the impact of consent in the private, intimate, and public spheres: consent cleans or purifies that to which the consent is given, and thereby insulates it from political critique as well as legal challenge. Questioning the value of that to which consent has been given is politically suspect—because it is unjustifiably paternalist, logically incoherent, or both.

Perhaps the hallmark of late twentieth-century critical legal studies (CLS) writing was the claim that this widely made inference from consent to value is simply unwarranted.[41] People's abilities to ascertain and act on their own self-interest are limited, the critical scholars argued. The capacity of countries, institutions, multinational corporations, social forces, or simply stronger parties to create in individual subjects a willingness to consent to transactions or changes that do not in fact increase their wellbeing is well documented.[42] "Consent" of the weaker can be manufactured to serve the interests of dominant parties, and when it is manufactured, it is not a good measure of the value to the weak of that to which consent was given. Neither skepticism regarding the good motives or knowledge base of the "paternalist," nor faith in the self-regarding preferences of the individual, justify the unexamined inference that a consensual change so extracted is a good one for all affected parties. The degree to which a consensual change is perceived as such is the degree to which it has been unduly legitimated by the consent that preceded it. The legitimation cost of consensual transactions, then, is the sometimes unwarranted belief in the increased value of the change to which consent was proffered.

Are these worries about the legitimating effects of either legal change on the one hand, or individual consent on the other, relevant to *Roe v. Wade*? Does the decision in *Roe*, even assuming the value of the right it created, carry legitimation costs? Placing the question in a historical context, one might recall that Catharine MacKinnon's early critiques of *Roe v. Wade* pointed to two important legitimating effects of that decision—one quite specific and the other more general. First, she argued, constitutionalizing a right to terminate a pregnancy broadly legitimates the

41 See generally Mark Kelman, *Choice and Utility*, 1979 Wis. L. Rev. 769 (exploring examples of choices that do not increase utility); Duncan Kennedy, *Distributive and Paternalist Motives in Contract and Tort Law, with Special Reference to Compulsory Terms and Unequal Bargaining Power*, 41 Md. L. Rev. 563 (1982) (defending paternalism in contract law on the grounds that consensual transactions do not necessarily increase utility); Robin West, *Authority, Autonomy, and Choice: The Role of Consent in the Moral and Political Visions of Franz Kafka and Richard Posner*, 99 Harv. L. Rev. 384 (1985) (critiquing the conflation of utility and consensuality).

42 See Kelman, *supra* note 41; West, *supra* note 41; see also Peter Gabel & Jay M. Feinman, *Contract Law as Ideology*, *in* Politics of Law, *supra* note 16, at 172, 183 (arguing that contract law today conceals the reality that "capitalism is a coercive system of relationships" in which "our functional roles produce isolation, passivity, unconnectedness, and impotence").

sex that produced the pregnancy—sex that might well have been less than fully consensual by both parties. It shifts the focus away from addressing the social and sexual imbalances that result in unwanted pregnancies to the unwanted pregnancy itself, and strongly suggests that the appropriate social and individual response to unwanted sex is to protect the decision to end the pregnancy. This has the effect of minimizing the social costs of sexual inequality for the strong and the weak both, rather than ending the sexual inequality itself. *Roe*, then, legitimates both unwanted sex and the hierarchies of power that generate it.[43] Second, MacKinnon argued, the privacy rationale of *Roe v. Wade* might have the pernicious effect of further insulating the already overly privatized world of intimate relations from either moral critique or political struggle. Men subordinate women, to a large degree, in private: in homes, in bedrooms, in hotel rooms, through pornography, prostitution, marriage, and sex. Extolling the privacy of these relations, and casting a constitutional wall of protection around them for the express purpose of warding off legal intervention or regulation, thus both insulates and valorizes—and hence legitimates—the subordination that occurs within them.[44]

These arguments, I think, were never answered satisfactorily by feminist supporters of *Roe v. Wade*. Completely unaddressed, however, was whether MacKinnon's critique went far enough. The question should have been not only whether MacKinnon was right to complain that *Roe v. Wade* might have the undesirable effect of legitimating, by privatizing, sexual violence, but also whether there are other legitimating costs of this decision, in addition to, and not reducible to, the problem of male sexual coercion.

I think there are such costs. The danger I want to highlight is that the individual right to terminate a pregnancy created by *Roe v. Wade* might have the effect not only of legitimating the coercive sex that might have led to it, but also of legitimating the profoundly inadequate social welfare net and hence the excessive economic burdens placed on poor women and men who decide to parent. As *Roe* and the choice it heralds to opt out of parenting become part of the architecture of our moral and legal lives, we increasingly come to think of the decision to parent, no less than the decision not to parent, as a chosen consumer good or lifestyle—albeit a very expensive one. As this shift in consciousness occurs, it may come to seem, at least for many, that the only role for a caring or just society, here as elsewhere, is to ensure that that consumer choice to parent or not parent is well informed. Making sure that choices are well informed, after all, exhausts the role of the state in regulating consensual affairs, particularly market-based ones, in a culture that valorizes consensual market transactions.

Consumers of the choice to parent or not to parent, from this "informed consent" model of the role of the just state, should know a few things. They should know that high-quality childcare can only be obtained at a very high cost. They should

---

43 Catharine A. MacKinnon, Feminism Unmodified: Discourses on Life and Law 94–95 (1988).

44 *Id.* at 96–102.

know that caring for a newborn, nurturing a toddler, and then raising a child, will interfere mightily with the parent's wage-earning potential in a working world that still valorizes the unattached laborer with no commitments to any earthly soul other than his employer.[45] They should know that the quality of public education is spotty—in communities where housing is affordable, the public education is abysmal, and vice versa—and that a purchased private education at elite private schools costs far more than most Americans' paychecks. They should know that publicly funded preventative (as opposed to emergency) healthcare for one's dependents is almost non-existent. They should know that once the decision is made to become a parent, there is no "exit," or turning back.[46] Parenting is not the sort of at-will employment from which an employee can simply walk away if the terms are not favorable; there are moral, emotional, and legal restraints on one's ability to do so. They should know all of this. All of this increases hugely the price of parenting.

If parenting is a choice, however—if it is a status entered freely, as might be a very long and very binding long-term contract—its expense is not a source of injustice or even a cause for worry, so long as the choice is made knowingly. Parenting is indeed expensive. But so are private jets and graduate degrees. If the potential parent—like the potential buyer contemplating whether to buy an airplane paid for in installments and that will require a lot of upkeep—is armed with enough information about her choices, then there is no further need for intervention into the various private markets for the support services—education, healthcare, childcare—from which she might choose when it comes time to employ those services. We now have a "choice" to end a pregnancy—when we parent, no less than when we do not, we have made our choice. And, since *Roe*, many of us do now view parenting in this way, and we so view it not just incidentally, but as a part of our fundamental, American, constitutional identity. As Americans, when we choose to parent, we should be well informed; we should make the choice knowing the price. At least here in the United States, that is no reason to publicly subsidize the choice. There is no further reason to help a poor mother pay for it than there is to help a would-be recreational sailor buy a boat that will allow him to sail around the world, or to help the aspiring scholar with the expense of yet another graduate degree. It is one lifestyle choice among several that happens to come with a hefty price tag.

Thus, constitutionalizing this particular right to choose simultaneously legitimates—in both of the senses noted above—the lack of public support given

45 See, e.g., Joan Williams, Unbending Gender: Why Family and Work Conflict and What To Do About It (2000) (exploring conflicts between work and family); Joan C. Williams, *Keynote Address: Want Gender Equality? Die Childless at Thirty*, 27 Women's Rts. L. Rep. 3, 3–4 (2006) (exploring the cost of mothering).

46 See Anne L. Alstott, No Exit: What Parents Owe Their Children and What Society Owes Parents (2004) (arguing that parents have no exit from parental work and obligations, and for greater public support of parenting).

parents in fulfilling their caregiving obligations. By giving pregnant women the choice to opt out of parenting by purchasing an abortion, we render parenting a market commodity, and thereby systematically legitimate the various baselines to which she agrees when she opts in: an almost entirely privatized system of childcare, a mixed private and public but prohibitively expensive healthcare system, and a publicly provided education system that delivers a product, the quality of which is spotty at best and disastrously inadequate at worst. Narrowly, by giving her the choice, her consent legitimates the parental burden to which she has consented. A woman who is poor and chooses to parent will exacerbate her poverty by so choosing, particularly if she "chooses" to parent without a partner. If she "chooses" to parent a special needs child, she will have little assistance for the extraordinary educational, health, and care needs of her child. If she chooses to parent without a partner while she herself lives in poverty, she likewise has so chosen. The choice-based arguments for abortion rights strengthen the impulse to simply leave her with the consequences of her bargain. She has chosen this route, so it is hers to travel alone. To presume otherwise would be paternalistic. The woman's "choice" mutes any attempt to make her claims for assistance cognizable.

More generally, the choice rhetoric of *Roe* undercuts the arguments for the development of what I have elsewhere called "caregiver rights"—the rights of caregivers, women and men both, to a level of public assistance for their caregiving work.[47] This has consequences for everyone who spends substantial parts of their adult lives caring for the needs of dependents, whether small children or the elderly, and who incurs substantial costs by virtue of so doing. Pregnant women, parents of small children, and the grown children of elderly parents, by virtue of their caregiving obligations, are not capable of the sort of independence that is so highly valued in a culture that prizes rugged individualism above all else. Caregivers are less independent, and therefore less autonomous, than those with no such obligations. Someone tied to the needs of others is that much less free to live the wealth-maximizing, self-regarding, autonomous life presupposed by, and valorized by, a free-market economy in the first place. The right to an abortion gives women a right not to be a caregiver, but at the cost of rhetorically making the difficulties of caregiving all the harder to publicly share, should she opt for it. For privileged women, this is not such a terrible trade-off: an economically secure woman gets a right to terminate a pregnancy, and can more or less put up with the bolstered legitimacy of an overly privatized system of health and child care. She can exit the paid labor market for a few years to raise her child, or she can split those obligations with a supportive spouse or partner and continue to work part-time, or she can delegate to others the caregiving work for substantially less than she herself earns so that she need not interrupt her own wage labor. She can, through one of these routes, simply absorb the expense of these choices. The woman only marginally capable of supporting even herself, however, faces

47 Robin West, *The Right To Care*, *in* The Subject of Care: Feminist Perspectives on Dependency 88 (Eva Feder Kittay & Ellen K. Feder eds., 2002).

a choice between parenting and severe impoverishment, on the one hand, and forgoing children on the other. Are we truly comfortable, morally, with a world that we have created, in which only rich people can parent satisfactorily? Is it a just world, in which poor people are told that perhaps they really should not have children, particularly if they cannot find someone to marry first? The sheer cruelty of this is what the legitimating rhetoric of choice, and of individual rights to privacy, liberty, and dignity, all mask.

B. Democracy

In the last 30 years, a growing body of scholarship from critical legal scholars and progressive political theorists has decried the political Left's heavy reliance on courts, rights, and constitutional law as vehicles for progressive victories, which might better have been secured through ordinary politics.[48] Several themes have emerged from this literature, some of it going back to early critiques of rights penned by the CLS movement,[49] some of it more contemporary and based in understandings of the workings of institutions.[50] Three themes in particular recur in this literature, which, I believe, are of relevance to *Roe*. I will quickly review these concerns, spell out the ways in which *Roe* is exemplary of them, and then suggest in a bit more detail a fourth.

The first concerns the logic of countermajoritarian, constitutional rights. Echoing Marxist critiques, critical scholars have argued for well over a quarter of a century that while constitutional rights in this country have indeed served the interests of minorities, as their celebrants claim, it has primarily been the interests, privileges, and entitlements of not particularly embattled property owners either to retain their wealth or to buy and sell assets on open markets for profit, against the wishes of those who would challenge them. What they have protected all that privilege against, primarily, is the majoritarian, democratically expressed wish of the less well off—peons, workers, renters, mobs, the poor, or the masses—for a bit of state-sponsored, democratically inspired, redistribution of wealth. With the advent of progressive rights-based movements in the nineteenth and twentieth centuries, this historical alignment of rights and privilege became mixed. Thus, whatever their propertied pedigree, rights have furthered the causes of abolition, suffrage, labor, and eventually racial justice and reproductive

48 See Kramer, *supra* note 30, at 227–41; Tushnet, *supra* note 29, at 154–63; Larry D. Kramer, *The Supreme Court, 2000 Term--Foreword: We the Court*, 115 HARV. L. REV. 4, 9 (2001); Jeremy Waldron, *The Core of the Case Against Judicial Review*, 115 YALE L.J. 1346, 1353 (2006); Robin West, *Ennobling Politics*, *in* EMPIRE OF FORCE (H. Jefferson Powell & James Boyd White eds., 2009).

49 See, e.g., Tushnet, *supra* note 8, at 1363–64 (developing four critiques of rights stemming from early CLS critiques: an instability critique, an indeterminacy critique, a false consciousness critique, and a legitimation critique).

50 See Kramer, *supra* note 30, at 251–52; Waldron, *supra* note 48, at 1386–90.

freedom. Nevertheless, purely as a matter of rhetoric and logic, rights are the coin of the realm of the relatively entitled, so to speak, and will likely always remain so. Regardless of content, then, rights and rights rhetoric (or "rights talk," as it used to be called) tend to protect pre-existing property entitlements to that which is owned, and contract entitlements to that which can be privately traded, even if just indirectly, by discrediting precisely the democratic, popular, majoritarian, and political deliberation and reform it would take to upend them. Rights generally protect entitlements against political encroachment rather than satisfy even dire need. Any progressive gains achieved by rights must therefore be understood as risking some degree of entrenchment of current distributions of power that favor a wealthy minority against majoritarian redistribution, simply because of the use of rights discourse.

Second, critical scholars argued forcefully that court-generated rights discourse in this country has tended to reinforce pernicious distinctions between the private and the public realms of social life, largely because of its cribbed insistence that injustice almost by definition emanates only from states and from state action rather than from private actors of any sort. What judicially discovered rights mostly give us is a way to ward off overly intrusive or irrational state involvement in our private lives.[51] There are two problems with this. The first has been much belabored: court-generated rights perversely protect rather than stand as a challenge to forms of oppression that are distinctively private, such as unfair employment or contract regimes, patriarchal privilege, or private sphere racism, all of which are accomplished by private actors in some "private" realm.[52] But second, and less noted, the valorization of the "private" realm comes at the expense of degradation of the "public." Consequently, the public/private distinction at the heart of rights discourse feeds a distrust of the machinations of public deliberation—including processes of government, of democracy, and collective action—the use of which is essential to any sort of genuinely progressive political movement against private injustice.[53] For this reason as well, particularly in the economic sphere, the result is an undue, and perhaps unwitting, regressive conservatism.

The third cost of court-created rights identified by rights critics stems from concerns about the methods of reasoning courts employ. Progressive victories secured through adjudication rather than politics must be or at least aim to be consistent with past practice—they must mesh more or less seamlessly with pre-existing precedent, policies, decisions, institutional arrangements, and forms. This makes the progressive victory achieved through the courts—including rights-based victories—relatively conservative, compared to what might be achieved politically: the restraint of integrity with the past makes it not even theoretically

51 See Kennedy, *supra* note 9, at 181–82; Tushnet, *supra* note 8, at 1382.

52 See, e.g., Horwitz, *supra* note 9, at 399–404; Tushnet, *supra* note 8, at 1392–93.

53 See Horwitz, *supra* note 9, at 402–03 (arguing that a "troubling aspect of natural rights discourse is its tendency to posit a sharp distinction between a public realm of coercion and a 'natural,' private realm of freedom").

possible that the victory will be a truly radical one. At the same time, the apparent gain in permanence, depth, certainty, or profundity that seemingly comes from the adjudicative victory being secured through law—the perception that the "right" so discovered is something that has always been deeply embedded in a system of law that has its own roots in antiquity, and is therefore truly there and secured against precipitous change—is an illusion. Rights found by courts can also be abandoned by courts. The right is hostage to the whims of the people on the Supreme Court rather than a working majority of a Senate. It is nevertheless just as much hostage to whimsy. It is a product of power, no less than any traffic ordinance passed by a city council, and just as subject to recall.[54]

These progressive critiques of judicially created rights, pressed in different ways by critical scholars over the past 30 years, all suggest limits to the progressive potential of *Roe v. Wade*. Let me take them in the order outlined above. First, the critics complained that constitutional rights, in spite of their occasional progressive potential, have tended to protect individuals' commodificationist rights to contract and property rather than to serve people's needs, and would likely continue to do so. The right created by *Roe* is no exception. *Roe*'s holding, whether couched in terms of liberty or privacy, did indeed quickly devolve into a bare negative contract right to buy a particular medical service—an abortion—free of moralistic intrusion by state legislators who would paternalistically intervene into that—or any other—consensual purchase. The right became a stick in a bundle of negative rights to our bodies and labor, that we wield in order to keep the state out of our sex lives: we have a right to birth control, a right to same-sex sex, limited rights to produce and consume pornography, and a right to engage in the commercial and medical consultation necessary to secure an abortion to end the pregnancies in which all that protected sex sometimes result.[55] It has furthered the cause of unfettered sexuality in open markets, for purchase and otherwise, by giving us a property right in the pregnancy and a contract right to purchase the means to end it. It has done nothing, however, to further the satisfaction of the positive needs—whether understood as rights or not—of either pregnant women or parents. By relentlessly celebrating negative rights as the route to women's liberty and equality, and thereby impliedly castigating politically secured legislation as the evil against which negative rights—and hence, liberty and equality both—are constructed, it has undermined the case for the very sorts of positive legislative schemes that might do so.

---

54 See Mark Tushnet, Red, White, and Blue: A Critical Analysis of Constitutional Law 46–57 (1988); Kennedy, *supra* note 9, at 202–06 (arguing that the Supreme Court's reversals on rights demonstrate the manipulability of rights arguments); Tushnet, *supra* note 8, at 1373–75 (arguing that courts can always reverse rights rulings by reinterpreting the background contexts).

55 See Thomas C. Grey, *Eros, Civilization and the Burger Court*, Law & Contemp. Probs., Summer 1980, at 83 (making this prediction).

Second, and as the rights critiques of the "public–private" distinction presaged, the libertarian rhetoric of the opinion has indeed focused attention on pernicious state intermeddling in women's lives, rather than either the private sphere appropriation of women's sexuality caused by male sexual aggression, or the appropriation of women's reproductive and parenting labor in that sphere, as the primary limit on women's equality and liberty. Catharine MacKinnon warned in her early critiques of *Roe* that the pro-choice community ran the risk that it would further obfuscate both the fact and nature of private sphere sexual subordination by aggressively shrouding that sphere, and the subordination that occurs within it, in a constitutionally protected veil of laudatory privacy.[56] The right to abortion, she argued, might further privatize the private by constitutionalizing it, and by so doing thicken the veil of privilege around intimate life, and therefore around the sexual subordinations that occur within it. Events have not proven her wrong to have so worried. The same is true, although she did not so argue, with respect to women's labor, no less than women's sexuality, and with respect to the economic sphere, no less than the sexual. Parenting is economic activity, as well as the consequence of sexual acts that may have been coerced. By insulating the private economic realm of parental choice against public critique and intervention, the economic deprivations occasioned by overly privatized parenting are further shielded against public intervention. The effect is not only the valorization of the "private" activities of sex and parenting, but also the denigration of the public sphere of politics. The public assistance that would be required to alleviate costs borne in private is cast as unwarranted intrusion into an exalted sphere of private economic life, rather than warranted assistance with an almost impossibly privatized burden.

And third, and just as a critical sensibility should have predicted, the right has indeed proven to be both relatively regressive and seemingly unstable. This right's genesis in "law" rather than "politics" has not yielded the permanence or security or respect that law promises. *Roe*, conceived as a "right" so as to withstand the whims of hostile political opinion that would upset it, still seemingly hangs by a legal thread. The Court can broaden it, narrow it, uphold it, or overrule it. Meanwhile, and ironically, the activity it primarily protects—legal and safe abortion in the first trimester of an unwanted pregnancy—enjoys strong majoritarian political support. Rendering legal abortion a constitutional right, rather than an ordinary political one, may not have made it any more secure than it otherwise would have been. We have seemingly gained the regressive features of constitutionalizing this right, without enjoying the gain of security or stability that constitutionalism promises.

There is, though, an additional and less appreciated cost to democracy of conceptualizing legal abortion as a judicially created right that the rights critics never touched on, but is worth addressing more expansively. This cost too has particular poignancy in the domain of abortion rights. When the Court claims privileged and even monopolistic access to the language of moral principle,

56 See Catharine A. MacKinnon, Toward a Feminist Theory of the State 184–94 (1989).

reasoned discourse, and civil dialogue, it suggests a lesser, distasteful view of the politics it thereby limits. Representative politics is routinely construed by liberal devotees of court-generated rights as the realm of bald power: whimsical, arbitrary, emotive, unprincipled, rent seeking, horse trading, reflective of the "interests" of a basically infantile constituency that does nothing but form arbitrary preferences for unprincipled—unthoughtful—reasons.[57] The public whose interests and preferences are so reflected in politics, in Congress, and in the legislative branches of state governments is portrayed as prone to hysteria, as a body that acts on whims and winds of political sentiment, and as given to unpredictable moments of mob mentality. Politics, as construed by the Court and its liberal devotees, is anything but the highest art of which the species is capable, and anything but deliberative. The Court, by contrast, expresses law—and when it does so, it speaks in the language of principle, reason, rationality, integrity, consistency with the past, and dispassionate concern for the future. It speaks with intelligence and wisdom both; it assimilates knowledge from history and judiciously weighs—rather than reacts to—the desires of the interested parties of the present. It takes the long view. It is attentive to enduring principles. It deliberates; it does not react. It engages in civil discourse. The Court, not the Congress, is the institution that permits rational and respectful dissent. It is the Court that keeps the civil conversation going in this country. Therefore, law, expressed through courts, is our highest and best form of politics. Meanwhile, our actual politics—what happens in Washington or Annapolis or Sacramento or downtown Wasilla—is everything this adjudicative conception of our highest politics is not. It is low life.

---

57 For some of the public choice literature that so argues, see ANTHONY DOWNS, AN ECONOMIC THEORY OF DEMOCRACY 28 (1957) ("[Politicians] act solely in order to attain the income, prestige, and power which come from being in office"); Gary S. Becker, *A Theory of Competition Among Pressure Groups for Political Influence*, 98 Q.J. ECON. 371, 371–74 (1983) (describing political action as competition among interest groups); and Sam Peltzman, *Toward a More General Theory of Regulation*, 19 J.L. & ECON. 211, 214 (1976) (theorizing regulators as driven by interest in attaining votes and dollars). But see Mark Kelman, *On Democracy-Bashing: A Skeptical Look at the Theoretical and "Empirical" Practice of the Public Choice Movement*, 74 VA. L. REV. 199, 202 (1988) (arguing that public choice theory views the democratic arena as an "arena of theft" marked by "stagnation, wasteful rent-seeking, and negative sum games"). Liberal constitutionalists also describe the representative political branches as less principled than the judicial, although not so baldly. See Ronald Dworkin, *A Reply by Ronald Dworkin*, *in* RONALD DWORKIN AND CONTEMPORARY JURISPRUDENCE 247, 270 (Marshall Cohen ed., 1983) (distinguishing, in a reply to Professor Donald Regan, legal from legislative rights, on the grounds that the former but not the latter must be consistent with principles provided by the best justification of the past). Frank Michelman famously described the Court, rather than Congress, as the political institution that best fits the civic ideals of equal participation in a democracy. Frank Michelman, *Law's Republic*, 97 YALE L.J. 1493, 1496–99 (1988); Frank I. Michelman, *The Supreme Court, 1985 Term--Foreword: Traces of Self-Government*, 100 HARV. L. REV. 4, 74–77 (1986).

Roe v. Wade and its progeny are not, of course, responsible for the degradation of politics that has become the natural counterpart of the institution of judicial review, its high-minded justifications, and the reverence we now accord it. It does, though, exemplify it. When the Court speaks of the hallowed right to privacy in which it locates abortion, it speaks of the sanctity of marriage and family,[58] of individual liberty,[59] of equality or dignity,[60] of respect, and of the great and deepest mysteries of life.[61] It speaks of the constituents of individual identity, and of what is most important to a well-led life,[62] of the grand promises of the Fourteenth Amendment,[63] of the importance of precedent to political and social order,[64] of the needs of all of us to be free of a "jurisprudence of doubt,"[65] and of the importance of consistency, integrity, and moral principle in decision-making and in our law. The contrast between what the Court and commentators say when speaking of this right, and what abortion rights advocates say in the public sphere when defending or addressing the need for legal abortion, could not be starker. When advocates speak of abortion in the public sphere and outside the courts, they do not talk, for the most part, about a "jurisprudence of doubt" or the importance of precedent or of principled judicial decision-making, of liberty, dignity, or even equality. Rather, they most often speak of women's bodies. They speak of the dangers to women's health that are posed by many pregnancies. They speak of the lives that have been lost to illegal abortion. They talk a lot about hemorrhaging, and of women and girls bleeding to death in botched back-alley abortions. They speak of fear and terror. They speak of lives shortened, or narrowed, or rendered mean and uncompromising by dangerous pregnancies, or too many unplanned pregnancies, or too many children, or too much mothering. They speak of shattered dreams, or girls with low or no expectations for their own futures. They often speak of abusive stepfamily members, of domestic violence, and child rape. They speak of intentional, deeply wanted pregnancies gone wrong: they talk about diseased

58 See Roe v. Wade, 410 U.S. 113, 152–53 (1973) (holding that the right to privacy extends to "activities relating to marriage," "procreation," and "family relationships"); Griswold v. Connecticut, 381 U.S. 479, 495 (1965) (Goldberg, J., concurring) ("[T]he rights to marital privacy and to marry and raise a family are of similar order and magnitude as the fundamental rights specifically protected").

59 Roe, 410 U.S. at 153 (arguing that the right to privacy is founded on personal liberty).

60 Gonzales v. Carhart, 550 U.S. 124, 157–60 (2007) (Kennedy, J.) (discussing the state interest in respecting the dignity of human life, while upholding the Partial-Birth Abortion Ban Act).

61 Planned Parenthood of Se. Pa. v. Casey, 505 U.S. 833, 851 (1992) (defining the heart of the liberty protected by due process as the "right to define one's own concept of existence, of meaning, of the universe, and of the mystery of human life").

62 See *id.* at 851 ("At the heart of liberty is the right to define one's own concept of existence, of meaning, of the universe, and of the mystery of human life").

63 *Id.* at 846–50.

64 *Id.* at 854–69.

65 *Id.* at 844.

fetuses, miscarriages, and tragic choices. They talk about stillbirths and life-threatening complications. They speak of the earthy, present, demanding, felt, fought-over need of women to control their bodies and fate.[66]

The contrast on the other side of this debate, between the rhetoric of the Court and commentators on the one hand, and activists on the other, is if anything even more stark, although it is beginning to narrow somewhat, at least if *Gonzales v. Carhart* is any guide.[67] In the public square, pro-life advocates speak, argue, petition, canvass, and beseech us to attend to the biological lives of unborn babies. They wield pictures of fetal life and body parts. They deploy sonograms and give voice to silent screams. They push their listeners to identify with the unborn, to open their sympathies and their hearts to the least of these, to pull fetal life into the human community, to recognize us in them and them in us. Conservative legal critics of *Roe v. Wade*, on the other hand, speak rarely if at all of any of this.[68] Rather, they speak of originalism,[69] of constitutional integrity,[70] of the close readings of texts, of plain meaning, and of the lack of the word "privacy" in the text of the Constitution.[71] They worry over the integrity, identity, and future of the Constitution. There is little talk, either on the Court or in the pages of scholarly commentary that is hostile to *Roe*, about fetal life, silent screams, or unborn babies, and even less about the struggles facing women with unwanted or dangerous pregnancies. The discussion is principled, constitutional, and historical. It does not stem from a visceral identification with or sympathy for the plight of murdered babies.

This momentous gulf in the substance of pro-choice and pro-life arguments on the street, versus pro-choice and pro-life arguments on the Court, is understandable:

66 In Webster v. Reproductive Health Services, the National Abortion Rights Action League (NARAL) made the strategic decision to file as amici what came to be known as the "Voices Brief" in that and subsequent Supreme Court abortion cases. Brief for the Amici Curiae Women Who Have Had Abortions and Friends of Amici Curiae in Support of Appellees, Webster v. Reprod. Health Servs., 492 U.S. 490 (1989) (No. 88-605), 1989 WL 1115239. The Voices Brief allowed women to speak to the issue of legal abortion in their own voices, and on the basis of their real concerns, rather than through the distorting lens of legal doctrine. For a general discussion, see Laura R. Woliver, The Political Geographies of Pregnancy 88–92 (2002), which discusses the Voices Brief and NARAL's "Silent No More" campaign. Both intended to present women's stories of illegal abortions to the public.

67 550 U.S. 124, 150–54 (2007) (describing partial-birth abortion, in graphic and morally charged detail).

68 There are of course exceptions. *See*, e.g., Paulsen, *supra* note 5, at 212 (comparing legal abortion with the Holocaust).

69 See Bork, *supra* note 6, at 143–60 (arguing for originalism).

70 See Ely, *supra* note 6, at 946–49 (arguing against the legality, as well as the correctness, of Roe v. Wade).

71 *Id.* at 927–29 (criticizing the inappropriate use of rights inferred from the Constitution).

the issue facing the Court, after all, is not the morality of abortion, but the power of the states to criminalize it. The contrasting substance of the arguments, however, is in turn reflected in contrasting styles and modes of discourse—and it is that contrast that I wish to problematize. The clerks and Justices of the Court craft arguments for and against legal abortion from the principles, precedent, and constitutional phrases found in the pages of past case law. They then make analogies from those principles and precedents. They reason closely or loosely from original texts—either of the Constitution or of the cases that interpret it. Public advocates of free and legal abortion as well as public advocates for criminalization of abortion speak in a different modulation entirely. They protest, march, yell, organize, canvass, petition, and carry posters depicting coat hangers and fetuses, dead women, and body parts. They make demands rather than arguments: that states either protect the least of us, or stay off our backs. And on both sides, the demands are visceral.

These contrasting modes of discourse around abortion—reasoned, from the bench, and impassioned, on the street—have fueled the perception that the Court, rather than the public square, is the necessary and proper place to decide the legality or criminalization of abortion. The Court epitomizes reason, dispassion, and principled discussion. The debate in the public square epitomizes the hysteria against which the Courts, law, and rights themselves do combat, with the sword of sweet reason. The Court and its product—opinions—jointly constitute and embody the nobility of law. The political branch that represents us, particularly at the local level, is ignoble.

Now, there is much to be said against this picture—most of it already said by the CLS scholars in the 1970s and 1980s. In a nutshell, they argued, the Court's reasoning is neither as rational nor as principled as might first appear.[72] True enough, but this argument missed and itself obfuscated what might be a more consequential point. The now-conventional division of labor spelt out above—that the Court exercises reason in the pursuit of principle, while the legislative branch is an escape valve for the emotive excesses of various publics and an arena for horse trading among their infantile interests and desires—is untrue, not only because it so discounts emotionality, infantilism, and horse trading on the Court, but also because it understates the seriousness, public mindedness, and capacity for reasoned discourse of legislators. Courts are less than fully reasonable, to be sure. And, Congress is more than emotive.

But even that friendly amendment understates the damage done by this liberal conception of judicial wisdom and legislative infantilism. The deeper harm is that it misstates the role of passion in politics. Politics at its best, not just its worst, is an admixture of passion and principle. Signs, pictures, and images that evoke empathy may be ingredients of mob un-think, but they are also necessary components of any movement that aims to broaden our moral compass—if we do not think of either women or fetal life as a part of us, we will not legislate, as a people, to

72 *See*, e.g., Tushnet, *supra* note 54, at 147–68.

protect them. Any politics, but certainly progressive politics, must seek to expand affective sympathies. The derogation of passionate politics, so deeply embedded in the jurisprudence of an activist, anti-majoritarian, and rights-oriented Court, systematically belittles precisely the sort of politics that is obviously not sufficient, but is likely necessary to any sort of expanded progressive political vision.

Finally, the traditional identification and elevation of reasoned discourse with the Court, which is at the heart of rights-oriented constitutionalism, not only pits the principled decision-making, of which the Court is so proud, against passion, but also pits itself against compromise. Principle cannot abide compromise, but politics cannot proceed without it. The public discussion of abortion has become as raw as it has, in part, because of that fact. When we battle this issue out in court as a clash of principles, we develop those martial arts of the mind that are necessary to that battle. We lose, though, the arts of political compromise. We lose the ability and willingness to craft deals we can live with, the nimbleness of giving a little and getting a little, the commitment to the project of living with and under the roofs that compromise creates. There is much to worry over, of course, in compromise, but there is also much to applaud: it is neighborly, civil, and inclusive.

Adjudicating abortion rights over the last quarter century and more may have dulled our capacities and appreciation for both impassioned, engaged politics and civil compromise. It is not at all clear that the result has been a stronger rather than weaker set of reproductive rights and liberties.

C. Aspiration

Roberto Unger famously complained of the truncated thinking that constitutes the core of canonical common and constitutional law texts.[73] The "weighing of policies" that informs common law cases in the absence of clear legal rules, for example, flattens even ordinary normative argument: policies are listed on each side, one side declared more compelling, and the case decided. This is a cartoon version of decent policy analysis. Principled decision-making fares no better. The same is true of what I call aspirational vision—arguments about what we should do now, based on a view of what we should ideally be, or aspire to become. Aspirational visions of what justice requires get truncated as they get litigated: they are cut to size so as to fit the demands of doctrine, of standing requirements, of what the fifth Justice might believe, and of the principles laid down by the past. Thus, *Brown* truncated the claims of racial justice that motivated those who brought the case: it was reduced to a bare right not to be irrationally discriminated against by the state on the basis of skin color. *Miranda* likewise: what was trimmed was an aspiration of a decent criminal justice system, not riddled by racism and contempt of criminal defendants. What remained after the trimming was a crude right to be "Mirandized."

73 Roberto Mangabeira Unger, *The Critical Legal Studies Movement*, 96 Harv. L. Rev. 561, 576–77 (1983).

Nowhere, though, has this truncating dynamic been more on display than in the context of abortion rights and the aspirational vision of which it was originally a part. The constitutional right to abort a fetus, and the right to be left alone on which it is built, is as hollow as it is in part because it represents just such a truncation of the aspirational feminist vision of reproductive justice from which it was forged. For most of the first two-thirds of the century just passed, legal abortion was understood by feminists who sought it as a component of a conception of women's equality that also included a demand for a robust public role in childcare, heightened protections against rape and domestic violence, equal employment opportunities, equal pay for comparable worth, and inclusion of women in the public spheres of politics and governance.[74] Abortion rights were a branch on a tree, the trunk of which was the aspiration of equal citizenship and whatever social reimagining of basic structures of work and governance would be necessary to achieve it.

At least according to contemporary social and legal historians of the time period, advocacy for legal abortion was in effect severed from its trunk largely because of the politics surrounding the Equal Rights Amendment (ERA) movement[75] and then transplanted into the quite different terrain of individual liberty. It then became its own "tree," rooted not so much in women's equality, but in marital, medical, and sexual privacy. Without second-guessing the then-compelling reasons for doing so, it is clear in retrospect that this re-rooting strategy carried costs beyond even the legitimation and democratic costs outlined above—it also carried costs for our understanding of what an abortion right is and why we should have one. Understood as one of a series of Supreme Court cases, *Roe v. Wade* and the right it articulates become a chapter in a narrative authored, developed, and controlled by the Court, rather than a part of a narrative of women's rights authored, developed, and controlled by feminists, progressives, or women's rights devotees. Abortion rights are a part of a story consisting of Supreme Court cases, not a part of a story consisting of political victories for women's equality, healthcare, or poor families.

And what is that story? Of course there are several narratives that can be told based on these cases, just as there are any number of patterned ways to assemble beads on a string. One might, for example, think of *Roe* as the first in a possible trajectory of future cases revitalizing a libertarian and anti-moralistic strand of

---

74 See Reva Siegel, *Constitutional Culture, Social Movement Conflict and Constitutional Change: The Case of the De Facto ERA*, 94 Cal. L. Rev. 1323, 1395–97 (2006) (arguing that abortion advocacy shifted to liberty and privacy rationales when abortion rights became disaggregated from the equality thrust of the ERA movement); *see also* Woliver, *supra* note 66, at 82 (arguing that the emergence of abortion in the 1960s transformed birth control, family planning, and women's health politics).

75 Siegel, *supra* note 74, at 1395–97. See generally David J. Garrow, Liberty and Sexuality: The Right to Privacy and the Making of Roe v. Wade 293–310 (1994) (describing the conception of abortion as an individual liberty right).

Lochner v. New York.[76] *Lochner* famously found a right to contract for labor in the Constitution that in turn trumped democratic control of labor markets, and *Roe* likewise found a right to contract for an abortion that trumped democratic control of markets for reproductive services. *Roe*, then, like *Lawrence v. Texas*,[77] might be sensibly viewed as a stepping stone toward a revitalized libertarian understanding of the relation between citizen, state, and contract. The libertarian and anti-moralistic language in *Lawrence* also supports such a reading, as commentators have noted.[78] Perhaps the extreme administrative and legal intervention into markets that characterized so much of the twentieth century, whether prompted by moralistic impulses or by redistributive impulses, is the anomaly. The norm may be an ecumenical understanding of the individual liberty protected by the substantive prong of the Due Process Clause—a liberty that arguably protects the sale and purchase of labor, contraception, abortions, subprime mortgages, high interest loans, prostitution services, surrogacy services, babies, gambling contracts, guns, or kidneys, and protects all of these contractual transactions against either moralistic or paternalistic intervention. That is one way to string the beads.

Another way to string the beads aligns *Roe* with other cases that establish what I call "lethal rights," or defensive rights to kill. On this understanding, *Roe* is part of a narrative that also prominently includes *District of Columbia v. Heller*.[79] Thus, the Court in *Heller* created, or discovered, a right to own a handgun, desired not only by gun enthusiasts and hunters, but also by citizens who worry that the state will not defend them against aggressors in their home or elsewhere. The right to own a gun, read in this way, is the complement to the Court's refusal to grant a positive right to a state's protection against private violence:[80] if you do not have a right to the state's protection against violence, but you do have a right to kill in self-defense, then it becomes quite natural that you must have a prior right to the arms necessary to exercise it. Viewed as a bead on that string, we might understand *Roe* as granting a right to kill fetal life, made all the more desirable by virtue of the state's refusal to create meaningful systems of health and child care, and the Court's refusal even to consider the possibility of creating a right to such assistance. A right to an abortion looks all the more desirable if one has no right to assistance in dealing with the economic stresses of parenting. It becomes

76 198 U.S. 45 (1905).

77 539 U.S. 558, 582–83 (2003) (striking down an antisodomy law in part because of the claim that a statute resting solely on moralistic condemnation is an unconstitutional infringement of liberty under the Equal Protection Clause).

78 Randy Barnett, *Justice Kennedy's Libertarian Revolution: Lawrence v. Texas*, 2002–2003 Cato Sup. Ct. Rev. 21 (2003).

79 128 S. Ct. 2783, 2793 (2008) (holding that the right to bear arms is historically a right to self-defense).

80 DeShaney v. Winnebago County Dep't of Soc. Servs., 489 U.S. 189, 195–97 (1989) (holding that due process does not impose any duty on a state to provide members of the general public with adequate protective services).

another "defensive" lethal right, necessitated, in part, by an excessively minimalist state.[81] The rights created by the Court in *Heller* and *Roe* have more than a slight family resemblance.

Of course, neither of these radically libertarian understandings of *Roe* are the narratives preferred by *Roe*'s pro-choice celebrants, or by the Court itself. Rather, the dominant narrative puts *Roe* in line with cases protecting sexual expression, not personal liberty, and not self-defense. On the dominant understanding, *Roe* is on a string of beads with *Griswold v. Connecticut*,[82] *Eisenstadt v. Baird*,[83] and *Lawrence*,[84] not with *Lochner*, and certainly not with *Heller*. What *Roe* does, along with *Griswold*, *Eisenstadt*, and *Lawrence*, is protect an individual's right to have nonreproductive sex. What is stressed, on this story, is the consequence for sexual freedom to be garnered from the right to be free of the risk of pregnancy.

There are undoubtedly other ways to read *Roe*. There are many ways to string a finite number of beads. Nevertheless, the class is not infinite. It is not possible, for example, to read *Roe* as protective of marital, as opposed to individual, privacy.[85] That is foreclosed by *Eisenstadt*. It is not possible, I believe, to read *Roe* as a part of an adjudicative, narrative movement toward a robust conception of reproductive justice. That is ruled out by the right's negativity. Reproductive justice requires a state that provides a network of support for the processes of reproduction: protection against rape and access to affordable and effective birth control, healthcare, including but not limited to abortion services, prenatal care, support in childbirth and postpartum, support for breastfeeding mothers, early childcare for infants and toddlers, income support for parents who stay home to care for young babies, and high quality public education for school age children. The Court is not equipped to mandate any of that, and has stated repeatedly that it is not inclined even to suggest that a citizen might have a right to a state that does so. The negative right that it has recognized suggests something very different: it suggests at best a right to nonreproductive sex, and at worst, a right to end a pregnancy by killing the fetus so as to free oneself of the burden of impossible parental obligations in an unjust world. Either way, it is not all that clear that women, parents, or children are the beneficiaries.

---

81 The controversial "right to die" might also be viewed as a right necessitated, in part, by the lack of a right to healthcare, including palliative care. See generally THE CASE AGAINST ASSISTED SUICIDE: FOR THE RIGHT TO END-OF-LIFE CARE (Kathleen Foley & Herbert Hendin eds., 2002) (including arguments for a right to assisted suicide as well as arguments for increased palliative care instead of a right to assisted suicide). For a criticism of the argument against assisted suicide, see Ani B. Satz, *The Case Against Assisted Suicide Reexamined*, 100 MICH. L. REV. 1380 (2002).

82 381 U.S. 479 (1965).

83 405 U.S. 438 (1972).

84 539 U.S. 558 (2003).

85 See Eisenstadt, 405 U.S. at 453 (making clear that privacy protects individual rather than marital privacy).

III. The Opportunity Costs of Constitutionalized Abortion Rights

Reproductive justice is a political and moral project. The Court-created abortion right is a judicial and constitutional one. How might the world be different, if the pro-choice community focused on the former a bit more, and the latter a bit less? What opportunities have been foregone, by virtue of the constancy of the gaze on courts? What are Roe's "opportunity costs"? This part outlines three: political, rhetorical, and moral.

A. Political Costs

First, movement toward a broadened reproductive justice movement could prompt a fresh look at the pro-life movement, which is different than it was 30 years ago, when it coalesced around the overriding goal of reversing *Roe*.[86] Feminist and progressive theorists and advocates routinely characterize the pro-life movement as aimed at reversing *Roe*, and as committed to the project of requiring women to carry pregnancies to term, primarily so as to enforce restrictive and Victorian roles of motherhood, femininity, and sexuality. This depiction, however, is dated. At least parts of that movement, as expressed both by its leadership and by its members, are not single-mindedly focused on overturning Roe or on criminalizing abortion, and are not particularly interested in using either pregnancy or motherhood as a way to punish premarital or extramarital sexual activity. Thus, a fair amount of pro-life feminist scholarship is now focused as much on increasing public support for parenting—both for its own sake, and as a means of minimizing the number of abortions—as with minimizing abortions by criminalizing them and incarcerating the doctors that perform them.[87] The change is just as clear outside of the law review pages. Websites such as MomsRising[88] seek to organize mothers—both pro-life and pro-choice, but the focus seems to be on the former—around what have to date been almost exclusively progressive-feminist goals: paid maternity leave, publicly funded childcare, more public assistance for single mothers, more support across the board for working families. These Internet-based movements express more interest in helping women and teens through their pregnancies and with their families, and less or no interest in punishing teenagers for premarital sex.

86 *See* Salmon, *supra* note 34 (reporting on the shift of several prominent pro-life leaders and groups against strategies focusing on criminalization of abortion, to a focus on reducing incidences through pregnancy prevention as well as lowering the cost of mothering).

87 *See*, e.g., Elizabeth R. Schiltz, *Should Bearing the Child Mean Bearing All the Cost?: A Catholic Perspective on the Sacrifice of Motherhood and the Common Good*, 10 Logos 15 (2007) (arguing for a blend of Catholic and feminist social thought on issues pertaining to support for child-raising).

88 MomsRising, http://www.momsrising.org (last visited March 11, 2009).

By putting legal abortion in its place—that is, putting it in the context of a reproductive justice agenda pursued in the legislative arena—pro-choice advocates might find common cause with pro-life movements that responsibly seek greater justice for pregnant women who choose to carry their pregnancies to term, working families, and struggling mothers. I do not mean to suggest that progressive-feminist advocates and scholars have not been actively seeking these goals. Of course they have, and for a good long while. But at the level of theory, the pro-choice movement exists in considerable tension with those goals.[89] And at the level of politics, the antipathy of pro-choice and pro-life advocates has veiled the possibility of coalitions on these issues, where interests are in fact aligned.[90] Pro-life and pro-choice movements have a common interest in reducing the incidence of abortion, both by minimizing the number of unintended pregnancies and lowering the cost of mothering. They should also have a common interest in protecting the ordinary legal rights and interests of pregnant women who complete their pregnancies—rights that also are threatened by a legal regime that generally neglects the demands of reproductive justice.[91] It might be time to give ordinary politics a chance to achieve common goals.

89 For an early statement regarding the tension between the negative logic of Roe and the struggles of drug-addicted mothers, see Dorothy E. Roberts, *Punishing Drug Addicts Who Have Babies: Women of Color, Equality, and the Right of Privacy*, 104 Harv. L. Rev. 1419, 1477–78 (1991) (arguing that the negative right of privacy created in *Roe* is not helpful to drug-addicted mothers).

90 Lynn M. Paltrow, Executive Director of the National Advocates for Pregnant Women, has decried the fragmentation and also has worked assiduously to bridge the gap from the pro-choice side. See Lynn M. Paltrow, *Towards a Real Culture of Life*, TomPaine.com, March 12, 2007, http://www.tompaine.com/articles/2007/03/12/towards_a_real_culture_of_life.php.

91 Both groups, for example, should have a joint interest in protecting the currently embattled rights of pregnant women to make choices regarding their modes of delivery, or of pregnant teenagers to a full education, of pregnant inmates not to be shackled during their deliveries, of new mothers to breastfeed, of mothers of children conceived in rape to be free of coercive pressures by their rapists, and of drug-infected pregnant women to be free of incarceration and have access to healthcare. On shackling female prisoners during pregnancy, see Geraldine Doetzer, *Hard Labor: The Legal Implications of Shackling Female Inmates During Pregnancy and Childbirth*, 14 Wm. & Mary J. Women & L. 363, 372–73 (2008) (arguing that shackling inmates during childbirth is unconstitutional). On protecting the rights of mothers to control their deliveries, see April L. Cherry, *Roe's Legacy: The Nonconsensual Medical Treatment of Pregnant Women and Implications for Female Citizenship*, 6 U. Pa. J. Const. L. 723, 732–36 (2004) (arguing that the structure of *Roe* has led to restrictions on pregnant women's medical choices in the later stages of pregnancy by creating a constitutionally protected state interest in the fetus).

B. Rhetorical Costs

Third, turning our attention away from the courts might prompt a profitable return to pragmatism and away from principle in the formulation of arguments for legal abortion. Principled argument on this issue, perhaps like any other, can take us only so far. It does not follow, though, that the alternative is unthinking chaos. There are pragmatic reasons that the power to make this decision should rest with the pregnant woman or girl: she is the one physically burdened for a substantial period of time by the pregnancy, she is the one faced with the decision to raise or relinquish a baby, she is the one to bear the burden of motherhood with little support from the public sphere should she carry the pregnancy to term, and so on. Giving this power over to husbands, fathers, or medical boards when the pregnant woman is the person who will bear the brunt of the decision, and when that "brunt" is as life-altering and as life-shrinking as it currently is, will result in injuries, stunted lives, and some deaths. We should be explaining the pragmatic reasons that women here and now must have control over their own reproductive lives, rather than focus as exclusively as we have on principled constitutional claims that purport to rest on timeless principle.[92] The need to shoehorn arguments for choice into constitutional form has not only forced the "right to an abortion" into its current truncated and negative form, with the costs noted above, it has also muted arguments for reproductive choice that are pragmatic and time-bound. De-constitutionalizing the case for legal abortion, and relocating the argument so as to appeal to legislative and popular audiences, rather than judicial ones, might re-center those claims.

C. Moral Costs

Finally, the focus on the abortion right has diverted resources not only from political and legal possibilities for promoting reproductive justice, but also from other forms of social persuasion, including moral argument, that might reduce the number of unwanted pregnancies women experience, whether they result in live births or not. Bluntly, if women and men were encouraged to be more sexually responsible, there would be fewer unintended pregnancies and less need for abortions or abortion rights. There are two moral constraints in particular on individual sexual behavior that seem particularly compelling, the case for which has been neglected, in part, because of an obsessive fixation on rights.

First, it would behoove the pro-choice community to acknowledge—and then insist—that opposite-sex partners who do not intend to conceive have a compelling

92 For an example of this sort of pragmatic, and explicitly time-bound argument that is clearly intended for a public rather than judicial audience, see Joan C. Williams & Shauna L. Shames, *Mothers' Dreams: Abortion and the High Price of Motherhood*, 6 U. Pa. J. Const. L. 818, 830–40 (2004), which argues that the high price of mothering should be understood as an argument for legal abortion.

moral duty to use birth control. The pro-choice community has focused hard on a right to use birth control and much less on the duty to do so. For purposes of contrast, look at another historical moment. At the height of the AIDS epidemic, the gay male community embraced a "condom code," the purpose of which was to influence, through moral persuasion, the use of condoms, so as to reduce the incidence of recklessly transmitted HIV.[93] In the straight community, there has been nothing even remotely comparable to the condom code with respect to undesired pregnancies. There ought to be. We need a moral code that makes clear that heterosexuals who do not wish to conceive have a duty to use birth control. We currently have none.

Second, a powerful array of societal forces still pushes heterosexual women and girls to have sex that they patently do not desire, some of which leads to unwanted pregnancies. Women who have sex they do not want may regard such sex as a duty, a hassle, a trauma, a bore, a mystery, a pain in the neck, or, perhaps, as something closer to rape—as the cost of staying free of violence. But whether traumatic or boring, unwanted sex that is not enjoyed is alienating to the woman who experiences it: she gives her body over—willfully, but still she gives it over—for use by a man, as a part of a bargain she has struck that gives her no pleasure. All of this, I have argued at length elsewhere, is a serious but largely unrecognized and deeply alienating harm.[94]

Should she then become pregnant, however, and consent to an unwanted pregnancy, the alienating harm is compounded: she now will have a comparable relation with an unwanted fetus that she initially had with the unwanted sex. Again, her body is being used for the service of another, rather than a part of an integrated self. This can be not just unpleasant but injurious down the road. When a woman who has endured an unwanted pregnancy must later reclaim use of her body, whether for remunerative market-based labor, or for sport, or even for relaxation, she might find it difficult to do. She might find that, having given one's body away against the sovereignty of one's own desire, it is not an easy path back. "Gifts" of one's body to sex and pregnancy are not joyous when they are deeply unwanted. The motion picture *Waitress*—in which unwanted sex leads to an unwanted pregnancy that then morphs into a wanted pregnancy, which eventually produces a loved child—was fiction.[95]

From this, I would argue that a girl or young woman owes a moral duty not just to herself but also to her future self not to engage in sex she does not want, and a boy or man has a duty not to engage in sex undesired by his partner. Our current sex education curricula—whether abstinence only or abstinence plus birth control—says nothing of this. Nor do the pro-marriage urban billboards that are one

93 For an excellent commentary on this development, see Marc Spindelman, *Sexuality's Law* (January 16, 2009) (unpublished manuscript, on file with author).

94 See Robin West, *Sex, Law and Consent, in* The Ethics of Consent: Theory and Practice (Alan Wertheimer & William Miller eds., 2009).

95 *Waitress* (Fox Searchlight Pictures 2007).

of the legacies of the Clinton and Bush administrations' war on welfare mothers: the "Marriage Works" and "Virgin: Teach your kids it's not a dirty word" and "I don't give it up and I'm not giving in" messages that now dot city landscapes, as a *quid pro quo* for block grants to aid poor families.[96] These abstinence-only curricula and personal responsibility-enhancing billboards all seemingly presuppose that teenagers universally desire vaginally penetrating sex, but that this sex they all want so intensely is bad, and for various unstated reasons they should not engage in it. We do not see billboards instructing the same population that there is no reason at all not to have sex if they want it—that fully desired sex is good—but that they should indeed abstain from sex they do not desire—that they have a duty to each other and to themselves to do so. We do not see billboards conveying the message that while sex is good, unprotected or unwanted sex is a moral wrong. Why not? A straightforward public relations campaign, aimed at teenagers and young adults, that sought to convey both norms—that while wanted sex is a human good, one has a duty to use contraception to avoid unwanted pregnancy, and a duty to say no to unwanted sex—could not hurt, and it might do a lot of good. It might also bring down the total number of unwanted pregnancies in the world.

IV. From Choice to Reproductive Justice

Pro-choice policies, from the outset, should have been generated by ordinary politics, respectful and reflective of a sex-friendly popular morality, and expressed ultimately in ordinary law. The community of advocates and scholars that held those commitments should have looked to the public, legislators, educators, and social structures, rather than to hoary constitutional principles expressed by not particularly trustworthy oracles, for their meaningful articulation, elaboration, and enforcement. The moment for developing such a politics without interference from the Court, however, has long passed. Nevertheless, both sides—pro-life as well as pro-choice—might yet reclaim at least a degree of such a focus, each from where they now stand. There are particularly compelling reasons for the pro-choice community to do so. Political arguments for reproductive justice, made in political fora and divorced from the adjudicative context, might not carry the specific costs of rights discourse theorized by critical writers and highlighted above. First, they need not rest on a commitment to negative rights and libertarian premises. Women need legal abortion not to ward off undue state interference, but in order to live better and more integrated lives in their families and workplaces both. And to live those better and more integrated lives, they require both reproductive choice

96 See Robin West, Marriage, Sexuality, and Gender 134–35, 173 (2007) (discussing the "Marriage Works" campaigns); Heather Harris, *Marriage Works. Or Does It?: A Pro-Marriage Campaign Pops a Lot of Questions but Provides Few Answers*, The Urbanite Magazine, September 27, 2006, http:// www.urbanitebaltimore.com/sub.cfm?ArticleID=461&IssueID=39&SectionID=4.

and better support for their caregiving obligations, as do the men with whom they might partner. Viewed as pragmatic needs for well-led lives, rather than principled demands for rights, better supports for childcare and legal abortion are both components of an as yet unrealized reproductive justice. Only when elevated to the level of constitutional and timeless principle does the argument for one component seem to undercut the case for the other.

Nor should these arguments be put forward in the context of appeals to individual anti-majoritarian rights that have the effect, whether intended or unintended, of undercutting the institutional structures of majoritarian democracy. Arguments for legal abortion have strong majoritarian appeal, and are at least as amenable to public deliberation, persuasion, and compromise as the ordinary fodder of political debate. Arguments for legal abortion in legislative and public arenas need not be made in ways that limit the movement for reproductive justice to this most individualistic and self-abdicating "right to an abortion." They need not be "truncated." Re-politicizing reproductive justice arguments, in other words, might not carry the costs of rights-focused constitutional rhetoric.

Finally, a shift in focus away from courts to more democratic fora might open the door to moral and political opportunities to which we have been blinded by the light of the promises of a living Constitution. We might recapture some of those heretofore-slighted opportunities. Most modestly, it might at least break the logjam that now frustrates any sort of coalition between parts of the pro-choice and pro-life communities that undoubtedly share many common interests and goals. Substantial parts of both sides of these movements have an interest in minimizing the demand for abortion through minimizing the cost of mothering, enforcing and strengthening the rights of pregnant women, advocating the responsible use of birth control, insisting upon sensible anti-rape policies, and discouraging unwanted sex. The reproductive justice that might be achieved through these coalitions—that is, achieved through ordinary modes of political persuasion—might prove more enduring than what we have garnered to date from the Court. It also might prove more deserving.

Chapter 2
The Price of Pleasure*

Shari Motro

Condoms break. Diaphragms malfunction. Even hormonal contraceptives are not 100 percent effective. More than three million American women become pregnant unintentionally every year,[1] and the rate of unintended pregnancy is especially high among young unmarried women.[2] What is the legal status of unmarried lovers who conceive?

Under current law, a woman who becomes pregnant with a man to whom she is not married is essentially on her own. Most states do require an unwed father to reimburse the mother of his child for certain birth and pregnancy-related medical expenses as part of his child support obligations or in connection with a paternity proceeding. But the law generally disregards the physical, financial, and professional toll pregnancy takes on the woman herself.[3] And where pregnancy ends in abortion, the man has no obligations whatsoever. The law thereby reinforces a fundamental gender imbalance: pregnancy is a woman's problem.

Thus far, the law's main answer to this imbalance has been to expand women's reproductive choices by ensuring their access to contraception and freedom to terminate an unwanted pregnancy. With reforms on these fronts, some have little sympathy for the accidentally pregnant. Sexual liberation comes with responsibility, the argument goes. A sexually active woman[4] who does not want babies should use protection. If she fails to prevent pregnancy, and chooses not to abort, she should deal with the consequences. Demanding that men support

---

* This chapter is an abridged adaptation of an article of the same title previously published in the Northwestern Law Review. *See* 104 Nw. U. L. Rev. 917 (2010).

1 Guttmacher Inst., Facts on Publicly Funded Contraceptive Services in the United States 1 (2009), *available at* http://www.guttmacher.org/pubs/fb_contraceptive_serv.pdf.

2 Stanley K. Henshaw, *Unintended Pregnancy in the United States*, 30 Fam. Plan. Persp. 24, 27 (1998), *available at* http://www.guttmacher.org/pubs/journals/3002498.pdf; Melinda Beck, *The Birth-Control Riddle*, Wall St. J., April 20, 2010, at D1 ("One out of every two American women aged 15 to 44 has at least one unplanned pregnancy in her lifetime. Among unmarried women in their 20s, seven out of 10 pregnancies are unplanned").

3 *See infra* pp. 62–65.

4 Because the focus of this chapter is on pregnancy, "sex" or "sexual relations" generally refers to penile-vaginal penetration. There are, of course, many other types of sex.

"irresponsible reproduction"[5] that they are powerless to prevent once conception occurs amounts to women wanting to have their cake and eat it.

Yet reproductive choice is not the answer, because contraception and abortion alike tend to harm women more than they harm men.[6] Effective birth control—like hormonal contraception—poses serious risks to women's health and wellbeing, as does abortion.[7] Women's freedom to choose between taking an unwanted pregnancy to term and terminating it, between the risks of condoms or of hormones, is hardly an unalloyed blessing. Only women bear the consequences on their own flesh.

At its core, the problem with the legal status quo is that it treats all sexual partners who conceive as legal strangers. In reality, though some pregnancies do result from casual encounters, others result from intercourse that happens in the context of a relationship in which the expectation is that the couple will deal with the consequences of pregnancy together. Between the two extremes lie connections in which parties' expectations are unclear or inconsistent. A legal regime that treats all conceptions as if they result from no-strings-attached sex fails to protect the more vulnerable party and sets up the wrong incentives. No-strings-attached sex isn't wrong in itself, it's only the wrong default.

This chapter argues that unless sexual partners explicitly agree otherwise, pregnancy should create a unique type of legal relationship. This relational default would come with certain obligations: in limited circumstances, a woman would be expected to communicate the fact of a pregnancy to the man with whom she conceived, and a man would be required to help support her during pregnancy and recovery. Child support obligations should kick in only once a child is born; until and unless this happens, a man's economic responsibility should be conceptualized as a responsibility toward the woman herself.

The goal of this chapter is to start a conversation about an issue that is critically relevant to our lives yet virtually absent from our laws. Commentary on current laws addressing the pregnancy-related obligations of "unwed fathers" is sparse and the scope of these provisions is uncertain. And while theorists have written extensively on rape, reproductive freedom, family leave policies, public funding for abortion, child support, and pregnancy discrimination in the employment context, virtually no one has focused on the legal relationship between unmarried sexual partners who conceive.

---

5 Linda C. McClain, *"Irresponsible" Reproduction*, 47 Hastings L.J. 339, 340 (1996) (defining "irresponsible reproduction" to include conception outside of wedlock and abortion).

6 Whereas both genders must contend with the risks of contracting a sexually transmitted disease, some studies indicate that women are more vulnerable to infection. *See*, e.g., Women's Health, STDs & Women: What Causes STDs?, http://www.womens-health.co.uk/www.std-women.html (last visited August 28, 2010) ("The reason women are more vulnerable to infection than men is because the surface area which is exposed is larger in women").

7 *See infra* pp. 65–69.

The precise parameters of the legal status governing sexual partners who conceive should be designed following a robust public discussion that has yet to commence. What I provide here is a preliminary sketch that I hope will be useful in beginning that discussion. I aim to reconceptualize a substantive issue; I do not address the ideal administrative mechanism for implementing the new paradigm I propose.

The first part lays out the problem. A fundamental gender imbalance hovers in the background of nonprocreative heterosexual sex: Women get pregnant, men do not. Women's alternatives—celibacy, chemically-induced sterility, or other, less effective contraceptive methods with abortion as a last resort—do not correct the imbalance. The current legal default is both unfair and inefficient. It imposes a rule that contradicts many people's expectations, it exacerbates vulnerabilities, and it gives men who assume their partner will terminate an unwanted pregnancy no external incentive to prevent conception.

The second part builds on the work of Robin West to identify the core problem underlying the current legal treatment of sexual partners who conceive. According to West, modern American jurisprudence views human beings as essentially separate individuals whose primary value is autonomy, when in fact human beings are essentially connected as well as separate. The law privileges autonomy and privacy but human happiness also demands relationship and mutual responsibility. Viewing the legal status quo through this prism reveals its essential flaw: the law treats lovers as strangers.

After introducing this framework, the second part of the chapter illustrates how the same individualistic framework that leaves a woman to deal with an unwanted pregnancy alone also gives her almost complete license to disregard a man's interest in the fate of his offspring. A woman has no obligation (outside the limited context of adoption) to notify the man with whom she conceived of conception, abortion, or the birth of his child. Pregnancy thus makes both men *and* women vulnerable—radically vulnerable—in radically different ways.

Finally, the third part proposes a new, relationship-centered paradigm for the legal treatment of sexual partners who conceive. Unless a pregnancy results from sexual fraud or coercion, or the parties agree to a no-strings-attached rule, pregnancy should create a legally cognizable relationship status. This status would require a minimal duty of communication and material support between sexual partners who conceive regardless of whether the pregnancy ends in birth, abortion, or miscarriage.

I. The Myth of Free Love

The typical American woman wants two children.[8] This means that she will spend "about five years pregnant, postpartum or trying to become pregnant, and three

8 Guttmacher Inst., *supra* note 1, at 1.

decades—more than three-quarters of her reproductive life—trying to avoid pregnancy."[9] But no birth control method is foolproof. Half of pregnancies are unintended, and half of these end in abortion.[10] How does pregnancy affect a woman's life and what are her sexual partner's responsibilities toward her? As we shall see, the conceptual paradigm undergirding the law's approach to pregnancy vastly underestimates its effects on women's lives.

The Mismatch Between Life and Law

Pregnancy's effects on women's lives

"[I]n sorrow thou shalt bring forth children."[11] Pregnancy as punishment—this is our story of origin. At the opposite extreme, modern culture tends to sentimentalize "expectant motherhood"—airbrushing away the pain and danger that are often bundled with its joys. None of these descriptions does justice to the complexities of gestation and childbirth, which vary dramatically from woman to woman. For most, pregnancy is neither an illness nor is it no big deal[12] (although some working women still feel pressured to pretend it is just that).

Pregnancy is often a profoundly transformative experience, an earthquake in a woman's life. And women report feeling many things at once during labor and delivery—empowered and terrified, ecstatic and exhausted, uplifted and radically vulnerable.[13] For many mothers, the joys of childbearing unquestionably outweigh its challenges. Indeed, some women report experiencing a "hormone high" during pregnancy and delivery, describing childbirth itself as orgasmic.[14] But all pregnancies, even wanted and overall enriching pregnancies, affect women's health, freedom, and professional capabilities in ways that temporarily diminish their ability to take care of themselves. As Sylvia Law put it:

> The power to create people is awesome. Men are profoundly disadvantaged by the reality that only women can produce a human being and experience the

9 *Id.*

10 *Id.* at 1, 4 ("About half of all pregnancies in the United States each year—more than three million—are unintended. By age 45, more than half of all American women will have experienced an unintended pregnancy, and about one-third will have had an abortion").

11 *Genesis* 3:16 (King James).

12 *See* Jennifer S. Hendricks, *Body and Soul: Equality, Pregnancy, and the Unitary Right to Abortion*, 45 Harv. C.R.-C.L. L. Rev. 329, 342 (2010) (suggesting that "the idea of a health exception [to abortion regulations] … incorporates an implicit distinction between normal pregnancy and the complications of pregnancy," and that the "distinction renders the inherent risks and physical burdens of all pregnancies invisible").

13 *See* Christiane Northrup, Women's Bodies, Women's Wisdom 477–94 (1998); The Business of Being Born (Barranca Productions 2008); Welcome to Orgasmic Birth, http://www.orgasmicbirth.com (last visited August 28, 2010).

14 For resources on the pleasure of birth, see Welcome to Orgasmic Birth, http://www.orgasmicbirth.com (last visited August 28, 2010).

> growth of a child in pregnancy. Pregnancy and childbirth are also burdensome to health, mobility, independence, and sometimes to life itself, and women are profoundly disadvantaged in that they alone bear these burdens.[15]

As we shall see, the law recognizes only a fraction of these burdens.

When a pregnancy progresses normally and is taken to full term without complications, its physical effects are relatively well known, though euphemisms used to describe them ("discomforts," "morning sickness," "the baby blues") are part of what some pregnant women see as the great conspiracy of silence around pregnancy.[16] Morning sickness is sudden, uncontrollable nausea and vomiting every day, sometimes *all* day, for months.[17] Other routine "aches and pains" include back and abdominal pain, chronic fatigue, anemia, insomnia, swollen feet, breast tenderness, leg cramps, shortness of breath, mood swings, headaches, dizziness, bleeding and swollen gums, heartburn, vulvar burning, urinary tract infections, constipation, and hemorrhoids.[18] When complications arise, pregnancy can be debilitating, even life-threatening. Pregnancy complications include gestational diabetes, heart disease, hemorrhaging, jaundice, severe nausea and vomiting leading to weight loss and dehydration, itching all over the body, and blood pressure so high it causes seizures.[19]

And every year hundreds of thousands of women worldwide die in childbirth.[20] The risks of death remain significant enough that surrogate mother contracts

15 Sylvia A. Law, *Rethinking Sex and the Constitution*, 132 U. Pa. L. Rev. 955, 955–56 (1984).

16 *See*, e.g., Lucy J. Puryear, *Understanding Your Moods When You're Expecting—The Conspiracy of Silence*, StorkNet, June 2008, http://www.storknet.com/cubbies/pregnancy/moods-silence.htm. Some courts have reinforced this trivializing view of pregnancy's symptoms. *See*, e.g., Dormeyer v. Comerica Bank-Ill., 223 F.3d 579, 583 (7th Cir. 2000); Troupe v. May Dept. Stores Co., 20 F.3d 734, 738 (7th Cir. 1994); *see also* Ann C. McGinley & Jeffrey W. Stempel, *Condescending Contradictions: Richard Posner's Pragmatism and Pregnancy Discrimination*, 46 Fla. L. Rev. 193 (1994).

17 Susan Renee Wilcox, *Pregnancy, Hyperemesis Gravidarum*, emedicine, January 13, 2010, http://emedicine.medscape.com/article/796564-overview.

18 *See generally* WebMD, Health & Pregnancy Guide, Common Pregnancy Pains and Their Causes, http://www.webmd.com/baby/guide/pregnancy-coping-with-discomforts (last visited August 28, 2010); Merck Manual of Medical Information, Risk Factors that Develop During Pregnancy, http://www.merck.com/mmhe/print/sec22/ch258/ch258c.html (last visited August 28, 2010).

19 *See* WebMD, Health & Pregnancy Guide, *supra* note 18; *see also* Eileen L. McDonagh, Breaking the Abortion Deadlock 69–71 (1996).

20 *See* Columbia University, Mailman School of Public Health, Averting Maternal Death and Disability, http://www.amddprogram.org (last visited August 28, 2010); UNICEF, The Progress of Nations 48 (1997), *available at* http://www.unicef.org/pon97; *see also* Bharati Sadasivam, *The Rights Framework in Reproductive Health Advocacy—A Reappraisal*, 8 Hastings Women's L.J. 313, 343 (1997) Amnesty Int'l, Deadly Delivery:

typically provide the woman carrying the fetus with life insurance.[21] But even "easy" births are rarely pain-free, including births in which pain-relief medication is administered—which itself comes with a host of risks.[22] Common experiences during vaginal labor and delivery (the least risky birth method) include abdominal cramping, hot and cold flashes, nausea, vomiting, indigestion, diarrhea, vaginal tears, and back, leg, perineal, and rectal pain. In many cases, the woman's vulva, perineum, or both are surgically cut to prevent delivery lacerations.[23] This routine procedure, called an episiotomy, may interfere with a woman's ability to enjoy sex after childbirth.[24]

More complicated births may require a cesarean delivery—major surgery that involves opening the woman's abdomen and sometimes temporarily removing her intestines before making an incision into her uterus.[25] Increasingly, C-sections are also performed when they are not medically necessary; today, one-third of births in the United States are by cesarean.[26] The risks of the operation to the woman include bladder or bowel injury; major infections of the uterus, kidneys, or lungs; opening up of the incision scar; blood clots; and uterine damage rendering future childbirth dangerous.[27] The risk of maternal death is five to seven times greater when a woman gives birth by cesarean rather than through normal vaginal birth.[28]

THE MATERNAL HEALTH CARE CRISIS IN THE USA, SUMMARY 3 (2010), http://www.amnestyusa.org/dignity/pdf/DeadlyDeliverySummary.pdf. *Id.*

21 *See infra* note 158 and accompanying text.

22 *See* WebMD, Health & Pregnancy Center, Pregnancy and Signs of Labor, http://www.webmd.com/baby/labor-signs (last visited August 28, 2010); Lewis E. Mehl-Madrona & Morgane Mehl-Madrona, The Medical Risks of Epidural Anesthesia (Epidurals), http://www.healing-arts.org/mehl-madrona/mmepidural.htm (last visited August 28, 2010).

23 WebMD, Episiotomy and Perineal Tears—Overview, http://www.webmd.com/baby/tc/episiotomy-and-perineal-tears-overview (last visited August 28, 2010).

24 The episiotemy "can impair sexual pleasure by irreversibly injuring clitoral muscles, replacing erectile tissue in the vulva with scar tissue, interfering with the capacity to produce natural lubrication, and making future intercourse painful." Susan Frelich Appleton, *Toward a "Culturally Cliterate" Family Law?*, 23 BERKELEY J. GENDER L & JUST. 267, 324 (2008). Appleton notes that despite these risks and the questionable efficacy of the episiotomy in aiding delivery, it remains "one of the most common medical procedures in the United States." *Id.* at 323–24.

25 D. Ashley Hill, *Cesarean Section*, CHILDBIRTH SOLUTIONS, 2000, http://www.childbirthsolutions.com/articles/birth/cesarean/index.php; WebMD, Health & Pregnancy, Cesarean Section—Topic Overview, http://www.webmd.com/baby/tc/cesarean-section-topic-overview?page=2 (last visited August 28, 2010).

26 Christiane Northrup, *A Woman's Nation: Reclaim Your Right to Birth Right*, HUFFINGTON POST, October 16, 2009, http://www.huffingtonpost.com/christiane-northrup/c-section-or-natural-birt_b_323422.html.

27 eMedicineHealth, Cesarean Childbirth, http://www.emedicinehealth.com/cesarean_childbirth/article_em.htm (last visited August 28, 2010).

28 Northrup, *supra* note 26.

After childbirth, a woman may need days, weeks, or months to recover.[29] She may also suffer from long-term medical problems like diabetes, urinary or fecal incontinence,[30] and uterine, bladder, or kidney infections.[31] On the psychological side, approximately 80 percent of women recovering from childbirth experience mood dips (the "baby blues") for up to two weeks following the delivery.[32] Hormonal changes during and following pregnancy can also produce more severe psychological symptoms which are now recognized as postpartum depression—a distinct clinical condition that manifests itself in prolonged sadness, panic attacks, paranoia, hallucinations, eating disorders, and, in the most tragic cases, suicide or infanticide.[33]

Pregnancy alters a woman's appearance as well. The rapid weight gain associated with pregnancy often leaves stretch marks and increases the risk of developing obesity.[34] Hormonal changes can produce acne, dark blotches on the skin, leaking breasts, rashes, brittle nails, thinning hair, and hair growth in unusual areas.[35] Pregnancy may also leave women with saggy breasts, varicose veins, and abdominal and vaginal scars.[36]

A pregnant woman also faces restrictions on her freedom. These range from the relatively benign, such as dietary restrictions, exclusion from certain sports,[37] and the inability to travel, to the life-altering, such as prescribed bed rest lasting

---

29 *Compare* WebMD, Health & Pregnancy, Cesarean Section—Topic Overview, *supra* note 25 ("[I]t may take 4 weeks or longer to fully recover [after a C-section]"), *with* Hill, *supra* note 25 ("Many women recover [from a C-section] surprisingly quickly and leave [the hospital] after a few days").

30 *See* Matthew D. Oldfield, *Long Term Prognosis of Women with Gestational Diabetes in a Multiethnic Population*, 83 Postgrad. Med. J. 426 (2007); Miranda Hitti, *Anal Incontinence Lingers After Vaginal Birth: More Common with Anal Sphincter Tear, Additional Births, and Increased Age*, WebMD Health News, December 10, 2004, http://www.webmd.com/baby/news/20041210/anal-incontinence-lingers-after-vaginal-birth.

31 WebMD, Health & Pregnancy, Postpartum Problems, http://www.webmd.com/baby/guide/postpartum-problems (last visited August 28, 2010).

32 University of Michigan Depression Center, Women and Depression, Postpartum Depression, http://www.depressioncenter.org/understanding/postpartum.asp (last visited August 28, 2010).

33 *Id.*; Kevin Caruso, *Postpartum Depression and Suicide*, Suicide.org, http://www.suicide.org/postpartum-depression-and-suicide.html (last visited August 28, 2010); Medline Plus, Postpartum Depression, http://www.nlm.nih.gov/medlineplus/postpartumdepression.html (last visited August 28, 2010).

34 Sally Ann Lederman, *Pregnancy Weight Gain and Postpartum Loss: Avoiding Obesity While Optimizing the Growth and Development of the Fetus*, 56 J. Am. Med. Women's Ass'n 53, 53 (2001).

35 Univ. of Maryland Med. Ctr., Pregnancy Guide, http://www.umm.edu/pregnancy/000214.htm (last visited August 28, 2010).

36 *See id.*; Andrea Thompson, *Breast-Feeding Isn't Such a Drag on Breasts*, MSNBC.com, November 2, 2007, http://www.msnbc.msn.com/id/21599854.

37 *See* Catharine A. MacKinnon, Sex Equality 395 (2d ed. 2007).

several months. In addition, the "fetal rights" movement's legal victories have undermined pregnant women's medical decision-making freedom during pregnancy and delivery.[38]

Finally, pregnancy transforms a woman's public identity. For some women, this transformation is exhilarating. For others, especially unmarried women whose pregnancy was unintended, it may bring shame. Pregnancy "is a sign of female sexuality," writes Catharine MacKinnon, "a brand of having had intercourse."[39] The derogatory term "knocked up" captures the many indignities to which unmarried pregnant women are subjected. In extreme cases, the change in public identity exposes women to more than just humiliation; pregnancy increases a woman's risk of being the target of violence.[40] One survey, for example, finds that pregnant women are 60 percent more likely to be beaten than women who are not pregnant.[41] Professor Reva Siegel captures some of the effects of pregnancy on a woman's personhood:

> A woman may find that pregnancy comes to embody her social identity to others, who may treat her with love and respect or, alternatively, abuse her as a burden, scorn her as unwed, or judge her as unfit for employment ... Pregnancy, and the period of lactation that follows it, are not merely burdensome, disruptive, or even consuming forms of work. They amplify the gendered judgments and constraints to which women are already subject, exposing them to material and dignitary injuries having nothing to do with the physiology of reproduction, and entangling them in relationships that profoundly define their identity and life prospects.[42]

---

38 Cynthia R. Daniels, At Women's Expense: State Power and the Politics of Fetal Rights (1993); Rachel Roth, Making Women Pay: The Hidden Costs of Fetal Rights (2000); April L. Cherry, *Roe's Legacy: The Nonconsensual Medical Treatment of Pregnant Women and Implications for Female Citizenship*, 6 U. Pa. J. Const. L. 723, 732–33 (2004); Martha A. Field, *Controlling the Woman to Protect the Fetus*, 17 L. Med. & Health Care 114 (1989); Dawn E. Johnsen, *The Creation of Fetal Rights: Conflicts with Women's Constitutional Rights to Liberty, Privacy, and Equal Protection*, 95 Yale L.J. 599, 612–13 (1986); Nancy K. Rhoden, *The Judge in the Delivery Room: The Emergence of Court-Ordered Cesareans*, 74 Cal L. Rev. 1951, 1986 (1986); Katherine A. Taylor, *Compelling Pregnancy at Death's Door*, 7 Colum. J. Gender & L. 85, 103–08 (1997); *see also In re* A.C., 573 A.2d 1235, 1253 (D.C. 1990) (vacating a lower court's judgment ordering a cesarean for a woman dying of cancer posthumously).

39 MacKinnon, Sex Equality, *supra* note 37, at 395.

40 *See infra* notes 116–119 and accompanying text; *see also* Planned Parenthood of Southeastern Pa. v. Casey, 505 U.S. 833, 889 (1992); MacKinnon, Sex Equality, *supra* note 37, at 395.

41 *See* Pan Am. Health Org., Domestic Violence During Pregnancy, http://www.paho.org/English/AD/GE/VAWPregnancy.pdf (last visited August 8, 2010).

42 Reva Siegel, *Reasoning from the Body: A Historical Perspective on Abortion Regulation and Questions of Equal Protection*, 44 Stan. L. Rev. 261, 374–75 (1992).

All of these effects—from the routine to the exceptional—mean that pregnancy tends to interfere with a woman's ability to provide for herself, if only temporarily.[43] Unpredictable bouts of nausea and vomiting, frequent urination, memory loss, and difficulties concentrating affect the most resilient, dedicated workers.[44] Self-employed women and those working on commission absorb the entire costs of the decline in their productivity. Pregnant employees may be in a better position, but not necessarily. Some employers accommodate their pregnant workers, others do not, and the Pregnancy Discrimination Act provides only limited protections.[45] Discrimination against pregnant women also is prohibited generally under Title VII as a form of sex discrimination,[46] but pregnant women continue to face exclusionary hiring practices,[47] pay decreases, demotions, and firings.[48] Every delivery also entails a recovery period, and few employers provide paid maternity leave.[49]

---

43 For a discussion of pregnancy and work, see Samuel Issacharoff & Elyse Rosenblum, *Women and the Workplace: Accommodating the Demands of Pregnancy,* 94 COLUM. L. REV. 2154 (1994).

44 *See* Saeed Ahmed, *Pregnancy Does Cause Memory Loss, Study Says*, CNNHEALTH.COM, February 5, 2008, http://www.cnn.com/2008/HEALTH/conditions/02/05/pregnancy.memory/index.html; Univ. of Maryland Med. Ctr., *supra* note 35.

45 For example, the Act covers only businesses with 15 or more employees, *see* EEOC, Facts About Pregnancy Discrimination, http://www.eeoc.gov/facts/fs-preg.html (last visited August 28, 2010), and even where it does apply, a plaintiff's chances of success in litigation over its protections are slim. A plaintiff bringing a discrimination claim bears the burden of proving a causal link between her pregnancy and the adverse treatment she received. She must also show that the adverse treatment resulted from a policy adopted *in order* to disadvantage her rather than in spite of its disadvantage to her. This renders many cases difficult to litigate. *See* Joanna Grossman, *A Marked Increase in Pregnancy Discrimination Claims and Other Key Developments Illustrate the Continuing Struggle of Pregnant Workers—Including Pregnant Attorneys: Part Two in a Two-Part Series of Columns*, FINDLAW, April 15, 2008, http://writ.news.findlaw.com/grossman/20080415.html.

46 42 U.S.C. § 2000e(k) (2006).

47 *See Jennifer Cunningham & Therese Macan, Effects of Applicant Pregnancy on Hiring Decisions and Interview Ratings, 57 SEX ROLES 497, 507 (2007); see also id.* at 497; Joanna L. Grossman, *Pregnancy, Work, and the Promise of Equal Citizenship*, 98 GEO. L.J. 567, 575 & n.37 (2010).

48 *See*, e.g., Rafeh v. Univ. Research Co., 114 F. Supp. 2d 396, 399–400 (D. Md. 2000); Wellborn v. Spurwink, 873 A.2d 884, 891 (R.I. 2005); *see also* Lesley Alderman, *When the Stork Carries a Pink Slip*, N.Y. TIMES, March 27, 2009, at B6.

49 The Pregnancy Discrimination Act requires that employers hold open a job for a pregnancy-related absence the same length of time that jobs are held open for other employees on sick or disability leave, but it does not mandate paid maternity leave. 42 U.S.C. § 2000e(k). Recent U.S. Department of Labor data show that just 8 percent of private sector employers nationwide provide paid family leave to care for newborns. INST.

In sum, the consequences of pregnancy go far beyond the monetary charges of visits to the obstetrician/gynecologist and of the delivery room. Whether conception occurs in the context of a loving partnership or a casual encounter, whether it is intentional or accidental, whether the woman is rich or poor, young or old, healthy or sick—pregnancy is hardly ever a minor undertaking. Pregnancy changes everything from a woman's pulse to the chemicals that influence her thoughts and feelings. It can present her with unparalleled opportunities for personal growth, healing, and joy and it can jeopardize her independence for years to come.

The current law of conception

Under the common law, men had no legal obligations toward the women with whom they conceived out of wedlock.[50] Today most states require unwed fathers to participate in at least a portion of the "reasonable expenses" of pregnancy.[51] Most cases dealing with the scope of these obligations focus on prenatal and birthing medical expenses.[52] But what about other costs? Should "reasonable expenses" include lost wages?[53] Forfeited tuition payments? What about childbirth classes?[54]

FOR WOMEN'S POL'Y RESEARCH, MATERNITY LEAVE IN THE UNITED STATES 3 (2007), *available at www.iwpr.org/pdf/parentalleaveA131.pdf.*

50 *See*, e.g., Jelen v. Price, 458 N.E. 2d 1267, 1270 (Ohio App. 1983); People *ex rel.* Lawton v. Snell, 111 N.E. 50, 51 (N.Y. 1916); *In re* Cirillo's Estate, 114 N.Y.S.2d 799, 801 (N.Y. Sup. Ct. 1952).

51 *See*, e.g., CAL. FAM. CODE § 7637 (West 2009); R.I. GEN. LAWS § 15-8-1 (2008); VA. CODE. ANN. § 20-49.8(A) (2009); State *ex rel.* Reitenour, 807 A.2d 1259, 1262 (N.H. 2002).

52 *See*, e.g., Coxwell v. Matthews, 435 S.E.2d 33, 33–34 (Ga. 1993); Sisneroz v. Polanco, 975 P.2d 392, 398–99 (N.M. Ct. App. 1999); State *ex rel.* Dep't of Health and Human Res. v. Carpenter, 564 S.E.2d 173, 176 (W. Va. 2002); Kathy L.B. v. Patrick J.B., 371 S.E.2d 583, 587 (W. Va. 1988); *see also* MASS. GEN. LAWS ANN. ch. 209C, § 9 (LexisNexis 2000 & Supp. 2010); N.D. CENT. CODE § 14-20-48 (2009); OKLA. STAT. ANN. tit. 10, § 7700-621 (West 2009); TEX. FAM. CODE ANN. § 160.621 (Vernon 2008); TEX. FAM. CODE ANN. § 160.636(g) (Vernon 2008); UTAH CODE ANN. § 78B-15-613 (2008); WASH. REV. CODE ANN. § 26.26.570 (West 2005); WYO. STAT. ANN. § 14-2-813 (2009; UNIF. PARENTAGE ACT § 621(d) (amended 2002), *available at* http://www.law.upenn.edu/bll/archives/ulc/upa/final2002.pdf.

53 Many jurisdictions have been silent on the issue, but Minnesota, Montana, and Ohio—whose statutes are modeled on the Uniform Parentage Act—do not include lost wages as part of the reasonable expenses associated with the birth. *See* Bunge v. Zachman, 578 N.W.2d 387, 389 (Minn. Ct. App. 1998); *In re* Paternity of W.L., 855 P.2d 521, 523–24 (Mont. 1993); *Jelen*, 458 N.E.2d at 1270. Lost wages are also not included in reasonable expenses of pregnancy in Arkansas. *See* Taylor v. Finck, 211 S.W.3d 532, 537 (Ark. 2005).

54 *See In re* Baby Girl D., 517 A.2d 925, 929 (Pa. 1986) (construing the "reasonable lying-in expenses" language to mean that Lamaze classes, prenatal care, and sonograms are not chargeable to the adopting parents to reimburse for expenses on behalf of the natural

Maternity clothes[55]—which can run to hundreds of dollars for a professional woman? A breast pump?

Judicial commentary on the scope of unwed fathers' pregnancy-related obligations is sparse, scholarship on the topic is virtually non-existent, and many state courts have been silent on the issue. What is clear is that almost all references to the question focus on expenses that directly benefit the future child. This is because states generally frame the obligations as an element of a man's child support obligations[56] or as part of a parentage order,[57] not as a duty toward the woman in her own right. The rationale behind this approach stems from the now widely accepted imperative that children of unmarried parents should not be relegated to the legal no-man's land of "illegitimacy."[58] All 50 states now require both parents to support their offspring regardless of their marital status.[59] Since a child's prebirth health cannot be disentangled from the health of his or her expectant mother, child support begins *in utero*.[60] Thus, even though the real costs of pregnancy go beyond expenses related to the health and wellbeing of the fetus,

---

mother). The court in *Taylor* relied on this holding in denying a birth mother reimbursement for such expenses from the birth father. 211 S.W.3d at 537.

55 *See Taylor*, 211 S.W.3d at 537 (holding that lying-in expenses "normally would not include items such as maternity clothes, lost wages, or counseling").

56 *See* 750 Ill. Comp. Stat. Ann. 45/14 (West 2009); Iowa Code Ann. § 600B.1 (West 2001); Ky. Rev. Stat. Ann. § 406.011 (1999); Me. Rev. Stat. Ann. tit. 19-A, § 1552 (1998 & Supp. 2009); Mass. Gen. Laws Ann. ch. 209C, § 9 (LexisNexis 2000 & Supp. 2010); Mich. Comp. Laws Ann. § 722.712 (West 2002 & Supp. 2010); Miss. Code Ann. § 93-9-7 (2004); Neb. Rev. Stat Ann. § 43-1407 (2008); N.J. Stat. Ann. § 9:17-45 (West 2002); N.C. Gen. Stat. Ann. § 49-15 (2009); Or. Rev. Stat. Ann. § 109.155 (2009); R.I. Gen. Laws § 15-8-1 (2003); Utah Code Ann. § 78B-15-305 (2008); W. Va. Code Ann. § 48-1-244 (LexisNexis 2009).

57 *See* Ala. Code § 26-17-636(g) (LexisNexis 2009); Ark. Code Ann. § 9-10-110 (2009); Ariz. Rev. Stat. § 25-809 (LexisNexis 2007); Cal. Fam. Code § 7637 (West 2009); Colo. Rev. Stat. Ann. § 19-4-116(3)(a) (West 2009); Conn. Gen. Stat. Ann. § 46b-172a (West 2009) (when a father comes forward as parent); Fla. Stat. Ann. § 742.031(1) (Supp. 2005); Haw. Rev. Stat. Ann. § 584-15(c) (LexisNexis 2005); Kan. Stat. Ann. §38-1121(c) (2009); Md. Code. Ann., Fam. Law § 5-1033 (LexisNexis 2006); Minn. Stat. Ann. § 257.66(3) (West 2007); Mo. Ann. Stat. § 210.841 (West 2004); Mont. Code Ann. § 40-6-116 (2009); Nev. Rev. Stat. Ann. § 126.161 (LexisNexis 2004 & Supp. 2007); N.D. Cent. Code § 14-20-57 (2009); Ohio Rev. Code Ann. § 3111.13 (West 2005); Tenn. Code. Ann. § 36-2-311 (2005); Tex. Fam. Code Ann. § 160.636(g) (Vernon 2008); Va. Code Ann. § 20-49.8(A) (2008); Wash. Rev. Code Ann. § 26.26.130 (West 2005); Wis. Stat. Ann. § 767.89 (West 2009).

58 Am. Law Inst., Principles of the Law and Family Dissolution: Analysis and Recommendations § 3.01 (2002).

59 *See* Jeffery W. Santema, Annotation, *Liability of Father for Retroactive Child Support on Judicial Determination of Paternity*, 87 A.L.R.5th 361, § I (2002).

60 *See* Coxwell v. Matthews, 435 S.E.2d 33, 34 (Ga. 1993).

a straightforward interpretation of many states' laws excludes many of these costs from the man's obligations.

These laws not only underestimate the burdens of pregnancy, but they also imply that pregnancy is a liminal state significant only by reference to the child it may—but will not always—produce. Additionally, because the man's pregnancy-related liability attaches only after paternity has been established, it is almost always retroactive: a reimbursement for expenses after the child is born rather than as the expenses accrue. Thus, the woman must bear the overwhelming majority of the costs during the nine months of pregnancy and beyond, until and unless a paternity proceeding is completed. If no child is born, a woman who can establish paternity during pregnancy[61] *might* still be entitled to some support under one of the statutes discussed above even if she eventually miscarries, but cases addressing this issue are rare.[62]

A minority of states extend a man's pregnancy-related obligations beyond the narrow scope guided by the best interests of the child to encompass duties to the woman *in her own right.* Most notably, Delaware's domestic relations statute dedicates an independent code section to the "[d]uty to support woman with child conceived out of wedlock." This provision empowers judges to allocate the costs of pregnancy and birth as they see fit:

> The duty to support a woman pregnant with child conceived out of wedlock rests first upon the person by whom she became pregnant. Such support may include her necessary prenatal and postnatal medical, hospital, and lying-in expenses incident to the pregnancy and to birth of the child, and such other relief as to the court shall seem reasonable.[63]

---

61 Though technological developments have made it possible to conduct genetic testing *in utero*, as of 2010—the publication date from which this excerpt is adapted—such testing posed a risk to the health of both mother and fetus. *See* Am. Pregnancy Ass'n, Paternity Testing, http://www.americanpregnancy.org/prenataltesting/paternitytesting.html (last visited May 29, 2010). For more recent developments see Andrew Pollack, *Before Birth, Dad's ID*, N.Y. Times, June 19, 2012; Shari Motro, *Responsibility Begins at Conception,* N.Y. Times, July 6, 2012.

62 *But see* C. v. L., 305 N.Y.S.2d 69, 72 (N.Y. Fam. Ct. 1969) (holding that the termination of pregnancy did not divest a woman of her right to proceed with such a claim and that the cost of a therapeutic (i.e. medically indicated) abortion can be awarded at the court's discretion as a "reasonable expense" in connection with pregnancy); *see also* Stockton v. Oldenburg, 713 N.E.2d 259, 266 (Ill. App. Ct. 1999) (Myerscough, J., concurring in part and dissenting in part) (arguing there is a broad scope to reasonable expense in connection with pregnancy that encompasses therapeutic abortion). *But see* Alice D. v. William M., 450 N.Y.S.2d 350, 353 (N.Y. Civ. Ct. 1982) (requiring actual birth as a predicate for reasonable expense award and differentiating itself from *C. v. L.* at 353: "mandating an actual birth as a predicate for relief in the Family Court is sound").

63 Del. Code Ann. tit. 13, § 504 (2009).

Yet despite this broad statutory language, there is little indication that Delaware courts have awarded pregnant women anything in excess of the amount typically available in other states under the child support rubric: reimbursement for medical expenses directly related to pregnancy and childbirth.[64] Delaware's Code also includes an alternative provision giving courts the authority to order a man to pay for prenatal, postnatal, and lying-in expenses as part of his *child support* obligations rather than as a financial obligation to the woman.[65]

Choice is Not the Answer

Recognizing the gap between pregnant women's needs and their entitlements, feminists have worked hard to secure women's rights to contraception and abortion.[66] Their efforts over the last few decades have ushered in dramatic expansions in women's reproductive freedom through watershed cases like *Eisenstadt v. Baird*[67] and *Roe v. Wade*.[68] These advances leave some with limited sympathy for the accidentally pregnant. Considering the panoply of contraceptive options available to women today, what excuse does a woman have for waking up pregnant? Many people believe that sexual freedom comes with responsibility for the consequences. A woman who engages in sexual relations assumes the risk that she might conceive. Even once she does "fall" pregnant, a woman has a choice. If she is unprepared to take on the hardships of pregnancy and childbirth, she can abort. If she chooses to take the pregnancy to term after all, she should take care of herself. By this logic, the asymmetry in choice (women's unilateral decision-making power over abortion) counterbalances the asymmetry in sexual risk (women's exposure to unwanted pregnancy). The two may be apples and oranges, but there is arguably a rough justice in the current rule.

This argument belittles the harms that come along with *all* of women's reproductive choices. The "problem with the rhetoric of choice," writes one author focusing on broader gender equity issues, "is that it leaves out power. Those

64 *See* Div. of Child Support Enforcement *ex rel.* Harper v. Barrows, 570 A.2d 1180, 1184 (Del. 1990); DCES/J.O'C. v. D.U., 2009 Del. Fam. Ct. LEXIS 3, at *6 (Del. Fam. Ct. Mar. 18, 2009).

65 Del. Code Ann. tit. 13, § 513(a)(3) (2009); *see also* DCES/J.O'C., 2009 Del. Fam. Ct. LEXIS at 5.

66 For discussions of sex-equality based arguments for reproductive freedom, see Catharine A. MacKinnon, *Privacy v. Equality: Beyond Roe v. Wade*, in Feminism Unmodified 93 (1987); Law, *supra* note 15, at 978; Donald H. Regan, *Rewriting* Roe v. Wade, 77 Mich. L. Rev. 1569, 1621–22 (1979); Siegel, *supra* note 42; Reva B. Siegel, *Sex Equality Arguments for Reproductive Rights: Their Critical Basis and Evolving Constitutional Expression*, 56 Emory L.J. 815 (2007).

67 Eisenstadt v. Baird, 405 U.S. 438, 453 (1972) (guaranteeing access to contraception regardless of marital status).

68 Roe v. Wade, 410 U.S. 113, 153 (1973) (guaranteeing a woman's right to a first trimester abortion).

who benefit from the status quo always attribute inequities to the choices of the underdog."[69] No form of birth control is foolproof, and effective contraception as well as abortion come at great costs, costs that are paid almost entirely by women.

For example, although pharmaceutical companies work hard to create the impression that hormonal contraception, commonly known simply as "the pill," is not only safe but good for you, its harmful side effects are incontrovertible. Documented risks include strokes, heart attacks, migraine headaches, cancer, diabetes, asthma, breast pains, vaginal dryness and infections, and loss of sexual desire.[70] According to some studies, newer "third generation" pills developed in the 1980s to reduce earlier pills' minor side effects like acne or facial hair actually double the risk of blood clots—which can result in a stroke, deep vein thrombosis, or pulmonary embolism.[71] Women who are aware of these risks presumably feel

---

69 Ann Crittenden, The Price of Motherhood 234 (2001). Crittenden's book provided the inspiration for the title of this chapter.

70 *See* A.A. Ewies, *Levonorgestrel-Releasing Intrauterine System—The Discontinuing Story*, 36 Gynecol Endocrinol 1 (2009); Chrisandra L. Shufelt & C. Noel Bairey Merz, *Contraceptive Hormone Use and Cardiovascular Disease*, 53 J. Am. C. Cardiology 221 (2009); Sasitorn Siritho et al., *Risk of Ischemic Stroke Among Users of the Oral Contraceptive Pill*, 34 Stroke 1575 (2003); Nat'l Cancer Inst., *Oral Contraceptives and Cancer Risk: Question and Answers*, May 4, 2006, http://www.cancer.gov/cancertopics/factsheet/Risk/oral-contraceptives (linking oral contraceptives to an increase in some forms of cancer and a decrease in others); *Oral Contraceptives Linked to Asthma Risk*, Reuters, March 27, 2009, http://www.reuters.com/article/healthNews/idUSTRE52Q6PA20090327; *Pros and Cons of the Pill Tricky For Black Women*, Reuters, June 30, 2008, http://www.reuters.com/article/healthNews/idUSTON07346120080630 (describing a study showing black women at a lower risk of heart disease and diabetes from oral contraceptives than white women); Geraldine Sealey, *Why I Hate the Pill*, Salon.com, May 3, 2010, http://www.salon.com/life/feature/2010/05/03/pill_pushback ("Although a libido-destroying pill does wonders to lower your pregnancy risk, it's also done a number on my relationships, self-esteem and emotional well-being").

71 Ads marketing the newest invention—the "ring" (a plastic device that releases hormones directly into the vagina)—are especially misleading. The ads—which feature the slogan: "Let Freedom Ring!"—emphasize the fact that the ring contains a lower dose of hormones than most oral contraceptives. This is true, but studies suggest that the mode of delivery may increase certain risks. Since the ring, like the patch, releases hormones directly into the blood stream, the net amount of hormones absorbed by the body may be higher than those absorbed by women taking hormones orally. The company that manufactures the ring is facing over 100 pending lawsuits. *See* Stephanie Mencimer, *Is NuvaRing Dangerous?*, Mother Jones, May/June 2009, http://www.motherjones.com/environment/2009/05/nuvaring-dangerous. Similarly, Bayer ads presenting the pill as a beneficial "lifestyle drug"—to combat acne, headaches, and anxiety—resulted in a lawsuit by the Food and Drug Administration and the attorneys general of 27 states claiming Bayer underplayed the drug's dangers. The case ended in a settlement requiring that the company launch a $20 million corrective ad campaign. *See* Natasha Singer, *A Birth Control Pill That Promised Too Much*, N.Y. Times, February 11, 2009, at B1.

the pill's benefits outweigh its potential harms, but in this trade-off most of the downsides fall on the woman (although men suffer too when their partners' libido and natural lubrication are inhibited, or when the women they love suffer from more drastic side effects).

Furthermore, hormonal contraception is not accessible to all women. Pill refills can cost up to $50 per month,[72] they require a prescription and repeated physician appointments, and they are often not covered by insurance.[73] A recent study has found that "many women have difficulty preventing unintended pregnancy simply because they cannot afford the more effective, prescription methods of contraception."[74] Despite all of the advances, birth control remains, as it was in Margaret Sanger's time, "a woman's problem."[75]

Abortions, likewise, are hardly good for women. Whether one considers a fetus to be a life or not, every woman understands that it is at least a potential life. The decision to terminate a pregnancy, even when it represents a woman's best alternative, can be a heart-wrenching ordeal.[76] And then, of course, there are routine physical side effects like abdominal cramping, irregular bleeding, nausea, vomiting, and diarrhea.[77] When an abortion causes an infection, the long-term

72 Planned Parenthood, Birth Control Pills, http://www.plannedparenthood.org/health-topics/birth-control/birth-control-pill-4228.htm (last visited August 28, 2010).

73 *See* Sharon Lerner, *Why Doesn't Health Care Cover Birth Control?*, DOUBLEX, November 12, 2009, http://www.doublex.com/section/news-politics/why-doesnt-health-care-cover-birth-control; Geraldine Sealey, *Erections Get Insurance; Why Not the Pill?*, ABC NEWS, June 19, 2002, http://abcnews.go.com/US/story?id=91538.

74 JACQUELINE E. DARROCH, JENNIFER J. FROST & LISA REMEZ, GUTTMACHER INST., IN BRIEF: IMPROVING CONTRACEPTIVE USE IN THE UNITED STATES 1, 6 (2008), *available at* http://www.guttmacher.org/pubs/2008/05/09/ImprovingContraceptiveUse.pdf.

75 MARGARET SANGER, WOMAN AND THE NEW RACE 100 (1920).

76 *See* Project Voice, http://www.theabortionproject.org (last visited August 28, 2010); WebMD, Emotional Reactions After an Abortion, http://www.webmd.com/hw-popup/emotional-reactions-after-an-abortion (last visited August 28, 2010). I do not mean to suggest that the emotional aspects of the procedure justify abortion restrictions. For discussions of debates surround the woman-protective rationale for restricting abortion, see Reva B. Siegel, *The Right's Reasons: Constitutional Conflict and the Spread of Woman-Protective Antiabortion Argument*, 57 DUKE L.J. 1641 (2008); Jeannie Suk, *The Trajectory of Trauma: Bodies and Minds of Abortion Discourse*, 110 COLUM. L. REV. 1193 (2010).

77 Am. Pregnancy Ass'n, Unplanned Pregnancy: Possible Physical Side Effects (2007), http://www.americanpregnancy.org/unplannedpregnancy/possiblesideeffects.html (last visited August 28, 2010); WebMD, Women's Health, Abortion—Before, During, and After an Abortion: When to Call a Doctor, http://women.webmd.com/tc/abortion-before-during-and-after-an-abortion-when-to-call-a-doctor (last visited August 28, 2010).

effects may include chronic pelvic inflammations, heightened risk of miscarriage or ectopic pregnancy, and infertility.[78] In rare cases, abortion is fatal.[79]

For many women, an abortion is also hard to obtain. Though *Roe v. Wade* made abortion legal, *Roe* and its progeny did little to guarantee access to abortions,[80] and many women still are unable to obtain a speedy, safe, and affordable abortion. The overwhelming majority of US counties do not have abortion providers. This means that women must travel, sometimes for hours, to the nearest clinic. Once they arrive, an abortion typically costs several hundred dollars, and public funding for abortions is limited. As a result of their difficulties reaching a clinic and raising the money for the procedure, pregnant women who are both poor and young are more likely to undergo later-term—and therefore riskier—abortions.[81]

No state requires a man to participate in either the direct or indirect costs of abortion. The expense of the procedure itself, the lost income associated with undergoing and recovering from it, and the costs of any complications it may produce fall squarely on the woman. As one feminist put it, "[a]bortion is the last in a long line of non-choices."[82]

Setting aside communication issues,[83] when lovers are married, we already recognize that there is no contradiction between a man's obligation toward the woman with whom he conceives and her right to choose. When husband and wife disagree over abortion, the wife has the final say over the decision.[84] And if she chooses to continue the pregnancy, she is entitled to no less support than had

78 *See* Elizabeth Ring-Cassidy & Ian Gentles, Women's Health After Abortion: The Medical and Psychological Evidence (2002). *See* Cunningham et al., Williams Obstetrics 247 (22d ed. 2005); Joel Brind et al., *Induced Abortion as an Independent Risk Factor for Breast Cancer: A Comprehensive Review and Meta-Analysis*, 50 J. Epidemiology & Cmty. Health 481 (1996); David A. Grimes & Mitchell D. Creinin, *Induced Abortion: An Overview for Internists*, 140 Annals Internal Med. 620 (2004).

79 Guttmacher Inst., Facts on Induced Abortion in the United States 2 (2010), *available at* http://www.guttmacher.org/pubs/fb_induced_abortion.pdf.

80 *See* Planned Parenthood of Southeastern Pa. v. Casey, 505 U.S. 833, 874 (1992) (holding that states may enact restrictions so long as these do not unduly burden women seeking an abortion); Webster v. Reprod. Health Servs., 492 U.S. 490, 511 (1989) (holding that non-life-saving abortions for women prepared to pay full cost may be banned in public facilities); Harris v. McRae, 448 U.S. 297, 316 (1980) (upholding a ruling allowing funding for medically necessary abortions to be denied unless the mother's life is in danger).

81 *See* Guttmacher Inst., *supra* note 79.

82 Germaine Greer, *The Backlash Myth*, New Republic, October 5, 1992, at 21. The reproductive choices relevant to this chapter relate to pregnancy prevention and termination. For a discussion of the harms associated with choices made possible by reproductive technologies (IVF and surrogacy), see Janice G. Raymond, Women as Wombs: Reproductive Technologies and the Battle Over Women's Freedom (1995).

83 *See infra* pp. 74–77 and pp. 82–83.

84 Planned Parenthood of Central Mo. v. Danforth, 428 U.S. 52, 71 (1976) (holding unconstitutional the Missouri statute requiring spousal consent to an abortion).

she followed her husband's preference. In other words, the law in all 50 states recognizes that a wife's right to choose does not cancel her spouse's duty of mutual support. Precisely because no matter what she chooses it is her body that will bear the consequences, the rough justice that the law effectively strikes in marriage is that a wife gets the final say and is entitled to support while her husband gets to not be pregnant. A similar logic applies in the nonmarital context. A duty of support and reproductive choice are both compatible and fair.

Sex Creates Relationship

Leaving a pregnant woman to care for herself does make sense in two very particular situations. First, men should have no obligations vis-à-vis their sexual partners when both parties clearly agree that they have no expectation of an ongoing relationship. This might happen in the case of an explicitly casual, no-strings-attached "hookup." It might also arise where a woman wants and intends to have a child alone and conceives with a friend with the clear understanding that he will bear no responsibilities to help support her through the pregnancy. Second, a man should not be required to help support a woman with whom he conceives if the woman engaged in foul play—for example, lying about birth control. (Currently, victims of sexual fraud have limited recourse against a deceiving lover,[85] though scholars have argued persuasively for reform in this area.)[86] But the one-night-stand or the case of sexual deception should not define the rule applicable to all sexual encounters.

Much of nonmarital sex happens in the context of good-faith relationships. Of course many people never articulate their expectations should they conceive

85 Stephen K. v Roni L., 164 Cal. Rptr. 618, 620 (Cal. Ct. App. 1980); C.A.M. v. R.A.W., 568 A.2d 556, 556 (N.J. Super. Ct. App. Div. 1990); Douglas R. v. Suzanne M., 487 N.Y.S.2d 244, 246 (App. Div. 1985). *But see* Barbara A. v. John G., 193 Cal. Rptr. 422, 431 (Cal. Ct. App. 1983); Alice D. v. William M., 450 N.Y.S.2d 350, 356–57 (N.Y. Civ. Ct. 1982).

86 Martha Chamallas, *Consent, Equality, and the Legal Control of Sexual Conduct*, 61 S. Cal. L. Rev. 777 (1988); I. Glenn Cohen, *The Right Not to Be a Genetic Parent?*, 81 S. Cal. L. Rev. 1115, 1158 (2008); Jill E. Evans, *In Search of Paternal Equity: A Father's Right to Pursue a Claim of Misrepresentation of Fertility*, 36 Loy. U. Chi. L.J. 1045, 1065–92 (2005); Jane E. Larson, "*Women Understand So Little, They Call My Good Nature 'Deceit'*": *A Feminist Rethinking of Seduction*, 93 Colum. L. Rev. 374, 380 (1993). Paula C. Murray & Brenda J. Winslett, *The Constitutional Right to Privacy and Emerging Tort Liability for Deceit in Interpersonal Relationships*, 1986 U. Ill. L. Rev. 779, 780; Michelle Oberman, *Sex, Lies, and the Duty to Disclose*, 47 Ariz. L. Rev. 871 (2005); Lea VanderVelde, *The Legal Ways of Seduction*, 48 Stan. L. Rev. 817 (1996); Joshua Kleinfeld, Comment, *Tort Law and In Vitro Fertilization: The Need for Legal Recognition of "Procreative Injury,"* 115 Yale L.J. 237, 239–40 (2005); Anne M. Payne, Annotation, *Sexual Partner's Tort Liability to Other Partner for Fraudulent Misrepresentation Regarding Sterility or Use of Birth Control Resulting in Pregnancy*, 2 A.L.R.5th 301 (1992).

accidentally. Surprisingly, although there is a vast body of literature on expectations surrounding what constitutes consent to sexual contact, none of the sources I have reviewed deal with consensual lovers' *ex ante* expectations vis-à-vis each other regarding the unintended consequences of their activity. (A small number of studies suggest that once pregnancy occurs, unmarried male partners remain at least partially involved.)[87] In light of the fact that most pregnancies result not from birth control failures but from repeated acts of unprotected intercourse,[88] it is hard to believe that *more* women get pregnant from anonymous one-night-stands than from sex with a steady partner. Thus, it is likely that many people's baseline expectations, while diverse, are significantly higher than our default lovers-as-strangers rule, including when it comes to the costs of abortion.[89]

But even if the current rule were shown to match widespread expectations, it is inappropriate as a normative matter. When heterosexual partners have sex for pleasure and pregnancy ensues, it is only fair that both parties take responsibility for the consequences. This is especially true when a gap in the parties' expectations corresponds to power imbalances within the couple.[90]

There are also utilitarian reasons for allocating the price of pleasure more equitably. This is not to say that the current rule turns all men into cads. Good guys don't need external incentives to do the right thing; they do their best to prevent pregnancy and, when their efforts fail, they don't leave their partner in

87 One study of unmarried parents in Oakland, California, revealed that most unmarried parents were romantically involved when their child was born and that about half were living together. Sarah McLanahan et al., Pub. Policy Inst. of Cal., Fragile Families One Year Later: Oakland, California 7 (2003), *available at* http://www.ppic.org/content/pubs/op/op_1002smop.pdf. Approximately 80 percent of the mothers in the survey "reported that the father had contributed financial support or helped in other ways (such as providing transportation) during the pregnancy." *Id.* at 10; *see also* Maureen R. Waller, My Baby's Father: Unmarried Parents and Paternal Responsibility 2–3 (2002) ("Approximately 33 percent of all births in the United States now occur to unmarried parents … [and] about half of these parents are living together at the time of their child's birth" (citation omitted)).

88 *See* Darroch et al., *supra* note 74, at 1; McDonagh, *supra* note 19, at 52–53.

89 Surveys of men in abortion clinic waiting rooms reveal that most men pay for some or all of the procedure. The studies make no mention of additional costs like lost wages. *See*, e.g., Arthur B. Shostak, Gary McLouth & Lynn Seng, Men and Abortion: Lessons, Losses, and Love 36 (1984); Jennifer A. Reich & Claire D Brindis, *Conceiving Risk and Responsibility: A Qualitative Examination of Men's Experiences of Unintended Pregnancy and Abortion*, 5 Int'l J. Men's Health 133, 145 (2006).

90 Such imbalances may often be gendered in nature. Hirshman and Larson argue that "[i]n heterosexual exchanges, the male and female sexual players start from a baseline of physical inequality of strength, size and vulnerability to pregnancy." Linda R. Hirshman & Jane E. Larson, Hard Bargains: The Politics of Sex 22 (1998). Accordingly, a just sex code should "establish baselines that moderate the downward spiral of unequal bargaining" by "shifting the burden of silence onto the stronger player." *Id.* at 2, 283. But even where the imbalance does not fall along gendered lines, the same principle holds: the baseline should protect the weaker party to the "sexual bargain." *Id.* at 267–68.

the lurch, even when their legal duties are minimal or nil. But for some men, the bottom line matters.

Studies show, for example, that adolescent men who expect to pay child support should their partner become pregnant have fewer partners, less frequent intercourse, and are more likely to use contraceptives.[91] But in some relationships men assume—sometimes reasonably—that a woman will terminate an unwanted pregnancy. How does the fact that abortion frees men not only of child support but also of any responsibility toward the woman figure into what happens in the bedroom?

Decisions about sex, contraception, and abortion take place in the shadow of the law's allocation of their attendant risks. It's only logical that one way to reduce unintended pregnancies might be to raise the stakes for men, to make sure *all* pregnancies have concrete consequences for both parties involved. Thus, increasing support for pregnant women regardless of the pregnancy's outcome will, over time, change abortion from a form of birth control that lets men off the hook into something both parties are invested in preventing. It may also reduce abortions obtained under the pressure of short-term economic considerations.[92]

This chapter does not suggest that conception should trigger a type of common-law marriage with robust long-term commitments. Rather, as explained further later in the chapter, when unmarried lovers conceive, the law should recognize their relationship as something that falls *in between* that of complete strangers and that of spouses,[93] unless they agree otherwise. A lovers-as-strangers rule is not inherently wrong; it is simply the wrong default.

---

91 *See* Chien-Chung Huang & Wen-Jui Han, *Child Support Enforcement and Sexual Activity of Male Adolescents*, 69 J. Marriage & Family 763, 772 (2007) [hereinafter Huang & Han, *Child Support Enforcement*]; *see also* Chien-Chung Huang & Wen-Jui Han, *Perceptions of Child Support and Sexual Activity of Adolescent Males*, 27 J. of Adolescence 731 (2004) (discussing empirical studies relating to teen sexual activity, use of contraceptives, and pregnancy).

92 A recent study suggests that child support enforcement decreases the incidence of abortion. Jocelyn Crowley, Radha Jagannathan, & Galo Falchettore, The Effect of Child Support Enforcement on Nonmarital Births and Abortion in the United States (unpublished manuscript) (on file with author). For data on the higher incidence of abortion among poor women, see Rachel K. Jones, Lawrence B. Finer & Susheela Singh, Guttmacher Inst., Characteristics of U.S. Abortion Patients, 2008, at 1, 9 (2010), available at http://www.guttmacher.org/pubs/US-Abortion-Patients.pdf; Annie Murphy Paul, *Is the Recession Causing More Abortions?*, Slate, May 15, 2009, http://www.doublex.com/section/health-science/recession-causing-more-abortions?page=0,0 (arguing that "financial hardship has been an ever-present motivation for ending a pregnancy").

93 For a broader argument that family law should recognize and support friendships that do not resemble marriage or marriage-like relationship, see Laura A. Rosenbury, *Friends With Benefits?*, 106 Mich. L. Rev. 189 (2007).

II. Reconceiving Conception

Before turning to alternatives to the current rule, a deeper look at its conceptual underpinnings may help us identify not only the symptoms but also the roots of the problem. This part suggests that the "lovers-as-strangers" rule stems from a jurisprudential orientation that views human beings as definitionally separate and distinct from one another. This bias casts us as free-floating individuals whose primary concern is maximizing privacy and autonomy. But human beings are also essentially connected to others. In disregarding our dual nature and privileging separation over connection, the law's approach to pregnancy misses something fundamental, causing both men and women to suffer.

After introducing this framework, this part illustrates its effects on another aspect of the current law of conception: communication between sexual partners. The corollary of the no-strings-attached default governing men's responsibility vis-à-vis the consequences of pregnancy is a rule that places virtually no obligation on women to communicate with their partners about conception, abortion, or childbirth.

Human Beings' Dual Nature: Connected and Separate

The current lovers-as-strangers paradigm exemplifies what Robin West sees as the hyper-individualistic starting point—the "separation thesis"—that underlies modern American jurisprudence.[94] This starting point, she argues, corresponds with a philosophical worldview that places autonomy as its supreme value.[95] Under this view, man is born alone and he dies alone. His most powerful craving is to be left alone.

West believes that the "separation thesis" is "essentially and irretrievably masculine."[96] Women, unlike men, "are not essentially, necessarily, inevitably … separate from other human beings … [Women] are 'essentially connected.'"[97] West locates women's essential connectedness in their "critical material

94 *See* Robin West, *Jurisprudence and Gender*, 55 U. Chi. L. Rev. 1, 2 (1988). A related theory has been advanced by Linda Hirshman and Jane Larson, who employ the term "libertinism" to describe the individualistic sexual ideology that has dominated sexual politics since the 1960s. *See* Hirshman & Larson, *supra* note 90, at 10, 211.

95 "[W]hat separates us," West quotes Michael Sandel as saying, "is in some important sense prior to what connects us … We are distinct individuals first, and *then* we form relationships and engage in co-operative arrangements with others." West, *supra* note 94, at 2. Thus, under the "separation thesis," "the inevitability of the individual's material separation from the 'other,' entails, first and foremost, an existential state of … freedom: because the individual is *separate* from the other, he is *free* of the other." *Id.* at 5.

96 *Id.* at 2.

97 West, *supra* note 94, at 2–3.

experiences," including pregnancy and breastfeeding.[98] Women value or define themselves in terms of connection, intimacy, and relationship. Their wellbeing can only be advanced through a system that recognizes this essential aspect of their existential reality. A jurisprudence that places autonomy as its supreme value will by definition leave women out in the cold.[99]

But West believes that men also value connectedness. Referencing critical legal theorists, she explains that men are also harmed by the separation bias of dominant legal categories, albeit in different ways. Whereas women are naturally and constitutionally connected to others, men *crave* connection because their original state (as liberal legal theory proclaims) is one of separateness. According to West, liberal theory is wrong when it assumes that men's primary aim is to preserve this separateness through guarantees of autonomy. Rather, men yearn to overcome their essential alienation and isolation through relationship.[100]

I do not know whether separation is essentially masculine or connection is essentially feminine, but I do believe that the ultimate conclusion West draws from these categories is crucial to the knot we are trying to unravel. Her most compelling insight is that connectedness expresses an important, undervalued truth that is critical to the happiness of both men and women. Though she emphasizes the differences between the sexes, West also thinks that both men and women are animated by both connection and separation. It is the *tension* between the two, she says, that is essential to our nature.[101]

Applying West's insight to unintended pregnancy, the notion that human nature is centrally defined by the tension between separation and connection reveals the core problem undergirding the current rule. True, only women get pregnant, only women are capable of containing another life. But both men and women begin, at conception, in ultimate connection, contained in the body of

---

98 *See* Robin L. West, *The Difference in Women's Hedonic Lives: A Phenomenological Critique of Feminist Legal Theory*, 15 Wis. Women's L.J. 149, 210 (2000).

99 *Id.* at 209–10.

100 *See* West, *supra* note 94, at 9–12; *see also* Allan G. Johnson, The Gender Knot: Unraveling Our Patriarchal Legacy 56 (1997).

101 *See* West, *supra* note 94, at 50–58 (referencing the position of critical legal theorists Roberto Unger and Duncan Kennedy that the essential human condition is defined by a fundamental contradiction between connection and separation); *see also id.* at 70–71. West argues that the separation thesis is drastically untrue of women and not entirely true of men either: "First, it is not true materially. Men are connected to another human life prior to the cutting of the umbilical cord. Furthermore, men are somewhat connected to women during intercourse … Nor is the separation thesis necessarily true of men existentially … [M]en *can* connect to other human life. Men can nurture life. Men can mother. Obviously, men can care, and love, and support, and affirm life … On the flip side, the 'connection thesis' is also not entirely true of women, either materially or existentially. Not all women become pregnant, and not all women are sexually penetrated. Women can go through life unconnected to other human life. Women can also go through life fundamentally unconcerned with other human life." *Id.*

another. Both are born in radical separation, separation rife with pain. And both go through life negotiating this contradiction, this duality—our connection to and our separation from the woman and the man who gave us life, our connection to and our separation from the lovers with whom we each play out our original script. Sometimes the Rule of Law embodies this essential contradiction,[102] our internal tug-of-war between connection and separation. But often, and certainly in the case of conception, the law is biased in favor of separation.

In short, treating lovers who have conceived as strangers is wrong because treating all human beings as strangers is wrong. Pregnancy and the intercourse that brings it about are the *ultimate* embodiment of our essential connectedness, of our vulnerability at the hands of another, of our lack of control in relationship. What do men and women want when we conceive? The law assumes that the most important things we want are autonomy, equality, and privacy. We value all of these, but *as importantly*, many of us *also* want not to be left alone.[103]

Separation and Secrecy

So far we have focused on the current rule's allocation of the material costs of pregnancy. The relational critique sheds light on another troubling aspect of the status quo: the almost non-existent communication duties that it places on sexual partners. The same individual-centered orientation that leaves a woman to deal with an unwanted pregnancy alone and puts minimal responsibilities on the man also gives him minimal entitlements. A woman may decide to undergo or forgo an abortion irrespective of her lover's preferences,[104] and with no obligation to communicate with him regardless of the nature of their relationship, including if they are married.[105] Not only may a woman keep her decision to abort secret, she may conceive, carry a pregnancy to term, and raise a man's child without ever informing him.[106] If she does inform him, she may receive retroactive child

102 *Id.* at 52.

103 Of course, not everybody wants the same thing. Critics of relational feminism have made this clear. *See*, e.g., JANET HALLEY, SPLIT DECISIONS: HOW AND WHY TO TAKE A BREAK FROM FEMINISM 58–76 (2006).

104 *See* 1 AM. JUR. 2D *Abortion and Birth Control* § 25 (2009).

105 *See* Planned Parenthood of Southeastern Pa. v. Casey, 505 U.S. 833, 887–98 (1992); Cecily L. Helms & Phyllis C. Spence, *Take Notice Unwed Fathers: An Unwed Mother's Right to Privacy in Adoptions*, 20 WIS. WOMEN'S L.J. 1, 20 (2005); Anne M. Payne, Annotation, *Parent's Child Support Liability as Affected by Other Parent's Fraudulent Misrepresentation Regarding Sterility of Use of Birth Control, or Refusal to Abort Pregnancy*, 2 A.L.R.5th 337, § 2(a) (1992). *But see* Kim Shayo Buchanan, Lawrence v. Geduldig*: Regulating Women's Sexuality*, 56 EMORY L.J. 1235, 1245 (2007); John Tierney, Op-Ed., *Men's Abortion Rights*, N.Y. TIMES, January 10, 2006, at A25.

106 For a discussion of women's limited obligations to notify their partners of a pregnancy, see Mary Beck, *Toward a National Putative Father Registry Database*, 25 HARV. J.L. & PUB. POL'Y 1031, 1061 (2002).

support reimbursements for years during which the father did not know that he had a child.[107] The only scenario in which the woman may be required to give notice is if she wishes to begin an adoption proceeding.[108] In general, however, a man has no legally enforceable right to be informed regarding his sexual partner's conception, pregnancy, or childbirth.

This rule seems reasonable insofar as it protects a woman's privacy, autonomy, and safety. But from a relational perspective, it comes at a price. This price is obliquely acknowledged in jurisprudence on the interests of men whose sexual partners decide independently to undergo an abortion. Reading two such cases through the lens of separation versus connection is instructive.

Planned Parenthood of Central Missouri v. Danforth concerns whether husbands may veto their wives' reproductive choices,[109] and *Planned Parenthood of Southeastern Pennsylvania v. Casey* concerns whether husbands are entitled to be notified prior to an abortion (among other issues).[110] Both cases reject the control and informational interests of husbands and instead protect the woman's individual reproductive rights, but *Danforth* goes further toward acknowledging the relational tensions at play, the challenge inherent when we recognize both separate and connected aspects of human nature. Both cases deal with married couples, but their holdings apply to unmarried couples as well—if the relational interests that flow from marriage are not enough to overcome a woman's individual right to choose and to hide pregnancy, extramarital relations command even less respect.

Danforth holds that a husband may not veto his wife's decision to terminate a pregnancy. The opinion does, however, acknowledge the tension between its "separation"-privileging result and the imperatives of "connection" by recognizing "the deep and proper concern and interest that a devoted and protective husband has in his wife's pregnancy and in the growth and development of the fetus she is carrying."[111] As the Court explains:

> [I]deally the decision to terminate a pregnancy should be one concurred in by both the wife and her husband. No marriage may be viewed as harmonious or successful if the marriage partners are fundamentally divided on so important

107 The statute of limitations for retroactive child support can be as long as 18 years from the birth of the child. State *ex rel.* Reitenour, 807 A.2d 1259, 1262 (N.H. 2002).

108 *See* Unif. Adoption Act § 3-404, 9 U.L.A. 11 (1994); Unif. Parentage Act § 403 (amended 2002), 10 U.L.A. 321; *see also* Lehr v. Robertson, 463 U.S. 248, 263–64 (1983).

109 Planned Parenthood of Central Mo. v. Danforth, 428 U.S. 52, 71 (1976).

110 Planned Parenthood of Southeastern Pa. v. Casey, 505 U.S. 833, 895 (1992).

111 *Danforth*, 428 U.S. at 69. The Court reasoned that "the marital couple is not an independent entity with a mind and heart of its own, but an association of two individuals each with a separate intellectual and emotional makeup. If the right of privacy means anything, it is the right of the *individual*, married or single, to be free from unwarranted governmental intrusion into matters so fundamentally affecting a person as the decision whether to bear or beget a child." *Id.* at 70 n.11 (quoting Eisenstadt v. Baird, 405 U.S. 438, 453 (1972) (internal quotation marks omitted)).

> and vital an issue. But it is difficult to believe that the goal of fostering mutuality and trust in a marriage … will be achieved by giving the husband a veto power … [W]hen the wife and the husband disagree on this decision, the view of only one of the two marriage partners can prevail. Inasmuch as it is the woman who physically bears the child and who is the more directly and immediately affected by the pregnancy, as between the two, the balance weighs in her favor.[112]

Danforth thus implicitly recognizes the competing pulls of connection *and* separation. Pregnancy affects both parties to a relationship. Ideally, therefore, decisions about it should be made collectively. It is only when consensus cannot be reached that the decision-making balance must necessarily tip in favor of one of the two individuals. *Danforth* favors the wife, but it recognizes that pregnancy implicates husbands' interests as well. A husband who becomes a father against his will or is powerless to prevent the abortion he opposes may suffer deep, long-term, financial, psychological, and spiritual harms. A wife has the final say not because the husband has *no* say but because he has marginally *less* say, due to the fact that he is not the one who "physically bears the child."[113]

This tripartite balancing of the lovers' interests as a couple, the man's interests as potential father, and the woman's interests as potential mother and carrier of the fetus is less prominent in the Court's reasoning in *Casey*. *Casey* struck down a state statute requiring a married woman seeking an abortion to notify her husband in advance.[114] I believe the outcome of *Casey* is correct: doctors who perform abortions should not be required to withhold their services from women who have not signed an affidavit indicating that they have notified their husbands. But the reasoning, while briefly recognizing the relational interests discussed in *Danforth*,[115] is overwhelmingly weighted toward separation.

Justice O'Connor's majority opinion focuses on evidence showing that a significant number of women do not notify their husbands of their decision to obtain an abortion in order to protect their own and their children's safety.[116] Though the statute at issue in the case exempted women who believed that notification would expose them to bodily injury, the exception was too narrow because it did not account for emotional harm or harm to children. Also, by requiring the woman to sign an affidavit implicating her husband, the statute was blind to the dangers that victims of domestic violence face when they report their abusers.[117] Thus, O'Connor concludes that "[f]or the great many women who are victims of abuse inflicted by their husbands … a spousal notice requirement

112 *Id.* at 71.

113 *Id.*

114 *Casey*, 505 U.S. at 901.

115 *Id.* at 895, citing *Danforth*, 428 U.S. at 69.

116 *Id.* at 877–79.

117 *See id.* at 893.

enables the husband to wield an effective veto over his wife's decision."[118] Therefore, "the notice requirement will often be tantamount to the veto found unconstitutional in *Danforth*."[119]

The threat of violence doubtless justifies a woman's secrecy, and Justice O'Connor does a great service by turning the Court's spotlight on the unacceptably high incidence of domestic abuse and its impact on pregnant women. But women who hide their pregnancies from the men with whom they conceive do so for a range of reasons. Many, as *Casey* reports, are victims of abuse. Others may hide for different reasons: because they don't care for the man; because they want to avoid the intimacy that the conversation will create; because they are involved with another man; because they do not want to be swayed toward or away from abortion; because they are afraid of being abandoned; because they don't want to ask for empathy or help when they suspect none will be given; because they feel guilty, ashamed, responsible. Not all of these reasons justify the harm that secrecy inflicts on men and on the relationship. *Casey* missed an opportunity to make clear that when revealing her pregnancy would *not* endanger a woman, hiding it from the man is often wrong because pregnancy has relational implications. It may not be practically possible to craft a law that exempts only women with good reasons for hiding their pregnancies from notifying their partners, but acknowledging the rough justice that the current rule strikes would have expressive value.

Again, some men may prefer a no-strings-attached arrangement, but others approach sex with different baseline expectations. Many men would like and actively demonstrate their desire to know of the fact of conception.[120] They are willing and ready to help support the woman through whatever decision she makes, but they also want an opportunity to share their feelings about the pregnancy. When partners' wishes regarding abortion are diametrically opposed, the woman should have the final say: it is in the end her body that will bear the consequences, and even in marriage the wife's final preference rules. But guaranteeing this right to women may not require shutting all men out of the process entirely.

To sum up, sexual partners who conceive are not strangers. We are all connected. In sex we enact the most radical manifestation of our interconnectedness. Sex is connection, a connection that is sometimes also a conception. How might the law handle the results with greater care?

III. Toward a New Law of Conception

By treating sexual partners who conceive as legal strangers, the law reinforces rather than mitigates the vulnerabilities of both men and women. The law does, however, provide an alternative form for couples who want the consequences of

118 *Id.* at 897.

119 *Id.*

120 *See* Reich & Brindis, *supra* note 89, at 135.

sex to be governed by a set of robust relational obligations. It is called marriage. The lovers-as-strangers paradigm makes a lot more sense when viewed as one element of a broader societal strategy aimed at channeling sex into an institution designed and improved over the centuries to deal with its consequences. But this strategy has brought a debatable degree of success over time, and some historians insist that the theory behind it is flawed. The central function of marriage, they argue, was to forge alliances around power and property rather than to regulate the vulnerabilities that come along with reproduction.[121]

In any case, channeling sex into marriage today is clearly ineffective. Most Americans—secular and religious alike—have nonmarital sex, and women aged 18–24 have the highest number of unintended pregnancies.[122] A new approach tailored to our "postvirginal world"[123] is due.

Marriage and Accidental Procreation

"[A]n orderly society requires some mechanism for coping with the fact that sexual intercourse commonly results in pregnancy and childbirth," wrote dissenting Massachusetts Supreme Court Justice Robert Cordy in *Goodridge v. Department of Public Health*[124] and "[t]he institution of marriage is that mechanism."[125] According to Justice Cordy, marriage should be limited to heterosexuals because the *raison d'être* of marriage—regulating accidental procreation—is a nonissue for gay and lesbian lovers.[126]

Cordy and those who follow his lead are correct that heterosexuals face unique risks; accidental procreation does demand regulation. But marriage is not the ultimate answer to the problem. Marriage fulfills many worthy functions, but as society's main mechanism for safeguarding the interests of the accidentally pregnant, it is failing.

Marriage does guarantee spouses a minimal level of mutual support. A pregnant woman married to the man with whom she conceives is thus marginally safer, as

121 *See* Stephanie Coontz, Marriage, a History 34 (2005); *id.* at 31; *see also id.* at 34–49. Nancy F. Cott, Public Vows 15 (2002); E. J. Graff, What is Marriage For? 61 (2004).

122 *See supra* note 2 and accompanying text.

123 Joan Jacobs Brumberg, The Body Project: An Intimate History of American Girls 143 (1997). Sociologists describe a "hookup culture" on college campuses that leaves students who do not participate in it on the margins of the social scene, describing themselves as "abnormal." Kathleen A. Bogle, Hooking Up: Sex, Dating, and Relationships on Campus 64–71 (2008).

124 Goodridge v. Dep't of Pub. Health, 798 N.E.2d 941, 995 (Mass. 2003) (Cordy, J., dissenting). The case held that a bar against same-sex marriage violated the state's constitution.

125 *Id.*

126 *See* Kerry Abrams & Peter Brooks, *Marriage as a Message: Same-Sex Couples and the Rhetoric of Accidental Procreation*, 21 Yale J.L. & Human. 1, 3–4 (2009).

a matter of law, than a pregnant woman who is unwed.[127] This *de jure* safety, however, does not always translate into *de facto* benefits, and marriage may lock a woman into a harmful relationship with the only alternative—divorce—having potentially devastating economic consequences.[128] But even if we bracket these dangers, marriage is not the answer to the special relationship that arises with conception because accidental conception also happens outside of marriage.[129] It happens despite the carrots privileging spouses over unmarried couples (such as marriage-based tax benefits)[130] and despite the sticks discouraging nonmarital sex (like social pressures in religious communities)[131] and sex under the age of consent (statutory rape laws).[132]

In any case, while marriage used to be "the only option for a socially sanctioned intimate relationship,"[133] most Americans today have sex outside of marriage[134] during their teens.[135] Even the abstinence movement within conservative Christian communities has delayed the age of first intercourse only marginally.[136] Some studies have shown that teens who take chastity pledges are also less likely to

---

127 Note however that economically dependent spouses generally have few mechanisms for enforcing their entitlements during marriage. *See* Alicia B. Kelly, *Money Matters in Marriage: Unmasking Interdependence in Ongoing Spousal Economic Relations*, 47 U. Louisville L. Rev. 113, 144–51 (2008); *see also* Katharine Silbaugh, *Turning Labor into Love: Housework and the Law*, 91 Nw. U. L. Rev. 1, 34 (1996).

128 *See* Martha Albertson Fineman, The Neutered Mother, The Sexual Family and Other Twentieth Century Tragedies 228–30 (1995) (arguing that marriage and the "sexual family"—i.e. a conception of family focused on sexual affiliation rather than on the mother/child relationship—perpetuate gender inequality); Appleton, *supra* note 24, at 296–97 (describing family law's failure to deliver on the presumed promises of marriage).

129 *See* Coontz, *supra* note 121, at 112.

130 Appleton, *supra* note 24, at 273 ; Shari Motro, Op-Ed., *Single and Paying for It*, N.Y. Times, January 25, 2004, at 15.

131 *See generally* Naomi Cahn & June Carbone, Red Families v. Blue Families 42–44 (2010).

132 For an overview of statutory rape law, see Russell L. Christopher & Kathryn H. Christopher, *Adult Impersonation: Rape by Fraud as a Defense to Statutory Rape,* 101 Nw. U. L. Rev. 75, 111–16 (2007).

133 Elizabeth S. Scott, *Marriage, Cohabitation and Collective Responsibility for Dependency,* 2004 U. Chi. Legal. F. 225, 225.

134 *See* Cahn & Carbone, *supra* note 131, at 60 ("Social science research … suggests that well over 90% of all adults engage in sex before they marry").

135 *Facts on American Teens' Sexual and Reproductive Health*, GUTTMACHER INST. *(Jan. 2010),* http://www.guttmacher.org/pubs/FB-ATSRH.html. For a related discussion, see Lawrence B. Finer & Stanley K. Henshaw, *Disparities in Rates of Unintended Pregnancy in the United States, 1994 and 2001*, 38 Persp. on Sexual & Reprod. Health 90, 92–93 (2006), *available at* http://www.guttmacher.org/pubs/psrh/full/3809006.pdf; Henshaw, *supra* note 2, at 27.

136 *See* Lauren F. Winner, Real Sex: The Naked Truth About Chastity 17 (2005); Heather D. Boonstra, *Advocates Call for a New Approach After the Era of "Abstinence-*

use birth control, presumably because "the use of birth control implies that one thought about sex beforehand; one *planned* for it."[137]

Not only does marriage fail to deter accidental procreation, but the solution it offers young people who marry *because* of an accidental pregnancy—the preferred fallback in conservative communities—may also be less than ideal. A "shotgun marriage" will guarantee the woman a baseline level of support, but early marriages (particularly those "compelled by an improvident pregnancy")[138] are more likely than other marriages to end in divorce.[139] Furthermore, the financial and emotional costs of dissolving a failed marriage may outweigh the temporary security it provides during pregnancy.[140] Thus when pregnancy is accidental, couples whose actual emotional relationship is not one of lifelong commitment may be better served by an intermediate status that is calibrated to their situation.[141] The "shotgun" practice is thus at best an incomplete answer to the problem.

Justice Cordy concludes that:

> [A]side from an act of heterosexual intercourse nine months prior to childbirth, there is no process for creating a relationship between a man and a woman as the parents of a particular child. The institution of marriage fills this void by formally binding the husband-father to his wife and child … The alternative, a society without the institution of marriage … would be chaotic.[142]

But since marriage does not always link intercourse, procreation, and responsibility, and since it does not always fill the void by binding a man to the woman with whom he conceived, the blinkered reliance on marriage to solve the problem is

---

Only" Sex Education, 12 Guttmacher Pol'y Rev. 6, 8 (2009), *available at* http://www.guttmacher.org/pubs/gpr/12/1/gpr120106.html.

137 *Id.*

138 Cahn & Carbone, *supra* note 131, at 60.

139 *See id.* at 26.

140 Marriage provides a useful way to formalize intimate relations between lovers who would choose to marry regardless of the risk of procreative accidents. By standardizing a basket of rights and responsibilities between adults who intend to unite for life, it absolves couples of the need to deliberate and negotiate over every aspect of their union. Its maximalist one-size-fits-all defaults designate spouses as each others' primary beneficiaries, caretakers, guardians, agents, and representatives in all aspects of life—financial, medical, spiritual. In this capacity, spouses replace parents and siblings as a person's most significant legal relation. Though pregnancy and co-parenting are life-altering undertakings, marriage binds people to a broader, more extensive commitment than is needed to protect lovers who conceive and their unplanned children.

141 *See* Cahn & Carbone, *supra* note 131, at 59; *see also* Hirshman & Larson, *supra* note 90, at 276. *But see* Scott, *supra* note 133, at 235.

142 Goodridge v. Dep't of Pub. Health, 798 N.E.2d 941, 996 (Mass. 2003) (Cordy, J., dissenting).

misplaced. A society without an institution that fulfills these critical functions is indeed chaotic. It is the society in which we now live.

Matching Love Law to Love Life

What might a fairer law of conception look like? In love law—as in love life—one size does not fit all. Relations between unmarried lovers who conceive might therefore be handled differently depending on the type of intercourse that produced the pregnancy. Again, this chapter is concerned with pregnancies that result from sex that is consensual and involves no fraud or deceit. For our purposes, two types of consensual, good-faith sex might be distinguished—consensual sex that creates a set of baseline relational obligations, and consensual sex in which the parties expect and intend for there to be no strings attached. The former might serve as the basis for our default legal sex code, a code premised on contractual or equity-based principles; the latter might inform an alternative for those who wish to opt for a lovers-as-strangers rule.

The relational default

Nonmarital intimate relationships used to inhabit a legal no-man's land. Over the past few decades, however, courts and legislatures have begun to recognize unmarried partners who live together as forming a unique type of relationship under theories that parallel contractual and equity-based theories of marriage. Where a couple formalizes their domestic partnership and then one partner abandons the other, relief to the abandoned partner may be granted under contract principles.[143] Where a couple has made no explicit agreement formalizing their commitment, many jurisdictions nevertheless recognize that a partnership was formed and provide protections when the relationship breaks down under either an implied contract theory[144] or an equity-based status approach.[145]

A similar logic might apply to sexual partners who conceive, whether or not they live together. From a contractual perspective, partners who conceive might be recognized under the rubric of a distinct legal relationship because, in many instances, an agreement to assume mutual obligations of support and communication can be inferred. Even where such an agreement cannot be inferred, sexual partners who conceive should be legally responsible toward each other as a normative matter.

---

143 *See* Scott, *supra* note 133, at 255.

144 *Id.* at 256–58; *see also* Shahar Lifshitz, *Married Against Their Will* 11–13 (Bar-Ilan Univ. Pub. L. and Legal Theory Working Paper Series, Paper No. 06-09, 2009), *available at* http://ssrn.com/abstract=1352043 (explaining two models of implicit contractual relationships between cohabitating couples).

145 *See* Ira Ellman, *"Contractual Thinking" Was* Marvin*'s Fatal Flaw*, 76 Notre Dame L. Rev. 1365, 1373 (2001); *id.* at 1372 n.39.

In general, the relationship status of sexual partners who conceive might be founded on two guiding principles: (1) communication obligations surrounding conception should take the parties' individual interests as well as their relational interests into account; and (2) responsibilities for the costs of pregnancy, childbirth, miscarriage, and abortion broadly conceived should be equitably shared by both partners. Again, the goal of this chapter is to start a conversation. What follows are a range of possible parameters for structuring a new relational default.

Communication

As we have seen, the lovers-as-strangers paradigm translates into a default that gives men almost no entitlement to be informed of conception. When sex takes place in the context of a good-faith nonviolent relationship, the law thus disregards a basic and legitimate relational value. The status quo is also problematic because of the distinctions it draws between rich and poor. The current rule gives financially independent women a carte blanche to hide pregnancy and birth while applying a mandatory disclosure policy to women who are unable to shoulder the costs of childcare alone.[146] While it is true that the policy requiring indigent women applying for public assistance to identify the father of their child is rooted in a concern for public funds, not for the relational interests of the father, the result effectively distributes privacy privileges based on economics.

Ideally, men and women who engage in the type of sex that results in pregnancy—usually repeated acts of unprotected intercourse—will either share a no-strings-attached understanding or they will both feel safe discussing an unintended pregnancy. But for many women, notifying their partner of conception spells danger.[147] It may also undermine a woman's right to choose if, once notified, the man pressures or coerces her to undergo or forego an abortion. Even if the woman faces no such dangers, placing all of the communication burden on her would require her to proactively contact a man who may have no legitimate interest in the matter—for example, a man who demonstrated no relational commitment beyond the sexual encounter. Nevertheless, a default that gives no consideration whatsoever to nonviolent men's interest in knowing about a pregnancy goes too far.

This chapter does not address the ideal mechanism for administering a "danger" exception, but it is worth noting that the challenges it poses are not novel. When indigent mothers apply for public assistance, they are often required to identify the father of their child as a condition for receiving benefits unless doing so would expose them to danger.[148] The Pennsylvania statute struck down by *Casey* also contained a similar exception for women in danger of bodily injury.[149] Unfortunately, these exceptions have been poorly crafted

146 *See supra* note 108 and accompanying text.

147 *See supra* notes 116–119 and accompanying text.

148 *See* Jacqueline M. Fontana, *Cooperation and Good Cause: Greater Sanctions and the Failure to Account for Domestic Violence*, 15 Wis. Women's L.J. 367, 368–69 (2000).

149 *See* Planned Parenthood of Southeastern Pa. v. Casey, 505 U.S. 833, 908–09 (2002).

and ineffectively applied.[150] Protecting pregnant women against violence is of paramount importance, but I am not convinced that the most effective way to do so over time is through the minimal support and communication defaults of the lovers-as-strangers paradigm. Even a minimally enforceable rule directing a woman to notify the man only if he makes the first proactive relational step (by remaining involved with her or contacting a public registry) and only if she subjectively believes doing so is safe and wise would carry a positive expressive value; it would replace the current disregard for a man's relational interests with a clear normative priority for connection over separation.

Support

Pregnancy's effects on a woman's health, career, and education produce real costs that, to the extent they are not supported by public funds, should be borne by both a woman and the man with whom she conceives. Quantifying these costs is difficult, but the alternative—effectively valuing them at zero—is unacceptable.[151] Two broadly conceived approaches to determining the extent of men's financial obligations might be considered. First, pregnancy-related obligcations might be based on the costs of each particular pregnancy. Alternately, pregnant women might be entitled to a standard award based on average pregnancy costs adjusting for certain objective variables like the length of the pregnancy. Either of these alternatives might integrate an additional element keyed to men's financial profile designed to increase their incentives to prevent pregnancy.

Both approaches present valuation challenges. Fortunately, we need not start our pregnancy-valuation discussion from scratch. Negligence awards in wrongful pregnancy cases in which a botched sterilization procedure leads to an unplanned pregnancy and surrogate motherhood compensation arrangements provide useful starting points. Naturally, many of the issues that determine the awards in the tort and surrogacy contexts are different from the issues affecting sexual partners who conceive. Wrongful pregnancies are the fault of negligent surgeons, while surrogate mothers volunteer to bear a planned child for another family—both are very different from the relational situation with which we are concerned. Nevertheless, the in-depth examinations of the real costs of pregnancy in these contexts are instructive.

Most jurisdictions' wrongful pregnancy recovery allowance covers prenatal and postnatal medical expenses, including expenses of any complications associated with the pregnancy or birth *as well as* the mother's pain and suffering during the pregnancy and delivery.[152] Some jurisdictions also allow recovery

---

150 *See id.* at 888.

151 *See generally* Katharine Silbaugh, *Commodification and Women's Household Labor*, 9 Yale J.L. & Feminism 81 (1997).

152 *See* Boone v. Mullendore, 416 So. 2d 718, 721 (Ala. 1982); Coleman v. Garrison, 327 A.2d 757, 761–62 (Del. Super. Ct. 1974), *aff'd*, 349 A.2d 8 (Del. 1975).

for lost wages during pregnancy, delivery, and a postnatal period.[153] Finally, in some jurisdictions women may be compensated for emotional distress[154] and any permanent impairment suffered by the mother as a result of the pregnancy, the delivery, or subsequent corrective procedures.[155] Wrongful pregnancy cases also provide for recovery if the woman chooses to terminate the pregnancy.[156]

Compensation agreements between surrogate mothers and intended parents account for the fact that the real costs to the woman exceed the actual medical bills she incurs during and immediately following the pregnancy by tens of thousands of dollars. In addition to compensation for the service of carrying the intended parents' child, surrogates often receive additional allowances to cover miscellaneous expenses associated with pregnancy, such as maternity clothing, childcare for existing children, lost wages, and meals.[157] The intended parents also generally cover all medical costs not reimbursed by insurance, as well as life insurance premiums for the birth mother.[158] When a surrogate mother miscarries or undergoes a medically necessary abortion, she is paid a prorated portion of her fee for the period of time during which she carried the fetus, as well as an additional amount for her pain and suffering.[159]

Because pregnancy and childbirth may bring a woman both emotional and physical joy,[160] a question arises as to whether these positive effects should offset her physical and emotional pain for valuation purposes. This poses obvious difficulties, but omitting pain and suffering entirely is also problematic, especially in the cases of women suffering from debilitating postpartum depression, women who miscarry, and women who undergo a traumatic abortion. Possible solutions include setting a standard limited award for the pain and inconvenience of pregnancy or to omit pain from the calculation except for in exceptional cases. In

153 *See* Kingsbury v. Smith, 442 A.2d 1003, 1006 (N.H. 1982); Beardsley v. Wierdsman, 650 P.2d 288, 292 (Wyo. 1982).

154 *See* Smith v. Gore, 728 S.W.2d 738, 751–52 (Tenn. 1987); Miller v. Johnson, 343 S.E.2d 301, 305 (Va. 1986). Indeed, in some cases even the woman's "struggle whether to rear, place for adoption, or terminate the pregnancy" is reimbursable. *Gore*, 728 S.W.2d at 752. *See also* White v. United States, 510 F. Supp. 146, 149 (D. Kan. 1981); Weintraub v. Brown, 470 N.Y.S.2d 634, 641–42 (Sup. Ct. 1973).

155 *See* Flax v. McNew, 896 S.W.2d 839, 843–45 (Tex. App. 1995). Jurisdictions differ, however, on whether the tortfeasor doctor may also be held liable for the costs of raising a child.

156 *See Gore*, 728 S.W.2d at 752.

157 *See* Surrogate Mothers, Inc., Approximate Expenses, http://www.surrogatemothers.com/expense.html (last visited August 28, 2010).

158 *See* Circle Surrogacy, Payment/Bills, http://www.circlesurrogacy.com/surrogate/faq.html#Payments (last visited August 28, 2010).

159 *See* Shelley M. Tarnoff, *When Things Go Wrong: Pregnancy Termination in Surrogacy*, Opts, June 1, 2010, http://www.opts.com/pgterm.htm; *see also* Alex Kuczynski, *Her Body, My Baby*, N.Y. Times Mag., November 30, 2008, at 42.

160 *See* Orgasmic Birth, *supra* note 14.

any case, even if pain and suffering are taken out of the picture entirely, the real costs of pregnancy will almost certainly exceed the child-support type paradigm currently in force.

Once the costs of a given pregnancy are calculated, they might be allocated based on an equal division principle or on a formula that accounts for differences in the parties' marginal utility of wealth.[161] The main advantages of equal division are its simplicity and predictability. Marginal utility-based division, by contrast, is cumbersome, but it has the potential to allocate costs more equitably than a rigid equal division standard. Because it keys each partner's obligation to his or her financial situation, the method ensures that both parties are significantly affected and it eliminates perverse incentives that may arise when parties differ in wealth.

But both of these methods presume that the diverse physical and psychic costs of pregnancy can be easily plugged into a formula. In reality, translating them into a dollar amount may be more of an art than a science, and some cases may present alternative, nonmonetary opportunities. A third alternative for allocating the subjective costs of a particular pregnancy is by using a judicial case-by-case discretionary approach similar to equitable distribution at divorce. Under this approach, judges would have the freedom to impose an equitable allocation based on their own consideration of relevant factors.

The pros and cons of this case-by-case method track the pros and cons of discretionary approaches to divorce.[162] The main advantage is that it would allow

---

161 The marginal utility method would lessen the woman's burden and increase the man's such that both suffer a *comparable* loss. The result would mitigate the woman's burden only to the point at which the man would "share her pain." For example, a wealthy woman's pregnancy-related costs expressed in dollars would typically be high because her low marginal utility of wealth makes her pain "worth more," so she requires more dollars to be made whole. But if she conceives with a man of modest means she would be entitled only to a small fraction of her total loss, an amount roughly balancing the parties' loss relative to their overall circumstance. A poor woman who conceives with a rich man would be entitled to an amount close to but never exceeding her experienced loss, which will be much lower in dollars than the loss of the rich woman. (The poor woman's high marginal utility of wealth means that she requires less to be made whole.) Only where both parties are equally wealthy will the payment equal half of the woman's loss.

This method would therefore increase the deterrence potential of the new default rule, protect poor men from the risk of devastating losses (should they accidentally impregnate a rich woman), as well as limit rich men's risk exposure in the face of gold-diggers. A woman who might be tempted to abuse the law in order to extract a large payment from a rich man will quickly realize that she will never be able to recover more than her own true costs.

162 For a discussion on the drawbacks of broad judicial discretion over divorce, see AM. LAW INST., PRINCIPLES OF THE LAW OF FAMILY DISSOLUTION: ANALYSIS AND RECOMMENDATIONS § 4.09 cmt. a (2000); *see also* Jana B. Singer, *Divorce Reform and Gender Justice*, 67 N.C. L. REV. 1103, 1119 (1989) ("[D]ivorce doctrines that allow for substantial judicial discretion generally operate to women's disadvantage … The absence of clear-cut legal standards also affects the negotiation process in ways that disadvantage the economically weaker party, generally the woman, in a divorce. Finally, the lack of

decision-makers to tailor a solution to the specific facts and circumstances of the case. Relevant factors might include the parties' age, dependents, and behavior leading up to and following the conception. The main disadvantage of the discretionary approach is that it creates an opening for the legal system's separation bias to creep back into the allocation through individual decision-makers.[163] It would also be highly uncertain, time consuming, and costly. These drawbacks could lower the chances that parties would seek to enforce their entitlements in the first place.

Finally, instead of attempting to value the costs associated with each pregnancy, miscarriage, and abortion, women could be entitled to a standard support allowance upon conception and continuing for the duration of the pregnancy. This allowance might be based on an estimate of the average costs of pregnancy, and it might vary based on objective factors like the length of the pregnancy and the woman's age. It might also take into account the parties' relative wealth, producing the same advantages discussed in this connection above without the burden of case-by-case valuations.

It is important to stress that neither the notification nor the cost sharing principle should change a woman's right to make the ultimate decision about whether to take a pregnancy to term. Just as a husband's objection to his wife's decision does not diminish his spousal support duties, the proposed duties triggered by consensual intercourse between unmarried partners should be unaffected if the parties' reproductive preferences diverge.

Opportunity to opt out

The relational default proposed above is clearly not appropriate for all sexual partners. Some partners want to have sex with the mutual understanding that nothing more is expected. Others wish to conceive but want no financial or legal relationship with each other. Partners who truly desire no-liability sex should be permitted to play by their own rules, but the onus should be on them to make these rules explicit.

At first glance, this suggestion may seem out of touch with reality. Many, perhaps most, casual partners' expectations regarding unintended pregnancy remain unarticulated for a range of reasons. Some do not want to think about the risks, others simply trust each other, and still others remain silent because they don't want to imply that they don't trust each other. As one colleague put it, talking about pregnancy before sex can be a "buzz kill."

But Internet dating culture tells a different story. Some sites, for example, are explicitly devoted to users looking for "casual encounters"[164] or "friends

---

precise standards … may drive up the costs associated with divorce, particularly attorneys' fees, which again penalizes the economically weaker spouse").

163 I credit Corinna Lain for this insight.

164 Craigslist hosts such listings under categories named "missed connections" and "casual encounters" for various geographical areas. *See*, e.g., Craigslist: Atlanta Classifieds

with benefits."[165] Dating sites with a more diverse membership base include preset options allowing users to signal the type of connection they are looking for. OKCupid's standard questionnaire, for example, includes: "Which of these options most closely describes what you're looking for in your next relationship? Someone to come home to. Someone to go out with. Someone for tonight." It also asks users to indicate whether they believe in monogamy and whether they believe contraception is "morally wrong."[166] And almost all dating sites and personals venues provide a space in which users can describe their preferences in their own words. The Urban Dictionary now includes definitions for euphemisms commonly used in such forums, including "NSA"—no strings attached.[167]

Thus, while the suggestion that casual partners make their expectations clear before sex may seem jarring at first, plenty of people are already doing just that. Indeed, as online dating grows and evolves, in addition to changing norms among its direct users it may create opportunities for new codes among those meeting offline as well. If a relational default becomes law, we may discover that people's capacity for clarity when it comes to intimacy is more developed than we have come to expect and accept.

Where expectations are not discussed, however, the default rule should reflect equitable norms by imposing the communication and support obligations described above. As in the premarital context, unconscionable opt-out agreements should be unenforceable as a matter of public policy. Importantly, the partners' decision to opt out of the relational default should not affect their responsibilities vis-à-vis their child.

---

for Jobs, Apartments, Personals, For Sale, Services, Community, http://www.atlanta.craigslist.org (last visited August 28, 2010).

165 *See* Friends with Benefits, http://findfriendswithbenefits.com (last visited August 2010).

166 *See* OKCupid, http://www.OKCupid.com/questions/ask (last visited May 30, 2010) (users must create an account to access this page). FriendFinder.com advertises itself as providing "personals for fun, friends, & love." Friendfinder: Have Fun, Meet People, & Find Love, http://www.friendfinder.com (last visited August 28, 2010).

167 *See* Urban Dictionary, NSA, http://www.urbandictionary.com/define.php?term=nsa (last visited May 27, 2010) ("No Strings Attached, but it doesn't refer to a type of relationship, but to the willingness/desire to have sex without the necessity of a relationship. NSA means lets have some fun without creating any obligations beyond the moment. We do what we do tonight and dont [*sic*] ever have to see each other again. But without the negative connotation of one-night stand, even if that is what it is." One of the examples supplied reads: "Single successful individual with no time to spend in the bars looks for NSA relationship.—*craigslist*").

Closing Remarks

I have suggested that sex creates a unique type of relationship, and that sex that results in pregnancy extends this relationship. But the law treats lovers as strangers. It treats nonprocreative sex through an ideological framework of separation rather than connection, of free love rather than mutual responsibility. The current default contradicts mainstream expectations about sex and basic intuitions about fairness. Instead, this chapter proposes a new relational paradigm that establishes minimal notification and support obligations between sexual partners who conceive.

The relational default requires further study before it can be implemented. In the meantime, however, we don't need the law to start changing our lives. Each one of us—as individuals and lovers, siblings and friends, teachers and parents—can start now by asking: what is our own personal law of conception? What do we want it to be? Have we chosen the rules that govern our love lives deliberately, or have we adopted them passively, unreflectively? These are difficult questions to ask. Going along without asking is easier. Going along doesn't ruin the moment, but each time we put on the blinders we drift further from our intuitive capacity to listen and to feel for the answers. Going along distances us; it distances us from ourselves and it distances us from our lovers.

Asking these questions and talking about them openly will not merely clear the air of misunderstandings. The process of asking and sharing has the potential itself to begin to sensitize us to our own and to our lovers' true desires. It may help us to identify what inspires and what deadens, what lifts and what oppresses, what heals and what injures. And it may lead us to be more mindful about our choices.

In life there are no guarantees. Men and women who do not want children have sex anyway despite the wild roll-of-the-dice that it entails. This is the fundamental risk at the heart of making love. This is the true price of pleasure, a price no law can erase. But the law can—indeed it inevitably does—set the baseline. It is up to us to decide where.

Chapter 3
Abortion Rhetoric and Child Custody Laws for Women Who Mother Through Rape

Shauna R. Prewitt*

I. Introduction

The controversy that erupted after senatorial candidate Todd Akin's statement that a woman's body is capable of preventing pregnancy in cases of "legitimate rape"[1] ignited not only fierce backlash against the candidate but also public interest in the custody rights surrounding rape-conceived children.[2] Over the weeks and even months that followed Akin's statement, the media fed the public interest by recycling the known statistics: pregnancy from rape occurs with "significant frequency;"[3] potentially 32,000 rape-related pregnancies occur annually; and 4.7 percent of all raped women become pregnant.[4]

---

* Portions of this chapter excerpted from Shauna R. Prewitt, Note, *Giving Birth To a "Rapist's Child": A Discussion and Analysis of the Limited Legal Protections Afforded to Women Who Become Mothers Through Rape*, 98 GEO. L.J. 827 (2010). © 2010, Shauna R. Prewitt.

1 *See* Tom Cohen, *Akin Defies Mounting Calls to Withdraw from Senate Race*, CNN POLITICS (Aug. 22, 2012, 7:36 AM), http://www.cnn.com/2012/08/21/politics/akin-controversy/index.html?hpt=hp_t2.

2 *See* Dana Liebelson & Sydney Brownstone, *Imagine You Were Raped. Got Pregnant. Then Your Rapist Sought Custody*, MOTHER JONES (Aug. 24, 2012, 2:00 AM), http://www.motherjones.com/politics/2012/08/rapist-seeks-child-custody-shauna-prewitt.

3 *See* Sarah Kliff, *Rep. Todd Akin is Wrong About Rape and Pregnancy, But He's Not Alone*, THE WASHINGTON POST (Aug. 20, 2012, 8:46 AM), http://www.washingtonpost.com/blogs/wonkblog/wp/2012/08/20/rep-todd-akin-is-wrong-about-rape-and-pregnancy-but-hes-not-alone/; *see also* Melissa M. Holmes et al., *Rape-Related Pregnancy: Estimates and Descriptive Characteristics from a National Sample of Women*, 175 AM. J. OBSTETRICS & GYNECOLOGY 320, 320 (1996).

4 Kevin Robillard, *Doctors: Todd Akin Pregnancy Claim Bogus*, POLITICO (Aug. 20, 2012, 2:43 PM), http://www.politico.com/news/stories/0812/79895.html. *See also* Holmes et al., *supra* note 3, at 322 (concluding that, based on a 1990 study estimating that 683,000 women over the age of 18 were raped in that year, conceivably 32,000 rape-related pregnancies occur annually); Felicia H. Stewart & James Trussell, *Prevention of Pregnancy Resulting from Rape: A Neglected Preventive Health Measure*, 19 AM. J. PREVENTIVE MED. 228, 228 (2000) (concluding that, given the decline in the incidence of rape, 25,000 pregnancies following the rape of adult women occur annually). The number

In addition, the public learned that many raped women give birth to and raise their rape-conceived children, which could lead to custody battles with their rapists.[5] One study found that 32.3 percent of raped women raised their rape-conceived children.[6] Another study, conducted in a separate year, concluded that of the 73 percent of raped women who carried their pregnancies to term, 64 percent raised the children they conceived through their rapes.[7] Although the number of rapists who seek custody rights is unknown, stories emerged regarding its incidence.[8] Yet, as reported by the media, shockinglyfew states—at the time only 19—had laws designed to terminate and/or restrict the custody privileges of rapists over their rape-conceived children.[9] Without such laws, a man who fathers a child through rape has the same custody and visitation privileges regarding that child as does the father of a child not conceived through rape.[10]

Despite the mass media surrounding this issue in the year since Akin's comments, what has been missing from the conversation is a meaningful discussion of the reason for the *absence* of these laws. *Why have so many states failed to act?* The purpose of this chapter is to fill the void. It argues that societal rhetoric depicting the prototypical raped woman as hating her unborn rape-conceived child and viewing her rape pregnancy as a continuation of her rape experience has limited the protections available to women who defy the prototype by raising and purporting to love their rape-conceived children. By way of comparison, Part II describes how odious societal rhetoric and images about rape generally have

---

of rape pregnancies that occur each year may be substantially higher given that both studies excluded adolescents from their consideration. "Approximately 30% of rapes involve women under age 18. [Although f]ecundity among very young adolescents is not as high as that of adult women … adult women are far more likely to be protected against pregnancy when raped because they are using hormonal contraception or are sterilized." *Id.*

5 Mike Beaudet & Kevin Rothstein, *Rapist Wants Visitation Rights; Teen Mom Fighting Back*, My FOX Boston (Sept. 26, 2012, 7:18 AM), http://www.myfoxboston.com/story/19628763/2012/09/24/rapist-wants-visitation-rights-teen-mom-fighting-back#ixzz2VCHHtCHp.

6 Holmes et al., *supra* note 3, at 322 (also concluding that 50 percent of women who became pregnant by rape underwent abortions and 5.9 percent placed their infants for adoptions).

7 Amy Sobie & David C. Reardon, *A Survey of Rape and Incest Pregnancies*, *in* Victims and Victors: Speaking Out About Their Pregnancies, Abortions, and Children Resulting from Sexual Assault 18, 19 (David C. Reardon et al. eds., 2000) (concluding that 26 percent of raped women underwent abortions and, of the 73 percent of women who carried their pregnancies to term, 36 percent placed their infants for adoption).

8 *See, e.g.*, Beaudet & Rothstein, *supra* note 5.

9 Liebelson & Brownstone, *supra* note 2.

10 For an extended discussion regarding the negative consequences of granting rapists custody rights of their rape-conceived children, *see* Shauna R. Prewitt, Note, *Giving Birth To a "Rapist's Child": A Discussion and Analysis of the Limited Legal Protections Afforded to Women Who Become Mothers Through Rape*, 98 Geo. L.J. 827, 831–36 (2010).

operated to deny a certain class of women protection from the law, namely those women whose rape experiences depart from the *stranger-rape prototype*.[11]

Part III suggests that there exists a *pregnant-raped-woman prototype*, which, like the *stranger-rape prototype*, has been constructed from invidious stereotypes that have been articulated in public discourse, largely in discussions about funding for abortion access. These societal constructions have created a prototype of the pregnant raped woman and of the prototypical rape pregnancy experience by which all raped women are judged.

Part IV argues that the *pregnant-raped-woman prototype*, like the *stranger-rape prototype*, limits the law's protection of women who defy the prototype. Betraying the prototype by deciding to raise their rape-conceived children, these women are viewed with suspicion. They then are denied legal protections, such as alternate custody laws, because, being viewed as "impostor" rape victims, it is thought that there is nothing special about them or their conceptions requiring any change in the manner in which custody and visitation determinations are made. They are viewed as liars, not as rape victims, and therefore, subject to the same visitation and custody presumptions as other women. Part IV also reviews the laws that currently exist to protect raped women who raise their rape-conceived children and concludes that the *pregnant-raped-woman prototype* explains both the current legal absence and why, even in the few states with rape-conception custody laws, the protections are largely illusory.

Part IV concludes by arguing that the *pregnant-raped-woman prototype*, like the *stranger-rape prototype*, operates on a normative, and potentially biased, level. As a result, it limits the law's reach and protection of women who go against the prototype and also reifies odious social hierarchies.

II. Societal Rhetoric's Role in Limiting Legal Protections

Societal rhetoric historically has played a strong role in limiting the scope of the protections afforded to various individuals under the law, particularly to raped women. For example, despite the widespread condemnation of rape, the conviction rate for rape is remarkably lower than the conviction rate for other

11 The *stranger-rape prototype* contends that the prototypical rape occurs when a black stranger attacks a white woman in public using overwhelming force. *See* Martha Chamallas, *Deepening the Legal Understanding of Bias: On Devaluation and Biased Prototypes*, 74 S. Cal. L. Rev. 747, 784 (2001). Rape studies indicate that this prototype fails to accurately depict the typical or most common case of rape, and as a result, it restricts legal protections for women whose rape experience departs from this prototype. *See infra* Part II.

serious crimes;[12] "[n]inety-eight percent of the victims of rape never see their attacker caught, tried and imprisoned."[13]

In explaining the disparity between the high condemnation of rape and the low incidence of rape reporting, arrests, and convictions, many scholars fault the "invidious societal stereotypes regarding rape victims,"[14] which have constructed a prototype of the rape experience and of the prototypical raped woman and offender that frequently fails to reflect reality. People use prototypes to "process[] information, draw[] conclusions, and … mak[e] sense of the world."[15] According to Martha Chamallas:

> [P]ersons use prototypes as "cognitive shortcuts" to help them categorize new cases and situations. When a person "reasons" from a prototype, whether by conjuring up a prototypical victim, offender, or event, he or she searches for a family resemblance between the new case and the prototypical case. The more the new case looks like the prototype (for example, by sharing common features of the prototype), the more likely it will be classified as falling within the category.[16]

Because all prototypes—by defining what is typical or normal—also implicitly suggest what is atypical, they "set the standard by which others are judged."[17] Thus, the criticism of the rape prototype is not in its failure to capture the full range of rape experiences.[18] Rather, the rape prototype is problematic because it is not statistically or descriptively accurate, and consequently, it is biased.[19] Despite statistics to the contrary, the "stock images, mental portraits, schemas, or cultural scripts"[20] concerning rape depict that the prototypical rape occurs when a black stranger attacks a white woman in public using overwhelming force.[21] Rape studies indicate that this prototype, known as the *stranger-rape prototype*, fails to

12 *See* Chamallas, *supra* note 11, at 782.

13 Christina E. Wells & Erin Elliott Motley, *Reinforcing the Myth of the Crazed Rapist: A Feminist Critique of Recent Rape Legislation*, 81 B.U. L. Rev. 127, 128–29 (2001) (citing Majority Staff of Senate Comm. on the Judiciary, 103d Cong., The Response to Rape: Detours on the Road to Equal Justice iii (Comm. Print 1993)).

14 *Id.* at 129 (citation omitted); *see* Chamallas, *supra* note 11, at 783.

15 Ronald Chen & Jon Hanson, *Categorically Biased: The Influence of Knowledge Structures on Law and Legal Theory*, 77 S. Cal. L. Rev. 1103, 1125 (2004).

16 Chamallas, *supra* note 11, at 778 (citation omitted).

17 *Id.* at 787.

18 *Id.* at 783–84.

19 *Id.* at 783.

20 *Id.* at 778.

21 *See id.* at 784; Susan Estrich, Real Rape 4 (1987) (identifying the many different rape contexts and noting that only violent stranger rapes consistently result in criminal charges).

accurately depict the typical or most common case of rape.[22] Instead, nearly eight out of 10 rapes are committed by someone the raped woman knows,[23] and nearly six out of 10 rapes occur in the raped woman's home or the home of a friend, relative, or neighbor.[24] Seventy percent of raped women report no physical injuries stemming from their rapes,[25] and in violent crimes against women, the woman and the perpetrator are of the same race 80 percent of the time for white women and 90 percent of the time for black women.[26]

As the statistics demonstrate, the rape prototype depicts the statistically atypical rape case—stranger-rape—as the prototypical, or most typical, rape case.[27] Because it depicts what societal rhetoric argues *ought* to constitute "real rape," instead of what typically and statistically constitutes the majority of rape experiences,[28] the rape prototype "constructs a line between normalcy and deviancy, between the acceptable and the unacceptable"[29] and "distort[s] decisions about whether specific instances belong in the [rape] category"[30] in a biased way. Moreover, it conveys that rape experiences differing from the *stranger-rape prototype* constitute harm that is not merely different but that *ought* to be treated as less "real," less "substantial," and less "worthy of legal redress."[31]

As a result of legislators and courts applying the *stranger-rape prototype* in making their decisions,[32] rape laws are crafted, interpreted, and enforced in a way that fails to criminalize the majority of rape experiences, resulting in the legalization of most acts that should be regarded as rape.[33] Susan Estrich explains:

---

22 Chamallas, *supra* note 11, at 783.

23 PATRICIA TJADEN & NANCY THOENNES, FULL REPORT OF THE PREVALENCE, INCIDENCE, AND CONSEQUENCES OF VIOLENCE AGAINST WOMEN: FINDINGS FROM THE NATIONAL VIOLENCE AGAINST WOMEN SURVEY 61 (2000), *available at* http://www.ncjrs.gov/pdffiles1/nij/183781.pdf.

24 LAWRENCE A. GREENFELD, U.S. DEP'T OF JUSTICE, SEX OFFENSES AND OFFENDERS: AN ANALYSIS OF DATA ON RAPE AND SEXUAL ASSAULT 3 (1997), *available at* http://bjs.ojp.usdoj.gov/content/pub/pdf/SOO.PDF.

25 NAT'L VICTIM CTR. & NAT'L CRIME VICTIMS RESEARCH & TREATMENT CTR., RAPE IN AMERICA: A REPORT TO THE NATION 4 (1992).

26 RONET BACHMAN, U.S. DEP'T OF JUSTICE, VIOLENCE AGAINST WOMEN: A NATIONAL CRIME VICTIMIZATION SURVEY REPORT 6 (1994). However, where interracial rapes do occur, "the black offender/white victim rape produces the strongest legal response, perhaps because it is the prototype." Chamallas, *supra* note 11, at 784.

27 *See* Chamallas, *supra* note 11, at 783.

28 *Id.* at 778.

29 *Id.* at 780–81.

30 *Id.* at 779.

31 *Id.* at 779–80.

32 *Id.* at 778, 803.

33 *See id.* at 779–80, 783–84.

> At one end of the spectrum is the "real" rape ... A stranger puts a gun to the head of his victim, threatens to kill her or beats her, and then engages in intercourse. In that case, the law—judges, statutes, prosecutors and all—generally acknowledge that a serious crime has been committed. But most cases deviate in one or many respects from this clear picture, making interpretation far more complex. Where less force is used or no other physical injury is inflicted, where threats are inarticulate, where the two know each other, where the setting is not an alley but a bedroom, where the initial contact was not a kidnapping but a date, where the woman says no but does not fight, the understanding is different. In such cases, the law, as reflected in the opinions of the courts, the interpretation, if not the words, of the statutes, and the decisions of those within the criminal justice system, often tell us that no crime has taken place.[34]

Thus, the *stranger-rape prototype* both initially and continuously "infect[s] legal judgments about criminality and victimization[,] ... prevent[ing] many date and acquaintance rapes from being classified as 'real rapes.'"[35] And, as a result, it has "transform[ed] rape from a pervasive phenomenon into an isolated one."[36]

Chamallas suggests that the biased *stranger-rape prototype* is promoted because it serves a functional goal: "to reinforce certain social hierarchies."[37] Chamallas first argues that, by operating to decriminalize some nonconsensual sexual experiences, the *stranger-rape prototype* "reinforces male dominance and female powerlessness by giving (some) men sexual access to women they know."[38] She suggests that the "balance of power in marriage[s]," employment settings, and other relationships are "skewed" against women if they believe that others will view their rape claims skeptically.[39] Second, the *stranger-rape prototype* strengthens patriarchal norms concerning the way women should behave.[40] Even though the vast majority of women are raped by an acquaintance in their home or the home of a friend, relative, or neighbor, one study found

34 Susan Estrich, *Rape*, 95 Yale L.J. 1087, 1092 (1986). Explained another way: "Police and others are more likely to believe a case is genuine: (1) if violence occurred and bodily harm resulted; (2) if the offender was a stranger; (3) if the event reported involved more than one assailant; (4) if the victim showed signs of resistance and cried out; (5) if the victim reported the crime promptly; (6) if weapons were involved; (7) if the victim was emotionally upset afterwards; (8) if the victim had a reputation for chastity, did not voluntarily participate, and behaved in an acceptable, reputable manner prior to the assault; and (9) if witnesses were present to corroborate the claim of rape or abduction." Sedelle Katz & Mary Ann Mazur, Understanding the Rape Victim: A Synthesis of Research Findings 210 (1979) (citations omitted).

35 Chamallas, *supra* note 11, at 778.

36 *Id.* at 784.

37 *Id.* at 785–86.

38 *Id.* at 786.

39 *Id.*

40 *Id.*

that many women apparently believe they can avoid rape by dressing modestly, "avoid[ing] preferred public activities if alone," and "going out at night with[] a male protector."[41] Thus, the prototype reinforces "patriarchal norms" by dictating that a woman should be "passive, modest, and under male protection."[42] Finally, Chamallas argues that the racialized prototype "reinforces white domination by using the threat of a charge of rape against black men to limit their freedom."[43]

III. Constructing the *Pregnant-Raped-Woman Prototype*: The "Necessity" of Abortion Access for Raped Women

The power of societal rhetoric to limit effective legal protections extends beyond the *stranger-rape prototype*. Societal rhetoric, images, and stereotypes—largely advanced in discourse concerning funding for abortion access—have also limited legal protections, this time to raped women who choose to raise their rape-conceived children.

Societal rhetoric and images concerning the plight of the pregnant raped woman began during the 1960s as the result of what some describe as a strategic attempt by proponents of abortion rights to create inroads on the path to the legalization of abortion.[44] Long before *Roe v. Wade*, a series of exposés were utilized to argue for the need for safe, legal abortions "without engaging the powerful value sets that surrounded it."[45] Primarily, proponents of abortion rights were battling against the view that women who sought abortions were making a choice against motherhood.[46] So, despite the fact that the motivating force behind the "uncountable thousands of illegal abortions" in the 1960s primarily was "the desire to control one's family, life-style, and economic status,"[47] many of the women in these exposés were cast as women who "had been raped" and whose pregnancies were depicted as exacerbating the grievousness of rape.[48] Proponents of abortion access used the image of the raped woman to challenge the public opinion that all women who sought abortions were making a *choice* "against motherhood."[49] They did this by depicting raped women as having no choice in seeking their abortions.[50] Instead, raped women were depicted as "unfortunates

---

41 *Id.* (citing Margaret T. Gordon & Stephanie Riger, The Female Fear 15–22 (1989)).

42 *Id.*

43 *Id.*

44 *See* Victims and Victors, *supra* note 7, at ix.

45 Celeste Michelle Condit, Decoding Abortion Rhetoric: Communicating Social Change 24 (1990).

46 *See id.* at 25–26.

47 *Id.* at 33.

48 *Id.* at 26.

49 *Id.*

50 *Id.*

who, through no fault of their own, were *forced* into an abortion"[51]—forced by the *necessity* of stopping the continuing violence of the rape against them and of avoiding giving birth to their "rapists' children."

Depicting abortion in the case of rape as a matter of necessity continues, even as the depiction of abortion as a matter of choice has gained favor in abortion rhetoric generally. Indeed, necessity is the motivating force behind how the plight of the pregnant raped woman is articulated today, most publicly in discussions regarding funding for abortion access.

A. The Hyde Amendment and the Pregnant Raped Woman

In 1976, Congress passed the Hyde Amendment, a rider to the annual Labor Health and Human Services Appropriation Act,[52] which prohibited the use of federal funds for abortions except in certain cases where the abortion was justified by an exceptional circumstance as articulated by Congress.[53] The Hyde Amendment predominantly affected Medicaid, "the program under which the federal and state governments share the cost of necessary medical … care" for qualifying poor Americans.[54] Prior to 1976, Medicaid funded nearly 300,000 abortions annually—33 percent of all legal abortions.[55] The ban created by the Hyde Amendment "represent[ed] one of the most effective means of reducing the number of abortions short of overturning *Roe*."[56] The list of exceptional circumstances permitting the use of federal Medicaid money for abortion has varied over the years, but it has often included pregnancies which result from rape or incest.[57] In 1993, Congress sought to reintroduce the rape exception into the Hyde Amendment, largely garnering support by means of necessity rhetoric similar to the abortion rhetoric of the 1960s.

51 *Id.* at 33 (emphasis added).

52 Pub. L. No. 94-439, § 209, 90 Stat. 1418, 1434 (1976); Dennis J. Horan & Thomas J. Marzen, *The Supreme Court on Abortion Funding: The Second Time Around*, *in* New Perspectives on Human Abortion 217, 218 (Thomas W. Hilgers et al. eds., 1981).

53 § 209, 90 Stat. at 1434.

54 Rachel Benson Gold, *After the Hyde Amendment: Public Funding for Abortion in FY 1978*, Fam. Plan. Persp., May–June 1980, at 131, 131.

55 Laurence H. Tribe, Abortion: The Clash of Absolutes 151 (1990).

56 *Id.*

57 *See* Pub. L. No. 103-112, § 509, 107 Stat. 1082, 1113 (1993) (providing abortion funding for the termination of pregnancies resulting from "an act of rape or incest"); Pub. L. No. 96-536, § 109, 94 Stat. 3166, 3170 (1980) (providing funding in cases where a woman was raped or made pregnant through incest, as long as she reported the crime to the proper authorities "within seventy-two hours"); Pub. L. No. 96-123, § 109, 93 Stat. 923, 926 (1979) (funding abortions in cases where a woman was raped or made pregnant through incest and "promptly" reported the crime); Pub. L. No. 95-480, § 210, 92 Stat. 1567, 1586 (1978) (same); Pub. L. No. 95-205, § 101, 91 Stat. 1460, 1460 (1977) (same).

For example, in arguing that federal money should be used to fund abortions in the case of rape, Senator Murray shared:

> My personal awakening on the abortion issue came when I was in college. A friend of mine was what we today would call date raped. Abortion was not legal at the time. However, those with enough money had the option to go abroad or were able to find a doctor who could provide them with a safe procedure. My friend did not have money. She was *forced* to obtain a back-alley abortion. The damage done during that procedure prevented her from ever having children … *Because of the laws of this country, my friend was never able to be a mother.*[58]

By stating that the laws of this country prevented her friend from ever being a mother, Senator Murray implied that pregnancy from rape does not result in authentic or "real" motherhood and ignored that her friend could have become a mother had she declined to undergo an abortion. Senator Murray's logic that an abortion ban, a ban designed to facilitate births, could somehow prevent a woman from giving birth goes unquestioned, however, because the notion that any child conceived through rape is not her mother's own child has become seemingly self-evident: pregnancy by rape does not result in "real" motherhood. An abortion in the case of rape is not a choice against motherhood then. It is an act of necessity: Senator Murray's friend was "*forced* to obtain a back-alley abortion,"[59] underscoring the necessity of abortion access for raped women.

B. The Kolbe-Lowey-Morella Amendment and the Pregnant Raped Woman

Having sought to enable pregnant raped women to get the abortions they desperately needed, Congress fought to ensure in 1995 that no state could prohibit these abortions by refusing to contribute state Medicaid funds to rape abortions. Because "[f]ederal contributions to abortion funding under the Medicaid program range from 50 percent to 90 percent of the total subsidy, with state funds making up the remainder,"[60] some in Congress were concerned that pregnant raped women would be unable to afford their rape abortions without the states' Medicaid contribution.[61] As a result, the Kolbe-Lowey-Morella Amendment to the Hyde Amendment was proposed, clarifying that any state receiving federal Medicaid money must provide state Medicaid money for abortions in the case of rape or incest.[62] Like support for the rape exception to the Hyde Amendment generally, support for the Kolbe-Lowey-Morella Amendment involved depictions of abortion access for the pregnant raped woman as a matter of necessity, not choice.

58 139 Cong. Rec. 22,627 (1993) (statement of Sen. Murray) (emphasis added).

59 *Id.*

60 Gold, *supra* note 54, at 131.

61 141 Cong. Rec. 21,925 (1995) (statement of Rep. Lowey).

62 *Id.*

In debating the amendment, many representatives underscored its necessity by depicting the unborn child as being solely an extension of the rapist father. Representative Lowey referred to the unborn child as the "rapist's baby."[63] Another representative asked, "Should [raped women] be forced to bear the child of a rapist?"[64] Others stripped the unborn child of any personhood, referring to the unborn child as merely an extension or after-growth of the rape itself. Representative Johnson stated:

> Think. Rape is someone grabbing you, assaulting you, overwhelming you with fear for your life and then violating you in the most deeply personal and destructive way. Please, leave to the victim the decision as to whether to carry or not to carry *any possible product of such violent, vicious and terrible act* as that of rape.[65]

Such depictions of the unborn child underscore the need for a raped woman's abortion access: she must be able to destroy the enemy growing within her womb. Indeed, Representative Maloney argued for the amendment by advocating that it was necessary to save the raped woman from "spend[ing] 9 months reliving the crime."[66]

By placing the unborn child exclusively in the rapist's genetic pool or by depicting it as prolonging the rape terrorization, this rhetoric underscores the necessity of abortion as a self-defense tool for the pregnant raped woman. The pregnant raped woman is depicted as needing an abortion, not to restore the reproductive *choice* denied to her, but to enable her to heal from the rape. Should any doubt linger as to whether necessity, and not choice, was the driving force behind the amendment, Representative Slaughter's comments foreclose such doubt. Representative Slaughter appealed for support by describing abortion in the case of rape as the most important medically *necessary* service provided by Medicaid.[67] She argued, "When this Medicaid statute was written, it was clear that Congress intended the program to cover all medically necessary … services … Is it possible to imagine a service more important … if you are a poor woman, or a girl, who has been raped … ?"[68]

---

63 *Id.*

64 141 Cong. Rec. 21,927 (1995) (statement of Rep. Hastings).

65 141 Cong. Rec. 21,925 (1995) (statement of Rep. Johnson) (emphasis added).

66 141 Cong. Rec. 21,926 (1995) (statement of Rep. Maloney).

67 *See* 141 Cong. Rec. 21,929 (1995) (statement of Rep. Slaughter).

68 *Id.*

IV. The *Pregnant-Raped-Woman Prototype*

The images concerning the pregnant raped woman, as articulated in public discourse concerning funding for abortion access, depict the typical or prototypical raped woman as someone who views her unborn child as an extension of her rapist; who views her rape pregnancy as perpetuating the violence against her; and whose hatred toward her unborn child is so natural that extraordinary measures are needed. The *pregnant-raped-woman prototype* that has developed from these depictions, like all prototypes, has "set the standard"[69] by which all pregnant raped women are judged. Unfortunately, just as the *stranger-rape prototype* has limited the legal protections afforded to many raped women, the *pregnant-raped-woman prototype* is responsible for the widespread absence of effective custody protections for raped women who raise their rape-conceived children.

A. The Limited Legal Protections to Women Who Mother Through Rape

Twenty-three states now have laws designed to terminate and/or restrict the custody rights of rapists over their rape-conceived children.[70] The remaining 27

---

69 Chamallas, *supra* note 11, at 787.

70 *See* ARK. CODE ANN. § 9-10-121 (West, Westlaw through 2013 Reg. Sess.); CAL. FAM. CODE § 3030(b) (West, Westlaw with urgency legis. through Ch. 526, except Ch. 352, of 2013 Reg. Sess., all 2013–2014 1st Ex. Sess. laws, and Res. Ch. 123); COLO. REV. STAT. § 19-5-105.5 (West, Westlaw through the 1st Reg. Sess. of the 69th Gen. Assembly (2013)); CONN. GEN. STAT. § 45a-717(g)(2)(G) (West, Westlaw with Public Acts of the 2013 Jan. Reg. Sess. of the Conn. Gen. Assembly); DEL. CODE ANN. tit. 13, § 724A(e) (West, Westlaw through 79 Laws 2013, chs. 1–185 (End)); FLA. STAT. § 39.806(m) (West, Westlaw through Ch. 272 (End) of the 2013 1st Reg. Sess. of the 23rd Legis.); IDAHO CODE ANN. § 16-2005(2)(a) (West, Westlaw through (2013) Chs. 1–354 (End)); 750 ILL. COMP. STAT. 45/6.5 (West, Westlaw through P.A. 98-486, with the exception of P.A. 98-455, P.A. 98-456, and P.A. 98-463, of the 2013 Reg. Sess.) (effective Jan. 1, 2014); LA. CIV. CODE ANN. ART. 137 (West, Westlaw through the 2013 Reg. Sess.) & LA. CHILD CODE ANN. ART. 1015(8) (West, Westlaw through the 2013 Reg. Sess.); ME. REV. STAT. ANN. TIT. 19-A, § 1658 (West, Westlaw with legislation through the 2013 1st Reg. Sess. and 1st Sp. Sess. of the 126th Legis.); MICH. COMP. LAWS SERV. §§ 722.25(2), .27a(4) (West, Westlaw through P.A.2013, No. 130, of the 2013 Reg. Sess., 97th Legis.); MO. REV. STAT. § 211.447.5(5) (West, Westlaw through the end of the 2013 1st Reg. Sess. of the 97th Gen. Assembly, pending corrections received from the Mo. Revisor of Statutes); MONT. CODE ANN. § 41-3-609(1)(c) (West, Westlaw through chs. eff. July 1, 2013, and the 2012 gen. election); NEV. REV. STAT. § 125C.210(1) (West, Westlaw through the 2011 76th Reg. Sess. of the Nev. Legis., and technical corrections received from the Legis. Counsel Bureau (2012));; N.J. STAT. ANN. § 9:2-4.1(a) (West, Westlaw with laws eff. through L.2013, c. 165 and J.R. No. 11); N.C. GEN. STAT. §§ 14-27.2(c), .3(c) (West, Westlaw through S.L. 2013-235 of the 2013 Reg. Sess. of the Gen. Assembly); OKLA. STAT. ANN. TIT. 10A, § 1-4-904(B)(11) (West, Westlaw with chs. of the 1st Reg. Sess. of the 54th Legis. (2013) eff. July 1, 2013); 23 PA. CONS. STAT. § 2511(a)(7) (West, Westlaw through Reg. Sess. Act 2013-72); S.D. CODIFIED LAWS § 25-

states and the District of Columbia have failed to explicitly address this issue.[71] Of the 23 states that authorize legal redress, 13 states[72] authorize the termination of the parental rights of the rapist father while nine states[73] merely strip custody and/or visitation privileges, leaving parental obligations intact. By stripping custody or visitation rights but not terminating parental rights altogether, rapist fathers in these nine states—plus Louisiana, which has statutes authorizing the restriction of parental rights *and* the termination of parental rights[74]—may be required to pay child or other economic support for their rape-conceived children.[75]

4a-20 (West, Westlaw through the 2013 Reg. Sess. and Sup. Ct. R. 13-08); Tenn. Code Ann. §§ 36-1-113(c), (g)(10) (West, Westlaw through end of 2013 1st Reg. Sess.); Tex. Fam. Code Ann. § 161.007 (West, Westlaw through the end of the 2013 3rd Called Sess. of the 83rd Legis.); Utah Code Ann. § 76-5-414 (West, Westlaw through 2013 1st Sp. Sess.); Wis. Stat. § 48.415(9) (West, Westlaw through 2013 Wis. Act 45, pub. 8/06/2013).

71 Even though 27 states and the District of Columbia do not have specific statutes restricting the parental rights of men who father through rape, these states might have laws that accomplish the same objective. For example, some states allow for the termination of parental rights as the result of a parent's incarceration. *See, e.g.*, Idaho Code Ann. § 16-2005(1)(e) ("The court may grant an order terminating the relationship where … the parent has been incarcerated and is likely to remain incarcerated for a substantial period of time during the child's minority."). On the other hand, the frequency of prison sentences for rapists may mean that imprisonment termination statutes are of little protection. Only 3 percent of rapists will spend "even a single day in prison." *See Reporting Rates, RAINN*, http://www.rainn.org/get-information/statistics/reporting-rates (last visited June 4, 2013). Moreover, given the fundamental right to parent recognized in *Troxel v. Granville*, 530 U.S. 57, 75 (2000), a statutory measure is often necessary to fully protect a raped woman, especially because courts are hesitant to terminate the parent-child relationship absent explicit statutory authorization. *See, e.g., S.J. v. L.T.*, 727 P.2d 789, 795 (Alaska 1986) (holding that the trial court erred in terminating a rapist father's parental rights and reasoning that "[i]nvoluntary termination of parental rights may not be accomplished absent some statutorily mandated procedure").

72 *See* Ark. Code Ann. § 9-10-121; Colo. Rev. Stat. § 19-5-105.5; Conn. Gen. Stat. § 45a-717(g)(2)(G); Fla. Stat. § 39.806(m); Idaho Code Ann. § 16-2005(2)(a); Me. Rev. Stat. Ann. tit. 19-A, § 1658; Mo. Rev. Stat. § 211.447.5(5); Mont. Code Ann. § 41-3-609(1)(c); Okla. Stat. Ann. tit. 10A, § 1-4-904(B)(11); 23 Pa. Cons. Stat. § 2511(a)(7); Tenn. Code Ann. § 36-1-113(g)(10); Tex. Fam. Code Ann. § 161.007; Wis. Stat. § 48.415(9)(a).

73 *See* Cal. Fam. Code § 3030(b); Del. Code Ann. tit. 13, § 724A(e); 750 Ill. Comp. Stat. 45/6.5; Mich. Comp. Laws Serv. §§ 722.25(2), .27a(4); Nev. Rev. Stat. § 125C.210(1); N.J. Stat. Ann. § 9:2-4.1(a); N.C. Gen. Stat. §§ 14-27.2(c), .3(c); S.D. Codified Laws § 25-4a-20; Utah Code Ann. § 76-5-414.

74 *See* La. Civ. Code Ann. art. 137 (denying visitation privileges) & La. Child Code Ann. art. 1015(8) (authorizing termination).

75 The termination of parental rights—as opposed to the mere restriction of visitation and custody privileges—generally erases child support obligations. However, in at least two states, legislators have authorized the termination of parental rights while keeping child support obligations intact. *See* Ark. Code Ann. § 9-10-121(c) ("A putative father to

The failure of more states to enact this legislation is unsurprising; it may even be said to be expected. This is because, by raising their rape-conceived children, women seeking protections under these laws have betrayed the *pregnant-raped-woman prototype* and, as a result, are viewed suspiciously. Public rhetoric does not account for the raped woman who loves her rape-conceived child, so she must be an "imposter," lying about her rape. Alternate custody laws then are unnecessary because there is no "legitimate" victim to protect. Indeed, not only the absence of these laws evidences the states' suspicions of these women, but even an examination of the laws that do exist reveal the full extent of the suspicions.

Of the 23 states that have laws designed to protect raped women and their children from the rapist fathers' child custody demands, 14 require a criminal rape conviction to trigger use of the termination or restriction provisions.[76] In the remaining nine states, no criminal rape conviction is explicitly required.[77]

---

a child conceived as a result of rape shall pay child support"); COLO. REV. STAT. § 19-5-105.5(8)(b) ("Termination of parental rights ... does not relieve the person of any obligation to pay child support or birth-related costs unless waived by the victim"). It unclear whether raped women who conceive would prefer to receive child or other economic support. Some raped women may feel that the money is tainted, that it is a monthly reminder of their rapes, or that it tethers them to their rapists. Others, however, might desire the additional economic support for their children. At least one state has placed the decision in the hands of the raped woman. *See* 750 ILL. COMP. STAT. 45/6.5(c) ("The child's mother or guardian may decline support and maintenance obligations from the father").

76 *See* ARK. CODE ANN. § 9-10-121; CAL. FAM. CODE § 3030(b); COLO. REV. STAT. § 19-5-105.5; CONN. GEN. STAT. § 45a-717(g)(2)(G); DEL. CODE ANN. TIT. 13, § 724A(e); ME. REV. STAT. ANN. TIT. 19-A, § 1658; MICH. COMP. LAWS SERV. §§ 722.25(2), .27a(4); MONT. CODE ANN. § 41-3-609(1)(c); NEV. REV. STAT. § 125C.210(1); N.J. STAT. ANN. § 9:2-4.1(a); N.C. GEN. STAT. §§ 14-27.2(c), .3(c); TENN. CODE ANN. §§ 36-1-113(c), (g)(10); TEX. FAM. CODE ANN. § 161.007; UTAH CODE ANN. § 76-5-414.

77 *See* FLA. STAT. § 39.806(m) ("The court determines by clear and convincing evidence that the child was conceived as a result of an act of sexual battery"); IDAHO CODE ANN. § 16-2005(2)(a) ("The court may grant an order terminating the relationship and may rebuttably presume that such termination of parental rights is in the best interests of the child where ... The parent caused the child to be conceived as a result of rape, incest, lewd conduct with a minor child under sixteen (16) years, or sexual abuse of a child under the age of sixteen (16) years"); 750 ILL. COMP. STAT. 45/6.5(a)(2) ("This Section applies to a person who has been found to be the father of a child under this Act and who ... at a fact-finding hearing, is found by clear and convincing evidence to have committed an act of non-consensual sexual penetration for his conduct in fathering that child"); LA. CIV. CODE ANN. ART. 137 ("In a proceeding in which visitation of a child is being sought by a natural parent, if the child was conceived through the commission of a felony rape, the natural parent who committed the felony rape shall be denied visitation rights and contact with the child") & LA. CHILD CODE ANN. ART. 1015(8) ("The grounds for termination of parental rights are ... (8) The commission of a felony rape by the natural parent which resulted in the conception of the child"); MO. REV. STAT. § 211.447.5(5) ("When the biological father has pled guilty to, or is convicted of, the forcible rape of the birth mother, such a plea or conviction shall be

Requiring a criminal rape conviction is problematic for several reasons. Not only is the criminal burden of proof—"beyond a reasonable doubt"—higher than the "clear and convincing" standard approved by the Supreme Court of the United States for parental termination proceedings,[78] but it is also inconsistent with the standard of proof typically required in these states to restrict or terminate parental rights on other grounds. For example, in Connecticut, a person's parental rights may be terminated if the court finds by "clear and convincing evidence" that the person has abused his or her child or has killed another of his or her children through a "deliberate, nonaccidental act".[79] Termination of parental rights may occur on the basis of these criminal concepts—child abuse and even murder—without criminal convictions for these acts having been secured or even sought. Yet, to terminate parental rights on the basis of rape conception in Connecticut, the petitioner must prove the rape conception via a criminal rape conviction.[80] The bias against raped women is apparent.

Requiring a criminal rape conviction is also problematic because only 9 percent of rapes in the United States are prosecuted and only 5 percent result in a criminal rape conviction.[81] Thus, a criminal rape conviction requirement fails to help the majority of raped women.

Even where a criminal prosecution is brought, a raped woman may be unable to secure a criminal conviction for the specific sexual act specified in these statutes. This is because prosecutors may allow rapists to plea bargain—that is, "plead[] guilty to a lesser related offense"—in order to avoid the lengthy, costly, and uncertain process of trial.[82] Indeed, this has occurred. In *Bobbitt*

---

conclusive evidence supporting the termination"); OKLA. STAT. ANN. TIT. 10A, § 1-4-904(B)(11) ("The court may terminate the rights of a parent to a child based upon the following legal grounds ... A finding that the child was conceived as a result of rape perpetrated by the parent whose rights are sought to be terminated"); 23 PA. CONS. STAT. § 2511(a)(7) ("The rights of a parent in regard to a child may be terminated after a petition filed on any of the following grounds ... The parent is the father of a child conceived as a result of a rape or incest"); S.D. CODIFIED LAWS § 25-4a-20 ("If it is in the best interests of the child, the court may prohibit, revoke, or restrict visitation rights to a child for any person who has caused the child to be conceived as a result of rape or incest"); WIS. STAT. § 48.415(9) ("Conception as a result of sexual assault ... may be proved by a final judgment of conviction or other evidence produced at a fact-finding hearing").

78 *See Santosky v. Kramer*, 455 U.S. 745, 769 (1982) (finding that "[a] majority of States have concluded that a 'clear and convincing evidence' standard of proof strikes a fair balance between the rights of the natural parents and the State's legitimate concerns" and holding that "such a standard adequately conveys to the factfinder the level of subjective certainty about his factual conclusions necessary to satisfy due process").

79 *See* CONN. GEN. STAT. § 45a-717(g)(2)(B), (F).

80 *Id.* at § 45a-717(g)(2)(G).

81 *See Reporting Rates*, *supra* note 71.

82 *See* LEE MADIGAN & NANCY C. GAMBLE, THE SECOND RAPE: SOCIETY'S CONTINUED BETRAYAL OF THE VICTIM 97–98 (1991).

v. Eizenga,[83] the Court of Appeals of North Carolina held that the trial court erred in dismissing the complaint of a convicted rapist who sought visitation rights of the child conceived during his attempted statutory rape. Although the father had plead guilty to attempted statutory rape, his conviction appears to have been the result of a plea bargain—the Court of Appeals itself noted the oddity of "how completion of the elements necessary to constitute the offense of *attempted* statutory rape resulted in the birth of a child."[84] Yet reasoning that the relevant statute only applies to first- or second-degree rape, the court held that the statute "d[id] not prevent a person convicted of attempted statutory rape that resulted in the conception of a child from claiming visitation rights to that child."[85]

Moreover, even when a criminal rape conviction is secured, these women may not be protected in these 14 states. Given that "a conservative estimate of the time from the date of the crime to the date of the sentencing is anywhere from six months to two years," a raped woman may be required to have her child interact with her rapist for months or even years if the custody determination proceeding precedes the criminal proceeding, as it is likely to.[86] Yet, only one of these 14 states—Colorado—explicitly has preempted this possibility by requiring that any custody hearing be stayed during the pendency of a criminal rape proceeding.[87] Without similar provisions in other states, a court may determine that it is not in the best interests of the child to terminate parental rights where the lengthy period of time between the child's birth and the rapist father's eventual rape conviction has allowed him to establish a parental presence.

Additionally, the mere requirement of a criminal rape conviction may produce unintended consequences. A raped woman, reluctant to gamble her and her child's future on an unlikely criminal rape prosecution, may choose to "bargain" with her rapist. State Representative Sam Ellis, who introduced the bill in North Carolina that prevents rapists from exercising custody and visitation privileges over their rape-conceived children, stated that his interest in the legislation[88] stemmed from

---

83 715 S.E.2d 613 (Ct. App. N.C. 2011).

84 *Id.* at n.1 (emphasis in original).

85 *Id.* at 615.

86 *See* Madigan & Gamble, *supra* note 82, at 96.

87 *See* Colo. Rev. Stat. § 14-10-124.3 ("If criminal charges alleging an act of sexual assault … are brought against the parent of a child alleging that a child was conceived as a result of the alleged sexual assault committed by that parent against the parent who is the alleged victim of the sexual assault, the court shall issue an automatic stay of any civil domestic proceedings … involving both the child and the parent who is the alleged perpetrator").

88 The original bill prevented rapists from using custody and visitation privileges to intimidate witnesses but was passed in an expanded form that terminates the parental rights of rapists who are found guilty of first- or second-degree rape. *See* N.C. Gen. Stat. §§ 14-27.2 to .3.

the stories of three women who had been intimidated by their rapists.[89] In each case, the rapist said he would terminate his parental rights in exchange for the raped woman's agreement to not press charges or to not testify.[90] One of the women asked, "What do I do? … Protect society or protect the [child]?"[91]

Because of the criminal rape conviction requirement, in 14 of the 23 states where statutory redress exists, raped women, in essence, are only protected if they are willing to gamble on a speedy, non-plea bargained, and unlikely criminal rape conviction—and succeed in their gamble. That no raped woman is likely to take this gamble—let alone prevail—is inconsequential. That a criminal rape conviction requirement is grossly out-of-step with the burden of proof generally required to terminate or restrict parental rights in other contexts is ignored. As a result, if a raped woman who betrays the prototype wants redress under the laws of these 14 states, she can have it—but only if she quickly can prove her entitlement by the highest standard of proof in the American legal system.

Further, the *pregnant-raped-woman prototype* also explains, if not predicts, why all but three of the remaining nine states have authorized the restriction of, as opposed to the termination of, the rapists' parental rights. As in the 14 states that require a criminal rape conviction, a woman seeking redress in the remaining nine states—other than Illinois, Louisiana, and South Dakota—can have it, but she will have to pay for it. Although she will not be required to secure a criminal rape conviction, she will have to forfeit all future child support payments in exchange for seeking to untether herself from her rapist. Again, the suspicion of these raped women is apparent.

B. The Pregnant-Raped-Woman Prototype*: Another Dangerous Prototype*

The *pregnant-raped-woman prototype*'s danger is not in its failure to capture the experiences of all pregnant raped women. Rather, the danger of the *pregnant-raped-woman prototype* is that it operates on an inappropriately normative level. As demonstrated, adopting prototypes that are either inherently, but avoidably, normative or biased, like the *stranger-rape prototype*, can be highly "influential in constructing a class of 'true' or 'real' or 'worthy' victims, making it harder for those who are injured or affected in ways that do not fit the prototype"—like those who are victims of "date" rape or those who choose to raise their rape-conceived children—"to have their interests understood or redressed in law."[92] The *pregnant-raped woman prototype* is inherently, but avoidably, normative, but it may also be biased.

---

89 Ruth Sheehan, *Rapists Lose Facet of Power*, News & Observer (Raleigh, N.C.), September 6, 2004, at B1.

90 *Id.*

91 *Id.*

92 *Id.* at 781.

Even if the *pregnant-raped-woman prototype*, unlike the *stranger-rape prototype*, is found to be statistically accurate in its depiction of the response of the typical raped woman toward her rape pregnancy and unborn child, the prototype remains problematic because it is inherently normative, although its normative character could have been avoided. Had society advanced a prototype depicting pregnant raped women as facing, not unwanted, but *unintended* pregnancies, there would be little potential for a raped woman to garner suspicion through the exercise of her *choice* to abort, place for adoption, or raise her rape-conceived child. Under a *pregnant-raped-woman prototype* informed by choice and not necessity, both the raped woman who gives birth to her rape-conceived child and the raped woman who aborts or places her child for adoption have acted consistently with the prototype: they have regained their reproductive freedoms by exercising a choice over whether or not to become mothers. Thus, regardless of whether the *pregnant-raped-woman prototype* is atypical, and thereby biased, it ought to be abandoned because it is inappropriately normative.

The danger of the *pregnant-raped-woman prototype*, like the *stranger-rape prototype*, may be amplified further, however, because its depiction of the rape pregnancy experience may indeed be biased. Just as the psychological response to rape varies, for example, "from 'lack of concern' to 'major emotional disturbances, including severe depression' or 'from fear, restlessness, tears and anger to smiling, calmness and composure,'"[93] the response of women to their rape-induced pregnancies also varies widely.

Perhaps surprisingly, the only research done to analyze the effects of pregnancy upon raped women has concluded that raped women are, above all, victims of rape, not pregnancy.[94] Thus, contrary to the *pregnant-raped-woman prototype*, which depicts the pregnant woman as suffering to a greater extent because of the "rapist's child" growing inside her, "it appears that the pregnant victim's problems stem more from the trauma of rape rather than from the pregnancy itself."[95] Only 19.2 percent of pregnant raped women stated that they needed to confront feelings of "resentment of the pregnancy" or "hostility towards [the] child."[96] Moreover,

93 Katz & Mazur, *supra* note 34, at 216 (citations omitted). The purpose of this section is not to argue that rape-induced pregnancy is a simple matter free from psychological and emotional impacts. Rather, it is to argue that the societal depiction of the pregnant raped woman has not only been too simplistic because it has entirely ignored the thousands of raped women who, each year, give birth to, raise, and love the children they conceived through rape, but it also may be inaccurate in its depiction of the reaction of the statistically typical pregnant raped woman. Further research is necessary to know how the statistically typical pregnant raped woman views her rape pregnancy.

94 *See* David C. Reardon, *How Abortionists Have Exploited the Victims of Rape*, *in* Victims and Victors, *supra* note 7, at 27, 41.

95 Sandra Kathleen Mahkorn & William V. Dolan, *Sexual Assault and Pregnancy*, *in* New Perspectives on Human Abortion, *supra* note 52, at 190.

96 Sandra K. Mahkorn, *Pregnancy and Sexual Assault*, *in* The Psychological Aspects of Abortion 53, 59, 61 (David Mall & Walter F. Watts eds., 1979). Thirty-seven individuals

only 14.3 percent responded that the pregnancy served as a "continual reminder of the rape event."[97] Also, an analysis of the attitudes of the 21 raped women whose pregnancies resulted in births revealed that 68.75 percent of the women either had "a positive viewpoint to begin with" or changed, through the course of their pregnancies, "from negative to more positive images, attitudes, beliefs, or feelings about the unborn child," and none of the raped women changed from a positive to a more negative image or attitude about the unborn child.[98]

Furthermore, it is too simplistic to rely solely on the numbers of raped women who abort or place their children for adoption to characterize the attitudes of raped women toward their pregnancies and children. Because all rape pregnancies are unintended, many raped women who choose abortion or adoption may be doing so because the pregnancy was unintended, not because of their negative attitudes toward the rape pregnancy or their rape-conceived children.

Even those who abort may be doing so for reasons that have nothing to do with their feelings toward their rape-induced pregnancies or children. One study found that "[o]pinions, attitudes, and beliefs of others about the rape and pregnancy [were] reasons most commonly mentioned by [pregnant raped women] as conditions or situations which 'make it most difficult for a woman who is pregnant as a result of sexual assault to continue her pregnancy.'"[99] Thus, just as public perceptions concerning what constitutes "real" rape have limited women's reporting of rapes that depart from the prototype, public perceptions articulating the necessity of abortion for raped women may cause them to choose abortion, even though their attitudes toward their pregnancies or unborn children depart from the prototype.

The *pregnant-raped-woman prototype* is also problematic because it unnecessarily reinforces odious social hierarchies. Depicting the unborn children in terms that suggest the children are exclusively extensions of the rapist fathers reifies many sexist and patriarchal ideas. Sandra Mahkorn argues that rhetoric which portrays the unborn child as "being the property of the rapist" derives from a "sexist mentality."[100] It is the mentality that views a woman as "merchandise to which a man can claim ownership," such that any offspring of that relationship are viewed as "the property of the owner, the father."[101] This "property" view not only allows for the illogic that a child conceived through rape is exclusively a genetic product of the rapist father, but also "de-legitimiz[es] [the] maternal genetic

participated in this study, and they were asked to participate after self-identifying as pregnant raped women seeking assistance from "various counseling and social welfare agencies that are known for assisting women through problem pregnancies." *Id.* at 57.

97 *Id.* at 60–61.

98 *Id.* at 63, 68.

99 *Id.* at 66.

100 Mahkorn & Dolan, *supra* note 97, at 191–92.

101 *Id.* at 192.

link,"[102] and thereby, "erase[s] all identity characteristics of the mother other than that as a sexual container."[103] For these reasons alone, the *pregnant-raped-woman prototype* ought to be abandoned.

V. Conclusion

The invidious stereotypes that have been articulated in public discourse, which depict raped women as hating their unborn children and as viewing their rape pregnancies as a continuation of their rape experience, have created a biased and inappropriately normative prototype by which all pregnant raped women are judged. Because women who raise their rape-conceived children depart heavily from the prototype, they are, as a result, viewed with great suspicion. Legal protections, such as statutorily mandated alternative custody or visitation rights, are then denied to them because, being viewed as suspicious in their rape-conception claims, it is thought that there is nothing special about their conceptions requiring any change in the manner in which custody and visitation determinations are made. This explains how the rape act, which is so heinous that even the child growing within the woman is repeatedly demonized in public discourse, can become so minimized that, after the birth of a "rapist's child," society's laws readily tether a raped woman to her rapist. It also explains why, even in the states with purported protections, the vast majority are illusory protections.

Combating the effects of the *pregnant-raped-woman prototype* requires conscious awareness of the way public and private discourse conceives of the pregnant raped woman. Utilizing *choice* rhetoric instead of *necessity* rhetoric in discourse concerning the pregnant raped woman would assist in reversing this trend and align abortion rights rhetoric across all pregnancies.

Indeed *choice* rhetoric of this type has been highly influential in prompting both pro-life and abortion rights advocates to work together. During the 2007 session of the Maryland General Assembly, Planned Parenthood of Maryland and Maryland Right to Life *joined together* in arguing that the parental rights of rapists over their rape-conceived children ought to be restricted. Maryland Right to Life testified that "women who *choose* to carry their pregnancies to term ought to be supported and protected from unnecessary burdens … [and] women who *choose* to carry their pregnancies to term should never feel coerced into abortion because of social concerns."[104] Planned Parenthood agreed and testified that a woman

---

102 R. Charli Carpenter, *Surfacing Children: Limitations of Genocidal Rape Discourse*, 22 Hum. Rts. Q. 428, 457 (2000).

103 Beverly Allen, Rape Warfare: The Hidden Genocide in Bosnia-Herzegovina and Croatia 87 (1996).

104 *Family Law—Denial of Paternity, Custody, and Visitation: Hearing on H.B. 648 Before the H. Judiciary Comm.*, 2007 Leg. Sess. (Md. 2007) (statement of Cathy McLeod, Maryland Right to Life).

pregnant through rape should be given the opportunity "to make the *choice* that is right for them [*sic*], without having to worry about how that choice may force her to interact at a later date with her perpetrator. If a woman *chooses* to carry her child to term it is important for her to feel supported and safe in her choice."[105]

By focusing on choice rather than necessity, a raped woman's autonomy is emphasized, not what her choice ought to be. It thus erases the stigma attached to the raped women who choose to raise their rape-conceived children because there is no longer an articulated public understanding of how pregnant-raped women respond to their pregnancies, or, more importantly, how they ought to respond. Freeing a raped woman from the stigma of being viewed as an "impostor" rape victim solely because of her decision to raise and love her rape-conceived child not only respects reproductive choice but also spurs greater legal protections for these women. Although the stigma concerning "real" rape remains, a piece of it—that which labels "real" rape as occurring only where a woman, pregnant from that rape, hates the unborn child growing within her—will be deconstructed. Such deconstruction is not only necessary to further erode the stereotypes underpinning "real" rape that continue to handicap rape laws, but it is the biggest barrier to addressing and redressing the rights of raped women who raise their rape-conceived children.

105 *Id.* (statement of Kate Canada, Director of Communications & Public Policy, Planned Parenthood of Maryland).

Chapter 4
Toward Common Ground on Policies Advancing Reproductive Justice

Dorothy Roberts

In February 2011, in honor of Black History Month, the nonprofit organizations Life Always and thatsabortion.com erected a giant billboard at the intersection of Sixth Avenue and Watts Street in New York City's Soho neighborhood.[1] The billboard displayed the image of a six-year-old African American girl beneath the words: "THE MOST DANGEROUS PLACE FOR AN AFRICAN AMERICAN IS IN THE WOMB." The message referred to the disproportionately high rate of abortion among black women: according to the Centers for Disease Control and Prevention, black women account for 36 percent of abortions in the United States, although blacks comprise less than 13 percent of the national population.[2] The New York City billboard appeared at the time of a nationwide campaign by toomanyaborted.com, launched by the Radiance Foundation, which placed more than 100 similar billboards targeting African American women in Arkansas, Atlanta, Chicago, Milwaukee, Los Angeles, and Texas.[3] When protest against the Life Always billboard ensued in New York, including objection by the mother of the little girl depicted on the billboard, Lamar Advertising took it down. The following month, however, Life Always put up billboards in Chicago displaying an image of President Barack Obama alongside the words: "Every 21 minutes, our next possible leader is aborted."[4]

Many pro-choice and women of color organizations, including SisterSong Women of Color Reproductive Justice Collective, argued that the billboard campaigns failed to address the societal causes of racial disparities in abortion

---

1 Lynette Holloway, *New York Latest Target of Black Anti-Abortion Billboards*, The Root (February 24, 2011), available at http://www.theroot.com/views/re-ppnyc-statement-abortion-billboard-targeting-african-americans-nyc (accessed on June 4, 2013).

2 Karen Pazol, et al., *Abortion Surveillance—United States, 2009*, available at http://www.cdc.gov/mmwr/preview/mmwrhtml/ss6108a1.htm?s_cid=ss6108a1_x.

3 Holloway, *supra* note 1; Miriam Zoila Perez, *Past and Present Collide as the Black Anti-Abortion Movement Grows*, Colorlines, March 3, 2011, available at http://colorlines.com/archives/2011/03/past_and_present_collide_as_the_black_anti-abortion_movement_grows.html (accessed on June 4, 2013).

4 Dawn Turner Trice, *Billboards that Highlight Black Abortion Disparity Spark Debate*, Chi. Tribune, April 19, 2011.

rates—poverty, lack of access to reliable contraception, and inadequate sex education—that result in unwanted pregnancies.[5] Instead, the anti-abortion messages demonized black women by blaming them for "genocide" against the black community and by suggesting they are incapable of making their own reproductive decisions. To me, the billboard's statement declaring black women's wombs unsafe was reminiscent of eugenicist rhetoric that advocated sterilization of women whose wombs were deemed unfit to bear children.[6] In both cases, the solution to perceived reproductive irresponsibility is to regulate socially marginalized women's decisions about their bodies. The billboard controversy brought to the forefront of the abortion debate the long legacy of images, rhetoric, and policies that devalue black women as equal and self-determining human beings.

This chapter examines the way in which debates about the morality of abortion are shaped by inequalities of gender, race, and class and seeks to find common ground around recognition of the equal moral status of all pregnant women. Examining the social context surrounding disagreements about abortion can help us recognize three crucial points we should all agree on. First, pregnant women have the moral status of self-determining human beings. Second, our society has historically and still values pregnant women according to an unjust reproductive hierarchy based on gender, race, and class. Third, we should collectively advocate for reproductive policies that help to eradicate this unjust hierarchy. Even if we can't come to agreement on the moral status of the fetus, we should agree that women are valuable human beings in their own right—and not only in relation to a fetus—and that all women are equally valuable.

Women's Moral Status

A central point of contention in the abortion debate is the moral status of the fetus. Opponents of abortion generally view developing fetuses as persons who have equal rights as individuals who are already born, including the right to support from a pregnant woman who does not wish to carry her pregnancy to term.[7] Supporters of the right to abortion generally view fetuses as having a different moral status as persons who are already born or (even if they have equal moral status) whose interests must be subordinated to those of pregnant women.[8] In the landmark US Supreme Court decision upholding the constitutional right to

---

5 Perez, *supra* note 3.

6 See Daniel Kevles, In the Name of Eugenics: Genetics and the Uses of Human Heredity (1985); Dorothy Roberts, Killing the Black Body: Race, Reproduction, and the Meaning of Liberty 56–89 (1998).

7 *See*, e.g., Randy Alcorn, Pro-Life Answers to Pro-Choice Arguments (2000).

8 *See*, e.g., Eileen McDonagh, Breaking the Abortion Deadlock: From Choice to Consent (1996); Judith Jarvis Thompson, *A Defense of Abortion*, 1 Phil. & Pub. Aff. 47 (1971).

abortion, *Roe v. Wade*, the Court rejected the argument put forth by the State of Texas that the fetus is a "person" within the language and meaning of the Fourteenth Amendment.[9] The Court concluded that the word "person," as used in the Constitution, does not extend to the unborn. In addition, the Court declined to decide the state's alternative claim that, apart from the Fourteenth Amendment, life begins at conception and is present throughout pregnancy. Instead, the Court resolved the issue of fetal status by recognizing the state's "important and legitimate interest in protecting the potentiality of human life."[10] The Court's legal resolution, however, did nothing to stem the vociferous debate over the moral status of the fetus that continues to fuel the abortion wars today.

The disagreement over the moral status of the fetus, however, need not disturb the moral status of women as self-determining human beings. Whether or not fetuses are rights-bearing persons, there is no question that women are. Opponents and supporters of the right to abortion disagree about the legitimate claims a fetus can make on the woman who is gestating it and about the legitimate use of state power to intervene in the lives and bodies of pregnant women to protect the fetus. But there should be no disagreement about the fundamental status of women as valuable persons whose interests deserve state protection.

Reproductive Hierarchy

We should also agree that all women are equally valuable and equally deserve state protection, regardless of social status. In the United States, however, the state has treated women unequally according to their social status, including race and class. Reproductive health policies have been shaped by and imposed a striking race and class hierarchy that values the childbearing of white and middle-class women more highly than that of poor women and women of color.[11] Regulating reproductive decisions has been a central aspect of racial oppression in the United States, beginning with slave masters' economic stake in coercing slave women to bear children; to the role of race in the eugenics movement during the 1920s and 1930s; to the massive sterilization abuse of black and Latina women as late as the 1970s; to policies that discourage immigrant women from having children in the United States.

Only two days after the US Food and Drug Administration approved the long-acting contraceptive Norplant, the *Philadelphia Inquirer* published a controversial editorial entitled, "Poverty and Norplant: Can Contraception Reduce

9 Roe v. Wade, 410 U.S. 113 (1973).

10 *Id.* at 162.

11 Roberts, *supra* note 6; Elena R. Gutierrez, Fertile Matters: The Politics of Mexican-Origin Women's Reproduction (2008); Lisa Sun-Hee Park, Entitled to Nothing: The Struggle for Immigrant Health Care in the Age of Welfare Reform (2011).

the Underclass?"[12] The editorial linked two recent news items: one announced the approval of Norplant; the other reported research finding that half of black children are born in poverty. It then went on to propose Norplant as a solution to inner-city poverty, arguing that "the main reason more black children are living in poverty is that the people having the most children are the ones least capable of supporting them."[13] The *Inquirer* was forced to print an apology when black advocates across the country expressed their outrage at the editorial's racist and eugenic overtones.[14] But many journalists and pundits came to the *Inquirer*'s defense. As the *Richmond Times-Dispatch* put it, Norplant "offers society yet another way to curb the expansion of an underclass most of whose members face futures of disorder and deprivation."[15]

Within two years 13 state legislatures proposed some 20 measures to distribute Norplant to poor women.[16] Some of these bills proposed pressuring women on welfare to use the device either by offering them a financial bonus or by requiring implantation as a condition of receiving benefits. Kansas Republican state representative Kerry Patrick, for example, touted his plan to pay welfare mothers to use Norplant as having "the potential to save the taxpayers millions of their hard-earned dollars" by reducing the number of children on the welfare rolls.[17] Republican representative Robert Farr echoed these sentiments when he proposed a similar bill in Connecticut, saying "It's far cheaper to give you money not to have kids than to give you money if you have kids."[18]

These twentieth-century proposals involving Norplant are part of a long and continuing legacy of state regulation of poor and minority women's reproductive decisions. A broad range of laws and policies permit state intervention in the lives of pregnant women. These include not only restrictions on access to abortion, but also compelled surgeries, prosecutions for substance abuse, coerced sterilizations, and welfare child exclusion laws.[19] Like eugenicist policies of the past, these modern-day policies serve an ideological function that benefits people in power: they pretend that we can solve social problems by curbing the reproduction of the victims of these problems. They try to make inequality seem like the product of nature rather than an unjust social structure. By identifying procreation as the cause of deplorable social conditions, they divert attention away from the need

---

12 Donald Kimmelman, *Poverty and Norplant: Can Contraception Reduce the Underclass?*, Philadelphia Inquirer, December 12, 1990, at A18.

13 *Id.*

14 Roberts, *supra* note 6, at 106.

15 *Journalistic Thought Police*, Richmond Times-Dispatch, December 27, 1990, at A12.

16 Roberts, *supra* note 6, at 109.

17 *Id.*

18 *Id.*

19 Id.; Gutierrez, *supra* note 11; Park, *supra* note 11; Gwendolyn Mink, Welfare's End (2002); Anna Marie Smith, Welfare Reform and Sexual Regulation (2007).

for social change. Proponents of such policies see the bodies of poor and minority women as appropriate subjects for social experiments and government supervision. The notion that these women should make their own reproductive decisions often escapes policy discussions entirely.

Deeply embedded stereotypes about poor women, women of color, and immigrant women as irresponsible reproducers fosters this reproductive surveillance. A disparaging mythology about black mothers links their maternity to sexual depravity. Dominant American culture is replete with negative icons of black maternity—the sexually licentious Jezebel that legitimated white slave masters' sexual exploitation of their female slaves; the Mammy who, although she cared for her masters' children, remained under the supervision of her white mistress and was alleged to be careless toward her own children; the Matriarch responsible for the disintegration of the black family; the Welfare Queen who bred children just to fatten her welfare check and then wasted the money recklessly on herself; and the pregnant crack addict who was supposed to lack maternal instinct and give birth to so-called "crack babies" who suffer not only permanent physical damage but are also destined to become social pariahs.[20] The myth of black female promiscuity created to excuse the sexual violation of enslaved women persisted after Emancipation, along with its corollary beliefs that black women procreate with abandon and then pass on a depraved lifestyle to their offspring.

The pregnant crack addict was added to the iconography of depraved black maternity in the late 1980s.[21] She was portrayed as a careless and selfish woman who puts her love for crack above her concern for her children. Reinforcing the link between black female sexual licentiousness and maternal irresponsibility, news stories often represented her as a prostitute who got pregnant after trading sex for crack. Unlike any other drug, the chemical properties of crack were said to destroy the natural impulse to mother. In other words, the pregnant crack addict is the exact opposite of a mother—promiscuous, uncaring, and self-indulgent.

Like his mother, the so-called "crack baby" was portrayed as uniquely monstrous, irreparably damaged, physically, psychologically, and socially. The media exaggerated the extent and nature of the harm crack causes and erroneously suggested that the problem of maternal drug use was confined to the black community.[22] They successfully transformed a public health problem that affects all racial, ethnic, and socioeconomic groups into a result of black mother's depravity that warranted harsh punishment.[23] Medical researchers have discredited this portrayal as scientifically unfounded: studies of adolescents exposed to crack cocaine *in utero*

---

20 Roberts, *supra* note 6, at 10–21; Patricia Hill Collins, Black Feminist Thought: Knowledge, Consciousness, and the Politics of Empowerment (2008); Melissa V. Harris-Perry, Sister Citizen: Shame, Stereotypes, and Black Women in America (2013).

21 Roberts, *supra* note 6, 154–59.

22 *Id.*

23 Assata Zerai, Dehumanizing Discourse, Anti-Drug Law, and Policy in America: A "Crack Mother's" Nightmare (2002).

have not found the dramatic effects predicted and researchers cannot determine authoritatively which of the hazards poor black babies experience caused outcomes originally attributed to crack.[24] But the caricature of the crack baby—trembling in a tiny hospital bed, permanently brain damaged, and on his way to becoming a criminal—seems indelibly etched in the American psyche, available to rationalize future infringements of black women's autonomy.

Movements for black uplift and liberation have also enlisted black women's bodies.[25] Control over reproduction and the discourse that frames reproductive health policy is a principal means for men to define the nation. Conversely, enlisting women's reproductive service for the sake of the nation helps to define gender and to inscribe sex inequality in the nationalist social order. Not only do women physically produce future members of the nation, but norms regulating which women may legitimately bear children and under which conditions contribute to the construction of national and gender identity. The birth control movement sparked a heated debate within the black community about the relationship between reproduction and racial advancement. Some blacks, including the nationalist leader Marcus Garvey, opposed birth control as a threat to racial survival and argued that a larger population would increase blacks' political strength. Others, such as the prominent civil rights leader W.E.B. DuBois, denounced "the fallacy of numbers" and endorsed birth control as a means of improving black maternal health and welfare. In the 1960s, many black nationalist men adopted the position that birth control was a form of racial genocide and that black women should bear more children "for the revolution."

Contrast the policies intended to deter poor women and women of color from having children with the popularity of the fertility business that assists more privileged women to bear more children. At a time when wealthy white women have access to technologies that assist them to have children who are not only genetically related to them or their partners but who are genetically screened, various laws and policies discourage women of color from having children altogether. As Rayna Rapp stated at a Radcliffe conference in October 2005, "Some women struggle for basic reproductive technologies, like a clinic where sterile conditions might be available to perform C-sections, while others turn to cutting-edge genetic techniques."[26] African American Studies scholar Marsha Darling similarly writes, "This stunning array of biotechnology is being directed at developing eugenical population control strategies especially for low income and poor women of color globally," while "reproduction enhancement options

---

24 Stacy Buckingham-Howes, Sarah Shafer Berger, Laura A. Scaletti, & Maureen M. Black, *Systemic Review of Prenatal Cocaine Exposure and Adolescent Development*, 131 PEDIATRICS E 1917 (2013).

25 ROBERTS, *supra* note 6, at 82–86, 98–103.

26 Madeline Drexler, *Reproductive Health*, RADCLIFFE QUARTERLY, Winter 2005, available at http://www.radcliffe.edu/about/news/quarterly/200501/feature_02.php.

under the rubric of 'choice'" are reserved "for economically and racially privileged women in the global North."[27]

While welfare reform laws aim to deter women receiving public assistance from having even one additional healthy baby, largely unregulated fertility clinics regularly implant privileged women with multiple embryos, knowing the high risk multiple births pose for premature delivery and low birth weight.[28] The public begrudges poor mothers a meager increase in benefits for one more child, but celebrates the birth of high-tech septuplets that require a fortune in publicly-supported hospital care.[29] The monumental effort, expense, and technological invention that goes into high-tech reproduction marks the children produced as especially valuable. It proclaims the unmistakable message that white children are precious enough to devote billions of dollars toward their creation. Black and Latina children, on the other hand, are the primary objects of welfare reform measures designed to discourage poor women from procreating.

Reproductive Justice

We should find common ground in advocating for laws and policies that dismantle the oppressive reproductive hierarchy that devalues women and children on the basis of gender, race, and class. Black women have consistently resisted state efforts to control their childbearing decisions and forged alternative approaches to reproductive freedom. Black women played a critical role in the early birth control movement of the 1920s and 1930s, both as advocates of women's right to regulate their childbearing and as opponents of coercive family planning programs. In the decades prior to World War II, a distinctive black discourse advocating birth control as a means of racial progress emerged in the black press, public lectures, and black women's fiction and poetry.[30]

Nor did most black women passively accept the male admonition to cast aside birth control and have more babies for the revolution. Rather, many re-articulated the relationship between birth control and liberation and demanded the inclusion of women's reproductive rights in the nationalist project. Shirley Chisholm, the first black woman in Congress, rejected the genocide argument against birth

27 Marsha Darling, *Gendered Globalization: State Interests, Women of Color and Marginalized Women*, available at http://www.gjga.org/conference.asp?action=item&source=documents&id=65.

28 Jessica Arons, *Future Choices: Assisted Reproductive Technologies and the Law* (2007); Frans M. Helmerhorst, Denise A.M. Perquin, Diane Donker & Marc J.N.C. Keirse, *Perinatal Outcome of Singletons and Twins after Assisted Conception: A Systematic Review of Controlled Studies*, 328 British Med. J. 261 (2004).

29 Lori B. Andrews, The Clone Age: Adventures in the New World of Reproductive Technology 55–61 (1999).

30 Roberts, *supra* note 6.

control as "male rhetoric, for male ears" and testified before a Senate committee about her female constituents' pleas for family planning services.[31] As head of the Black Women's Liberation Committee of the Student Nonviolent Coordinating Committee (SNCC), Frances Beal wrote in 1969: "Black women have the right and the responsibility to determine when it is in *the interest of the struggle to have children or not to have them and this right must not be relinquished to any* … to determine when it is in *her own best interests* to have children."[32] Similarly, black women organized a Trust Black Women campaign against the billboards erected in their communities that blamed them for high abortion rates and portrayed their wombs as dangerous.[33]

Women of color have developed an alternative approach to reproductive policy and ethics that contests the unjust reproductive hierarchy and advocates for the equal moral worth of all women.[34] Recognizing that reproductive decisions are made within a social context, reproductive justice addresses the relationship between birth control and abortion and racial injustice, gender inequality, and economic disadvantage. Advocates for reproductive justice call for greater access to reproductive health services, but also condemn the deplorable social conditions that constrain women's ability to have healthy children as well as the coercive use of family planning as a means of population control. An ideology that encourages abortion as a solution to social problems is equally guilty of falsely attributing disadvantaged social status to reproduction instead of to systemic and institutionalized inequality.

We must replace the traditional understanding of reproductive rights with a vision that centers on the experiences of the most oppressed rather than the most privileged; that encompasses the full range of reproductive health and reproductive decisions, not just termination of pregnancy; and that emphatically rejects the use of birth control as a tool of social regulation rather than self-determination. The fight for reproductive freedom must be part of a broader struggle to create a more just, humane, and egalitarian society. I believe this requires recognizing women's right to terminate an unwanted pregnancy and to access publically supported reproductive health services, including abortion. But I also believe we can work toward common ground on treating all women as equally valuable human beings.

---

31 Roberts, *supra* note 6, at 100–101.

32 Roberts, *supra* note 6, at 100.

33 SisterSong Women of Color Reproductive Justice Collective, Trust Black Women, available at http://sistersong.net/index.php?option=com_content&view=article&id=41&Itemid=78.

34 Jael Silliman, Marlene Gerber Fried, Loretta Ross, & Elena Gutierrez, Undivided Rights: Women of Color Organizing for Reproductive Justice (2004).

Chapter 5
Finding Common Ground in the Disability Rights Critiques of Selective Abortions

Elizabeth R. Schiltz

The philosopher Alasdair MacIntyre, in an essay fittingly entitled "Intractable Moral Disagreements," offers some interesting suggestions for advancing conversations like those presented in this book: conversations involving seemingly intractable disagreements among "intelligent, perceptive, and insightful agents" on basic moral issues.[1] MacIntyre asks "what rationality requires of us in situations in which we confront others who are in radical moral disagreement with us."[2] Of course, the first step is to deliberate together, in a free, open, unthreatening, noncoercive exchange.[3] But, MacIntyre concludes, even such deliberation might not result in agreement. So MacIntyre asks: "When we have reached this point, how should we proceed further? The urgent practical question will have become that of how we may most effectively find common ground with at least some of those with whom we are in continuing and irremediable disagreement."[4] MacIntyre quotes John Henry Newman in describing this sort of impasse: "'Controversy, at least in this age,' said Newman, 'does not lie between the hosts of heaven, Michael and his Angels on the one side, and the powers of evil on the other; but it is a sort of night battle, where each fights for himself, and friend and foe stand together.' What Newman said of his age remains true of ours."[5]

This observation about the complexity of the battle lines is especially apt in the context of one particular argument in the frustratingly intractable abortion debates. It is the argument framed by some disability rights advocates who are generally fully committed to abortion rights, but who nevertheless assert that there is something morally problematic about abortion after prenatal diagnosis of a disability (an argument often referred to generally as the "disability rights

1 Alasdair MacIntyre, *Intractable Moral Disagreements*, *in* Intractable Disputes about the Natural Law: Alasdair MacIntyre and Critics 1 (Lawrence E. Cunningham ed., 2009).

2 *Id.* at 3.

3 *Id.* at 18–24.

4 *Id.* at 4.

5 *Id.* at 328 (quoting John Henry Newman, Fifteen Sermons Preached before the University of Oxford 201 (1997)).

critique").[6] The debate on both sides of this argument is particularly intractable for a number of reasons. It involves two different foundational ethical precepts: the fundamental equality of all human beings (regardless of their disabilities), and the contested "rights" of either "life" or "choice." In addition, it juxtaposes two common—but incompatible—intuitions about the morality of abortion.

On the one hand, there seems to be widespread consensus that a diagnosis of a disability is one of the least morally problematic justifications for abortion. Indeed, it was publicity surrounding situations in which women were likely to have disabled babies (such as the discovery that the widely prescribed sleeping aid and anti-nausea drug Thalidomide caused birth defects, and an epidemic of rubella, a disease associated with disabilities in fetuses whose mothers are infected) that catalyzed much of the public support for liberalizing abortion laws in the United States in the 1960s.[7] Even those who oppose abortion sometimes argue for exceptions for women who learn that their child would be born with a disability.[8]

On the other hand, though, there also seems to be widespread consensus that people with disabilities have as much a claim to "human dignity" as people without disabilities, and that therefore there is something problematic about singling out fetuses with disabilities for abortion. This is the intuition that tells us that Nazi eugenic practices with respect to people with disabilities were repugnant. This is the intuition that tells us that the Supreme Court's decision in *Buck v. Bell* was wrong, and that causes us to reject Justice Holmes's justification for the forced sterilization of a woman identified as mentally retarded with the phrase: "Three generations of imbeciles are enough."[9] This is the intuition that would cause general discomfort with an effort to legislatively mandate prenatal testing and forced abortions for a disability such as Down syndrome.

In this chapter, I will explore how these conflicting fundamental premises and intuitions complicate the debate about the disability rights critique of abortion after a prenatal diagnosis of a disability. In an attempt to open up some space where "friend and foe" in the abortion debates might work together in this area, I will differentiate between two different categories of arguments in the disability rights critique: the autonomy-based argument and the expressivist argument. I will argue that while the former argument does not provide much room for common ground, the latter does. However, the expressivist arguments against selective

6 An excellent introduction to the complexities on both sides of this debate can be found in Prenatal Testing and Disability Rights (Erik Parens & Adrienne Asch eds., 2000). This book publishes the results of a two-year project by The Hastings Center exploring the disability rights critique of prenatal testing for genetic disability.

7 Samuel R. Bagenstos, *Disability, Life, Death, and Choice*, 29 Harv. J. L. & Gender 452, 437 (2006); John F. Muller, *Disability, Ambivalence, and the Law*, 37 Am. J. L. & Med. 469, 485 (2011).

8 Judith F. Daar, *Selective Reduction of Multiple Pregnancy: Lifeboat Ethics in the Womb*, 25 U.C. Davis L. Rev. 773, 813–15 (1992).

9 274 U.S. 200, 207 (1927).

abortion tap into a deep and uncomfortable ambivalence toward disability that is manifest in both the discourse about and the legal framework of disability law, as well as in both the discourse about and the social practices governing selective abortion. While a handful of scholars recently have begun to openly address this ambivalence, it will be difficult for many participants in the social discourse on this difficult topic to achieve the level of trust that would be necessary to openly address the consequences of this ambivalence in concrete debates about related policies. However difficult achieving such trust may be, I believe it offers the only way forward in the search for common ground on this issue.

Two Strands in the Disability Rights Critiques of Abortion After a Prenatal Diagnosis of a Disability

Two legal scholars have recently published particularly insightful observations about the participation of the disability rights community in public debates about beginning-of-life issues. In Samuel Bagenstos's 2009 book, *Law and the Contradictions of the Disability Rights Movement*,[10] he addresses what he identifies as an internal inconsistency in the positions taken by the disability rights movement in two public debates: decisions of parents to withhold food, water, or medical treatment from infants born with disabilities (often referred to as "selective non-treatment"), and decisions of parents to abort fetuses after receiving a prenatal diagnosis of a disability (often referred to as "selective abortion"). John Muller's 2011 article, "Disability, Ambivalence, and the Law,"[11] addresses the same inconsistency. Both authors note that, in the public debate about the 1982 decision of the parents of a child born with Down syndrome and a blocked esophagus (the "Baby Doe" case), the disability rights community joined forces with the pro-life community in vocally opposing the parents' decision, and in supporting subsequent efforts of the Reagan administration to prohibit such decisions, through regulatory and statutory initiatives.[12] In contrast, both authors note, the disability rights community has not joined forces with the pro-life community in a similarly united front to support any restriction of the right to an abortion after a prenatal diagnosis of a disability.[13]

The arguments raised by the disability rights community in both of these debates fall into two different categories: autonomy-based critiques, and an expressivist critiques. Neither Bagenstos nor Muller make such a distinction, and they both tend to focus most of their analytical attention on the autonomy-based arguments of the disability rights critique, rather than the expressivist arguments. In large

10 Samuel R. Bagenstos, Law and the Contradictions of the Disability Rights Movement (2009).

11 Muller, *supra* note 7.

12 Bagenstos, *supra* note 10, at 97–100; Muller, *supra* note 7, at 473–75.

13 Bagenstos, *supra* note 10, at 102–104; Muller, *supra* note 7, at 476.

part, this focus reflects the fact that the autonomy arguments fit more neatly into the existing categories of the dialogue about abortion, and are the arguments more readily presented by the disability rights community in the concrete realities of amici briefs or statements in support of specific legislation. However, I believe that appreciating this distinction helps us understand which aspects of the disability rights critique offer the possibility of common ground. Let us begin by describing the two different categories of arguments.

The Autonomy-Based Disability Rights Critique of Selective Abortions

The autonomy-based disability rights critique of selective abortion focuses on the validity of the consent of the parent choosing the abortion.[14] The basic argument begins with an affirmation of one of the core principles of the disability rights movement—the right of each person to determine her own destiny, and to live, work, and participate in society with as much autonomy and self-determination as possible.[15] This principle, in theory, should justify any person's choice of a selective abortion. However, the argument goes, in practice the choice of a parent to abort a child after a prenatal diagnosis is most often not, in fact, a genuinely free choice. In reality, parents faced with a prenatal diagnosis of a disability are typically in mental states of extreme stress and vulnerability, often exacerbated by pressure from the medical professionals advising them to make decisions quickly. In these situations, parents naturally tend to rely on the specialized knowledge of the genetic counselors and physicians advising them. However, the argument continues, recent studies tend to show that "many members of the health professions view childhood disability as predominantly negative for children and their families, in contrast to what research on the life satisfaction of people with disabilities and their families has actually shown."[16] This unduly negative, prejudicial, and factually unjustified perspective of the medical profession tends to have a disproportionate influence on the choice of the parents in these situations, effectively coercing parents into making a decision that reflects biases against people with disabilities.[17]

Both Bagenstos and Muller point out that this same basic argument is made by disability rights activists in debates about withholding treatment for infants born with disabilities. In that context, disability rights activists have argued that

---

14 The following discussion of the autonomy-based critiques of selective abortion summarizes a more complete description in Elizabeth R. Schiltz, *Hauerwas and Disability Law: Exposing the Cracks in the Foundations of Disability Law*, 75 L. & Contemp. Probs. 23, 44–47 (2012).

15 For a discussion and critique of some aspects of this core principle, see *id.* at 30–33.

16 Bagenstos, *supra* note 10, at 104 (citing Erik Parens & Adrienne Asch, *Disability Rights Critique of Prenatal Genetic Testing: Reflections and Recommendations*, *in* Prenatal Testing and Disability Rights, *supra* note 6, at 20).

17 Schiltz, *supra* note 14, at 46 n.111 and sources cited therein.

"societal stigmas and other social pressures, often presented by professionals without disabilities, effectively coerce people into making decisions that reflect biases against people with disabilities. Given that reality, regulation of the particular form of killing at issue is arguably not restrictive of free choice, but instead is necessary to preserve true freedom of choice."[18] However, in that context, the disability rights community has actively advocated for the legal prohibition of the decision of parents not to treat the newborn. In contrast, in the abortion context, the disability rights movement does not argue for a restriction on abortion. As Bagenstos writes, "They aim, instead, to persuade medical professionals to provide pregnant women with full information—including information about the positive aspects of living (and parenting a child) with a disability—before offering prenatal tests and suggesting selective abortions."[19]

The Expressivist Disability Rights Critique of Selective Abortions

The disability rights advocate most closely associated with the expressivist arguments against selective abortion is Adrienne Asch. She is fully committed to "reproductive choice for all women."[20] However, she argues that selective abortion is morally problematic in a way that other abortions are not. Two distinct arguments can be identified as part of the expressivist critique of selective abortion.

The any/particular expressivist argument

The first is the argument that there is a morally significant distinction between aborting a child for no reason and aborting a child for a specific reason—if that reason is the child's disability.[21] In the first instance, the act of abortion is simply a reaction to some particular circumstance in the life of the mother that makes her not want to have any child at this time. In the second instance, the act of abortion is expressive of a morally problematic judgment about the value of that particular child's life.

Asch explains, "What differentiates abortion after prenatal diagnosis … from … other abortions is that the abortion is a response to characteristics of the fetus and would-be child and not to the situation of the woman."[22] Selective

---

18 *Id.* at 44.

19 Bagenstos, *supra* note 10, at 104; *see also* Muller, *supra* note 7, at 477.

20 Adrienne Asch, *Reproductive Technology and Disability*, *in* Reproductive Laws for the 1990's 70 (Sherrill Cohen & Nadine Taub eds., 1989).

21 Although the issue of sex-selective abortions involves many of the same concerns as disability-selective abortions, my focus in this chapter is on disability-selective abortions. As Muller points out, "The threat to disability rights from disability-selective abortion … is arguably greater than the threat to women's rights from sex-selective abortion; the rate of disability-selective abortion is in a different league." Muller, *supra* note 7, n.79 and accompanying text.

22 Asch, *supra* note 20, at 82.

abortion, she argues, "expresses negative or discriminatory attitudes not merely about a disabling trait, but about those who carry it."[23] This message, she explains, is that "a single trait stands in for the whole, the trait obliterates the whole … The tests send the message that there's no need to find out about the rest."[24] Asch describes this distinction as the "any/particular" distinction. She argues that it is *not* morally problematic for a woman to abort because she does not want *any* child at this time; however, it *is* morally problematic for a woman to abort because she does not want *this particular* child, based on a trait identified in a prenatal test.[25]

The social message expressivist argument

The second argument is that the act of screening to prevent the birth of disabled children concretely affects the lives of living, existing people with disabilities, because it not only expresses, but also reinforces and socially validates, the view that people with disabilities are less valued than people without disabilities. Furthermore, the consequence of this screening is a smaller number of people with disabilities being born, resulting in fewer advocates for the rights of people with disabilities, and a decrease in social support for those with disabilities and those who care for them.

Asch argues that screening for preventing the birth of disabled babies ultimately "disparages the lives of existing and future disabled people."[26] This disparagement hinders the wider social acceptance of people with disabilities, and it concretely affects society's willingness to support the lives of those with disabilities. She explains:

> If the majority continues to see disability as a form of human difference that is worse than other types of difference, it is no wonder that the majority will resist social changes that would incorporate people who have these negatively valued characteristics. The goal of the disability rights movement is to persuade the majority to recognize that people with those disabilities are not lesser than others because of those variations; they are not lesser in what they have to offer and what they can contribute to family and social life. If we truly believed that it was acceptable to have a disability, we would subsidize more disability-related expenses than we do as a society.[27]

23 Parens & Asch, *supra* note 16, at 13.

24 *Id.*

25 Adrienne Asch, *Why I Haven't Changed my Mind about Prenatal Diagnosis*, *in* Prenatal Testing and Disability Rights, *supra* note 6, at 236.

26 Asch, *supra* note 20, at 81.

27 Asch, *supra* note 25, at 253.

Assessing the Possibility of Common Ground in the Disability Rights Critiques of Selective Abortions

Bagenstos and Muller offer different explanations of and prescriptions for resolving the inconsistencies between the positions of the disability rights community in the context of selective treatment of disabled infants and selective abortions. A careful look at their contrasting explanations and prescriptions illustrates both why the autonomy-based disability rights critique does not afford much common ground for abortion opponents and advocates, and why the expressivist disability rights critique might be more promising.

Autonomy-Based Critiques of Selective Abortion Afford Little Room for Common Ground

Bagenstos points out:

> Current constitutional doctrine relating to abortion is rooted in a principle of autonomy. The Supreme Court has held, most notably in *Planned Parenthood of Southeastern Pennsylvania v. Casey*, that a choice of such profound moral and practical significance for a woman must be made by her, freely. But the Court also has recognized—in the mode of the disability rights critique—that private as well as public pressures can inhibit free choice. Accordingly, it has upheld regulations of abortion that are justified as removing obstacles to women's authentic choice.[28]

If it were accepted that most abortions occur under conditions of effective duress, but that this duress is so subtle that it cannot be reliably detected in any individual case, then women's choices in these situations are never truly free, and an absolute prohibition on abortion might be justified. Both in his book and in an earlier article on the same topic, Bagenstos argues against this conclusion, searching instead for some way to "endorse the disability rights critique while at the same time adhering to support for broad abortion rights."[29] He suggests "gender equality" as a possible curb, a brake on the "kinds of (publicly or privately imposed) constraints that we are going to treat as rendering a choice unfree."[30] One could accept the theory that "many abortions that result from prenatal testing are effectively coerced by social stigmas filtered through powerful professional cultures," but also believe that

> any prohibition of a particular class of abortion will be abused to harass women who seek abortions more generally. Such a prohibition might also chill doctors from performing abortions, particularly if its terms are vague. If those

28 Bagenstos, *supra* note 10, at 104–105.

29 Bagenstos, *supra* note 7, at 457.

30 *Id.* at 451–2.

> risks outweigh the risk that disability-selective abortions will occur and harm disability equality—or if nonregulatory means such as public education can effectively address the harms caused by such abortions—then abortion should not be regulated, even if one accepts the critique.[31]

Bagenstos goes on to argue: "Indeed, I would wager that most disability rights activists who support abortion rights—including those who support assisted suicide—would favor informed consent requirements for disability-selective abortions, if they believed those requirements would not be used simply as part of a campaign to deny women the right to choose abortion."[32]

This would be, I think, the strongest autonomy-based argument against selective abortion that one could accept, while still preserving the right to abortion generally. Let us examine the premises underlying this argument. The starting premise for this argument is that the right to abortion is essential to women's equality. The argument is that when the risk that some people with disabilities will be aborted because of prejudicial social stigma is weighed against the risk that some women or physicians might be dissuaded from getting or performing abortions, the latter risk is greater than the former. Since (according to the starting premise) women's equality depends on unhindered access to abortion, in this situation, gender equality must trump the disabled fetus's right to be born (often based on a conviction that the taking of a potential life cannot be equated with the taking of an actual life). But most abortion opponents reject the starting premise of this argument: that women's equality depends on access to abortion. Instead, they start from the premise that at some point after conception, the right of the developing fetus to be born trumps all other considerations, including any potentially negative effect on women's equality or autonomy (often based on a conviction that society should be reformed to ensure that giving birth to a child does *not* necessarily precipitate such a negative effect).

Clearly, the autonomy-based disability rights critique offers a very slender plot of common ground for parties approaching the issue from such incommensurable starting points. As Bagenstos suggests, perhaps there is some room for agreement on initiatives to ensure more informed decision-making in connection with a prenatal diagnosis of a disability, such as the Prenatally and Postnatally Diagnosed Conditions Awareness Act of 2008[33] (commonly referred to as the "Kennedy-Brownback Act", after its bipartisan sponsors). However, if the "common goal" of more informed decision-making actually starts to significantly influence women's decisions to abort fetuses with disabilities, those convinced that women's equality depends on unfettered access to abortions are likely to perceive these measures as posing an obstacle to that goal. The "friend and foe" in any particular skirmish on

---

31 *Id.* at 457.

32 Bagenstos, *supra* note 10, at 113.

33 Prenatally and Postnatally Diagnosed Conditions Awareness Act of 208, Pub. L. No. 100-374, 122 Stat. 4051 (codified as amended at 42 U.S.C. § 280g-8 (2008)).

abortion that is being waged on these terms, who might find themselves standing together in some night battles about a specific measure to related to consent, are likely to turn on each other as soon as the measure begins to have an appreciable effect on parents' decisions.[34]

Muller's Argument for Acknowledging and Embracing Ambivalence about Disability Suggests that the Expressivist Critiques May Offer More Common Ground

Muller's analysis of what he characterizes as the disability community's "opposition to selective non-treatment but acquiescence in selective abortion"[35] provides additional insight into the limits of the autonomy argument. Muller suggests that the many contradictions and inconsistencies in matters related to disability law—including this one—stem from a largely unacknowledged ambivalence about disability that "hinders our capacity to confront disability honestly and forthrightly in the law."[36] He argues that "the law should express this ambivalence rather than strive for abstract conceptual clarity."[37] Although Muller does not make this argument, for the reasons discussed below, I believe that the autonomy-based disability rights critique of selective abortion tends to be shaped by notions of "abstract conceptual clarity" that in fact do not reflect the more honest ambiguity that underlies the discourse. The expressivist disability rights critiques, on the other hand, provide a more natural platform for acknowledging the ambiguity shared by all the participants in the debate, thus offering a more promising possibility for forging common ground.

What is the ambivalence that Muller identifies? He introduces it with reference to what he characterizes as "a pair of tired descriptive models" used by scholars speaking about disabilities:

> The medical model casts disability as a biological impairment synonymous with illness. By this view, disability is an undesirable deviation from normal human functioning. The social model, by contrast, casts disability as a social construction like race. By this view, cultural practices transform differences into disabilities. Neither of these descriptive models necessarily incorporates a particular norm of justice or a particular notion of the value of disability. It has long been clear, however, that adherents of the social model tend to cast

---

34 *See*, e.g., Deborah Pergament, *What Does Choice Really Mean?: Prenatal Testing, Disability, and Special Education without Illusions*, 23 Health Matrix: J. of Law-Med 55, 80–83 (expressing concerns about the potentially chilling effect of the Kennedy-Brownback Act's measures on "women's access to choices").

35 Muller, *supra* note 7, at 479.

36 *Id.* at 470.

37 *Id.*

> disability *as a difference we should celebrate*, and that adherents of the medical model tend to cast disability as a *difference we should eliminate*.[38]

The core dilemma ignored by both of these two dichotomous models is that human disabilities are neither solely biological impairments, nor solely social constructs. They are a complex blend of both. In fact, disabilities present neither solely valued differences, nor solely devalued differences. As Martha Saxton writes, "the experience of disability does not neatly reflect the experiences of [other socially stigmatized groups such as women, people of color and gay people] for whom negative judgments about their personal characteristics have been exposed as resulting solely from oppression."[39] Adrienne Asch adds, "The inability to move without mechanical aid, to see, to hear, or to learn is not inherently neutral. Disability itself limits some options."[40]

Muller argues that the legal regimes resulting from impoverished discourse based on the two common descriptive models are flawed. He uses the contradiction in the disability community's approach to selective non-treatment and selective abortion as a case study for his argument. He writes:

> Selective non-treatment and selective abortion raise variants of the same basic question: is it acceptable for prospective parents to choose death for their nascent offspring rather than life with a disability? The disability community has responded quite differently in these two contexts. With respect to selective non-treatment, it has answered no, advancing a vision of disability as a valued difference. With respect to selective abortion, it has answered yes, accepting a vision of disability as a devalued difference.[41]

Muller acknowledges that there may be many reasons for the disability community's different positions in these two situations, such as the distinction between a newborn and a fetus, or differences in the legal and political contexts in which the two different issues have arisen.[42] However, these reasons do not explain "the different visions of disability endorsed by disability advocates in discussions about these two issues."[43] Muller examines in detail how these conflicting sentiments about disability have been reflected in the public discourse on both of these issues.[44]

---

38 *Id.* at 470 (emphasis added).

39 Marsha Saxton, *Why Members of the Disability Community Oppose Prenatal Diagnosis and Selective Abortion*, *in* Prenatal Testing and Disability Rights, *supra* note 6, at 147, 150.

40 Asch, *supra* note 20, at 73.

41 Muller, *supra* note 7, at 472.

42 *Id.* at 479–80.

43 *Id.* at 479.

44 *Id.* at 481–89.

Without express acknowledgment of this ambiguity, Muller argues that the resulting legal outcomes in both situations only obliquely accommodate it. The Baby Doe controversy ultimately resulted in the enactment of the Child Abuse Amendments of 1984,[45] which require all infants (including those with disabilities) to be given medically indicated treatment unless such treatment would be futile. Muller points out, however, that the explicit legal prohibition of selective non-treatment has little practical impact. The sanction for noncompliance is limited to "withdrawal of a miniscule set of federal funds."[46] Enforcement is virtually non-existent; in practice, "physicians tend to deliberate about difficult treatment decisions amongst themselves and present a unified front to acquiescent parents."[47] In other words, the ambivalence expresses itself in a legal prohibition of selective non-treatment, but an unspoken social consensus that permits lack of enforcement of the prohibition.

The legal outcome with respect to selective abortion reflects the same ambivalence, oriented in the opposite direction: no legal prohibition, but significant moral sanction. Despite the absence of any legal prohibition of selective abortion, Muller notes, "The social ritual around prenatal testing … reflects a powerful ambivalence about testing and selective abortion."[48] Prenatal testing is routinely offered as a means of ensuring the health of the child, without any advance discussion of the real dilemma posed by the results of such testing—the choice between abortion or a child with a disability.[49] What little legal regulation of the area there is comes from cases considering the torts of wrongful birth and wrongful life, a troubled area of the law in which courts continue to "express[] profound unease with both forms of action," with even states recognizing the causes of action "proceed[ing] with trepidation."[50] The only relevant statutory enactment is the Kennedy-Brownback Act, which "expresses social concerns about selective abortion in general terms, yet … skirts the ethical questions at the issue's core."[51] Indeed, Muller contends, "Like the delicate dance conducted by physicians and expectant women, the Act limits its concern to testing and makes no mention of abortion … More than anything else, the Act provides a public statement of moral uncertainty that we may privately ignore."[52]

Muller argues that legal regimes resting on an unacknowledged ambivalence such as this can be dangerous for two reasons. The first is what he calls the "problem of conscious embrace": "denials of ambivalence lead to the embrace of a conscious view of disability that distorts our genuine concern … To deny the

45 42 U.S.C. § 5106g (2006).

46 Muller, *supra* note 7, at 485.

47 *Id.*

48 *Id.* at 487.

49 *See infra* notes 77–85 and accompanying text.

50 Muller, *supra* note 7, at 487.

51 *Id.* at 489.

52 *Id.*

mixed sentiments that inform our reactions to disability obscures the substance of the decisions before us."[53] Indeed, this is arguably precisely the dynamic exposed in the dialogue about the autonomy-based disability rights critique. If we deny the ambivalence in our reactions to disability, we must embrace either one or the other view of disability—either disability as a valued trait (leading to the view that the disabled fetus's right to life must trump the woman's right to abort) or disability as a devalued trait (leading to the view that the woman's right to abort must trump the right of the disabled fetus to survive).

The second danger that Muller sees in a legal regime resting on an unacknowledged ambivalence is what he calls "the problem of expressed suppression." He explains: "Suppression of one or both of two competing sentiments is rarely stable; the suppressed sentiment may either emerge, amplified, in behaviors we neither expect nor understand, or it may give rise to behaviors, once again amplified and neither expected nor understood, that reinforce the conscious view."[54] In the specific context of selective non-treatment and selective abortion, Muller suggests the following possible dangers:

> Under the regime espousing a view of disability as a valued difference, the law would encourage parents and prospective parents to choose life in situations where life is against the best interests of the parties involved. Suppressed negative valuations of disability could give rise to guilty uncertainty about this choice; they could also provoke eruptions of anger and resentment directed toward the child, the medical profession, or society more broadly. Under the regime espousing a view of disability as a devalued difference, the law would encourage parents and prospective parents to choose death in situations where death is against the best interests of the parties involved. Suppressed positive valuations of disability could give rise to uncertainty about these choices and similar eruptions of anger and resentment, albeit toward different targets. For example, parents and prospective parents might direct these eruptions toward living individuals with disabilities or children without disabilities.[55]

Muller proposes that the law should attempt to minimize the dangers identified above in two ways. It should not embrace unequivocally either a view of disability as wholly positive, or wholly negative. Moreover, it should consciously expose and accentuate this ambivalence, to ensure that policy prescriptions adopted through such legislation do not have unintended adverse consequences for people with disabilities.[56] Muller ultimately concludes that the current regimes governing both selective non-treatment and selective abortion do serve these two goals to a large extent. With respect to selective non-treatment, "The law's

53 *Id.* at 497.

54 *Id.*

55 *Id.* at 499–500.

56 *Id.* at 500.

formal condemnation preserves social mores [against infanticide], yet non-enforcement allows decisions against treatment. Moreover, the threat of social or legal sanction focuses responsibility for individual decisions."[57] With respect to selective abortion, "the law should allow selective abortion yet raise moral doubts about the practice."[58] The inconsistency in the positions with respect to the two different situations is explained (and justified), Muller argues, by the difference in our existing background legal presumptions regarding infanticide (generally prohibited) and abortion (generally permitted).[59] Although the existing legal schemes thus structurally accommodate the expression of our ambivalence toward disability, Muller argues that being more explicit about the fact that the legal scheme is structured to express this ambivalence might permit us to *actually* express it more directly. We will return to some of his specific suggestions for how this might be done later in this chapter.

Muller's proposal clearly acknowledges the expressive function of laws. His proposal also clearly rejects the primacy of the two incommensurable starting premises underlying the autonomy-based disability rights critiques. He is suggesting, instead, that both pro-life and pro-choice participants in the debate actually share the same set of fundamental starting premises: that the situation faced by parents who have received a prenatal diagnosis of a disability is fraught with ambiguity; that the actors in such a scenario most likely view the disabled fetus as both *valued* and as *devalued*; and that these conflicting views should all be taken into account in deliberations about the ultimate decision. I believe that a careful look at the expressivist disability rights critique suggests that Muller's insights might be applied to offer some possibility for forging the common ground that eluded us in considering the debate about the autonomy-based disability rights critique.

Do the Expressivist Critiques of Selective Abortion Offer Some Possibility of Common Ground?

Recall the two different dangers that Muller identifies in suppressing the ambivalence we feel about disabilities: the problem of conscious embrace, and the problem of expressed suppression. I have argued above that the problem of conscious embrace helps explains the lack of common ground among people on differing sides of the abortion debate in discussions framed by the autonomy-based arguments of the disability rights critique of selective abortion.[60] The problem of expressed suppression is directly related to the core concern underlying the expressivist disability rights critique. In both its forms, the expressivist disability rights critique is concerned about the effects of suppressed valuations of disability

57 *Id.* at 502.

58 *Id.* at 507.

59 *Id.* at 503, 506.

60 pp. 127–128, *supra*.

(both positive or negative) that might lead to negative consequences for people with disabilities. If both sides of the debate about this critique could more directly confront the dangers of suppressing expressions of ambivalence in their valuation of disability, perhaps the debate could proceed on a more productive path. Let us examine two common exchanges in debates about this critique, to consider how this might play itself out.

The slippery slope objection to the any/particular expressivist argument

The most common criticism of Asch's first expressivist argument, the any/particular argument, is a "slippery slope" argument: the any/particular distinction "calls into question the morality of virtually all abortions."[61] The decision to abort any fetus can be easily recast into a decision to abort this particular fetus, for some reason. For example, the decision of the mother of three children to abort her fourth child could be characterized as a decision to abort any child who happened to come along after she already had three children; or, it could be seen as a decision to abort that particular child because of her "trait of being fourth-born." Critics of Asch's argument fail to see why traits such as "fourth-bornness" can be distinguished from other disabling traits.[62] Anthropologist Nancy Press argues that such arguments fail to acknowledge the "important nuance" of Asch's argument, one that is based on women's experience of pregnancy.[63] Press explains:

> For Asch there is, virtually from its inception, a perceived difference between a wanted pregnancy and one that is not wanted at that time. In the first case there is an immediate, imaginative sense of carrying a baby; in the latter, the pregnancy remains a fetus. For Asch, the negative message of selective abortion for disability is that it is a decision to terminate a pregnancy, which was previously experienced as wanted, on the basis of knowing only one new fact about that baby—that it will have some sort of disability. To Asch this is fundamentally different from the termination of a pregnancy that was always unwanted based on characteristics of the woman's life at the time.[64]

61 Prenatal Testing and Disability Rights, *supra* note 6, at 15.

62 *Id.* at 15–16; James Lindemann Nelson, *The Meaning of the Act: Reflections on the Expressive Force of Reproductive Decision Making and Policies*, *in* Prenatal Testing and Disability Rights, *supra* note 6, at 201–05.

63 Nancy Press, *Assessing the Expressive Character of Prenatal Testing: The Choices Made or the Choices Made Available?*, in Prenatal Testing and Disability Rights, *supra* note 6, at 215. Press also argues that "fourth-bornness" "is not an intrinsic attribute of that child, but rather of that pregnancy. Put up for adoption and raised in another family, the fourth-born, biological child may become the first-born, adopted child. But a disability is intrinsic to the child. A fetus definitively diagnosed with a disability will have that disability, whatever family raises it." *Id.*

64 *Id.*

Press's observation emphasizes that the *particular* reason for the change in the parent's attitude toward the fetus is the concern of this critique. It is *precisely* the fact that the parent's decision is based on the category of disability that makes it problematic. The proponents of this argument would not embark on the slippery slope suggested by the fourth-born argument, because they are not entrenched in the all-or-nothing debate of the autonomy-based argument, where women's equality is pitted and balanced against the right to life. Instead, they are attempting to open a discussion that acknowledges a more nuanced, delicate balance of the ambiguities of the situation, and permits some discussion of both the valued and the devalued nature of the difference about this fetus revealed by the prenatal diagnosis.

In such a nuanced discussion, the disability rights critique proponents would be free to counter the parents' concerns about the negative value of the disabled fetus's life with arguments about the positive value. They might, for example, offer a civil-rights analogy that could serve as a response to this "slippery slope" critique of the any/particular distinction. Bagenstos discusses this argument in another section of his book, dealing with critics of the Americans with Disabilities Act (the "ADA")[65] who attempt to distinguish it from other civil rights laws on account of its accommodation requirements. The ADA does not simply forbid discrimination because of disability; it requires employers and providers of public services to make positive (and sometimes costly) accommodations to a person's disability. Bagenstos argues, however, that these accommodations are justified under the same rationale that justifies all of the antidiscrimination provisions in our civil-rights laws. He argues that antidiscrimination laws "seek to dismantle a system of group-based subordination and patterns of occupational segregation that support that system."[66] This is supported by the fact that our traditional civil-rights laws do not prohibit all irrational discrimination, but instead prohibit *only* discrimination against people in particular groups identified as having been the subject of group-based subordination. We are free to discriminate against our fellow human beings for all sorts of irrational reasons. We could arbitrarily refuse to hire people who have red hair, because we were jilted by a red-haired person when we were 16 years old. We could arbitrarily refuse to rent apartments to people who are exactly 5'6" tall, because we are locked in an extreme case of sibling rivalry with our 5'6" tall sister. But our civil-rights laws forbid irrational discrimination against people who belong to certain protected classes, classes defined by race, sex, religion, and disability. Indeed, even when such discrimination might be entirely rational, the laws still prohibit it. Even if an employer could empirically prove that employees of a certain racial group are less productive than employees of another, our laws would still prohibit discrimination on such grounds.[67] We have enacted these laws because we, as a society, have identified that particular protected class

65 The Americans with Disabilities Act of 1990, Pub. L. No. 101-336, 104 Stat. 328 (1990); *see* Bagenstos, *supra* note 10, at 55–75.

66 *Id.* at 57.

67 *Id.* at 63.

as having been systemically subordinated. We think that discrimination based on membership in one of these historically subordinated groups is much more dangerous, resulting in much more serious social harm, than discrimination based on personal idiosyncracies like resentment of a red-haired object of our unrequited love, or the trait of "fourth-bornness."

The ADA not only adds people with disabilities to the category of protected persons, but it goes even further than many civil-rights laws. It not only forbids discrimination against people with disabilities, but it sometimes mandates accommodation of people with such disabilities to enable them to access public facilities or to perform certain jobs. And that additional requirement of accommodation, with all its attendant costs and obligations, is justified for the same reason as the antidiscrimination provisions. People with disabilities are recognized as a group of people who have been systemically subordinated, and some accommodation, no matter how costly or inconvenient, can be mandated, because it "serves the goal of equal access to societal opportunities by helping to dismantle a structure of subordination."[68] That is the same rationale behind the Supreme Court's decision in *Olmstead v. L.C.*,[69] which required the state of Georgia to house people with mental disabilities in community settings, rather than in institutions, regardless of the greater cost this might entail. That is also the rationale behind the Individuals with Disabilities Education Act,[70] giving children with disabilities the right to be educated in our schools, despite the cost.

This argument potentially offers a response to the "slippery slope" criticism of Asch's first expressivist argument against abortion after a prenatal diagnosis of a disability. The civil-rights laws as characterized by Bagenstos provide a venerable model for the view that an act that might not be morally problematic if done for no particular reason might be morally problematic if done for some particular reason. In light of the overwhelming evidence of the systemic structure of subordination to which people with disabilities have been subjected in the history of the United States, and the overwhelming evidence of the effect of a prenatal diagnosis of a disability on the number of people with disabilities being born,[71] it is arguably legitimate to consider abortions after a prenatal diagnosis to be particularly morally problematic, even if one supports a woman's right to an abortion generally. It is this "systemic structure of subordination" that the disability rights critique considers to be suppressing the positive evaluation of disability in this situation; this is a subtle, but powerful systemic force, recognized as such in a significant body of civil-rights laws that most of us support—such as the ADA and IDEA.

Of course, in such a debate, the proponent of the disability rights critique would have to be equally appreciative of arguments that could only be raised by

68 *Id.* at 64.

69 527 U.S. 581 (1999).

70 20 U.S.C. §§ 1400–82 (2006) (originally enacted as the Education for all Handicapped Children act of 1975).

71 Schiltz, *supra* note 17, at 49 n.120 and sources cited therein.

interlocutors who trust the sincerity of the shared starting premise that accepts the ambiguities inherent in decisions about selective abortion. Even if the civil-rights analogy effectively addresses slippery slope concerns, it does not address counter-arguments based on the dangers of suppression of the negative valuation of a disability. In such debates, then, the proponent of the disability rights critique would have to productively engage counter-arguments such as the distinctions between race and disability identified by disability rights scholars such as Asch,[72] and distinctions between granting people with disabilities access to our workplaces, neighborhoods, and schools, and granting people with disabilities access to our wombs and our homes. But a debate about the correct balance between the more concrete dangers of suppressed expression of particular aspects of the negative and positive valuation of people with disabilities is at least directly focused on the concerns of the disability rights critique. This would be a more difficult, but more productive, dialogue than one focused on the conversation-stopping contention that the any/particular distinction places us on a "slippery slope" to questioning the morality of all abortions.

Objections to the social message disability rights critique

Critics of Asch's social message argument (that selective abortion to prevent the birth of disabled children disparages the lives of existing and future children, by diminishing the numbers of such people and hindering their wider social acceptance) commonly argue that individual acts by the parents choosing selective abortions cannot be attributed with any such message. Some argue that actions can only convey the conscious meaning intended by the actor. Selective abortions are typically *not* intended by the parents choosing them as intentional disparagements of people with disabilities, and thus cannot be attributed with such an expressive effect.[73] Others concede that actors might send messages without being fully conscious of the expressive effect, but argue that the circumstances "in which broad cultural agreement about the symbolic meaning of an act means that the act can send a specific message" are rare, limited to instances such as "flying the Confederate flag over a public building in the southern United States."[74]

Press points out, though, that these critics might be misinterpreting the expressivist argument by implicitly assuming that

> the "message" is having an abortion and the "sender" is the woman/couple who terminate the pregnancy. But this is only one possible way to construct the message to which those with disability may be reacting, and, I would contend, it is not the most useful way. Another way of thinking about it is that the offer

72 *See supra* notes 38–39 and accompanying text.

73 Press, *supra* note 63, at 214 (citing bioethicist Allen Buchanan).

74 *Id.* at 214–15 (citing James Lindemann Nelsons).

> of prenatal testing itself is the message and the institutional structures through which the offer is made constitute the senders of the message.[75]

Press's suggestion emphasizes that the concern of the social message disability rights critique is *not* the intent of any particular parent making a selective abortion decision. Adopting Muller's suggestion, this critique is best understood as coming from a perspective in which the honest ambivalence of the actors is accepted as a shared common presumption. The critique is not an argument that parents choosing a selective abortion are expressing a simplistically negative message about the perceived value of the life of the fetus with a disability.[76] Instead, it is an argument about a social structure that has developed around the process of prenatal testing that raises the specter of expressed suppression—that is, suppression of positive valuations of disability in discussion of the practices of selective abortion.

Press has conducted extensive research on the routinization of noninvasive prenatal screening for birth defects.[77] This research has led her to conclude that the more routine such testing has become, the more obscure the actual meaning and purpose of such testing has become, both in conversations with women about such testing as "under the rubric of routine postnatal care,"[78] as well as in scientific literature about such testing.[79]

Press surveyed pregnant women and test providers in California, which in 1986 mandated that all healthcare providers offer such testing to all their pregnant patients.[80] In particular, she focused on the maternal serum alpha fetoprotein (MSAFP) screen, a test involving analysis of the amount of a particular substance produced by the developing fetus that is found in the mother's blood. The MSAFP involves analysis of blood drawn from the mother, rather than the more invasive procedures such as amniocentesis, which involve drawing amniotic fluid from the mother's womb. The women Press interviewed had come to consider the MSAFP screening as part of "routine prenatal care," to the extent that it was sometimes "described in terms of helping to protect the fetus. The actual purpose of the MSAFP screening—to find cases of untreatable birth defects in order to allow women and couples the opportunity to terminate a pregnancy—appeared to be obscured from view."[81] Indeed, obscuring the connection between the test and

75 *Id.* at 217.

76 Indeed, Press's research has also revealed striking evidence of this ambivalence in the pregnant women surveyed in the MSAFP study. While they tended to express extremely positive attitudes about the lives of people with disabilities in general, when questioned about a possibility of disability in a child of their own, they expressed extremely negative attitudes toward the potential life of such a child. *Id.* at 225–29.

77 *Id.* at 218–30.

78 *Id.* at 219.

79 *Id.* at 221–22.

80 *Id.* at 218.

81 *Id.* at 219.

the most common outcome of tests that show fetal anomalies—abortion—was an intentional goal of the test providers. Press reports that:

> Health care providers in our study, and state officials who had created informed consent materials for the California MSAFP program, were often quite open about the fact that the link between abortion and prenatal screening was intentionally avoided. They cited as reasons behind this omission both political conflict over abortion and the observed discomfort of pregnant parties when abortion was mentioned in this context.[82]

Press notes the same approach in the scientific literature on this subject. She observed that the only literature that openly confronts the centrality of abortion to prenatal screening are cost–benefit analyses of selective abortion, comprising "up-front calculations of the minimum number of pregnancy terminations that can be done before screening ceases to be cost effective."[83] In more general articles, the goals of MSAFP screening are rarely discussed openly. In the brief statements of goals often contained in the introductions to such articles, Press identifies two types: "societally approved goals" and "controversial goals." The "societally approved goals" include reassuring the pregnant woman, providing information to doctors about the state of the pregnancy and possibilities for special preparations for the birth or *in-utero* treatment, and providing information to parents to prepare psychologically if the screening reveals an anomaly. Press notes that these goals focus on benefits to the people involved, on the joint interests of the mother and the fetus, and, generally, on "life." She also notes, however, that they are ancillary goals,

> in that they apply to statistically rare situations, involve information that could be found out in other ways, or describe either future situations or ones for which no guidelines for action currently exist. Fundamentally, they are ancillary because it is so unlikely that the MSAFP test would have become routinized if they were the only, or even the major, goals.[84]

In fact, the "controversial goals" are the ones that are "central to the public health purposes that make population-based prenatal screening viable": the ability to terminate the pregnancy when the testing reveals an anomaly, and the resulting cost savings to society. Yet, Press notes, these goals are so controversial that even when they are addressed, the obliqueness of the language used verges on "newspeak."

82 *Id.* at 221.

83 *Id.* at 221 n.18 (citing sources).

84 *Id.* at 222.

For example, one article contends that "MSAFP screening has proved to be a … cost-effective way of improving pregnancy outcome."[85]

Press describes the danger of obscuring the true stakes in dialogue about prenatal testing in language that invokes the social message disability rights critique:

> Such encoded language is explicable by the fact that, in opposition to the societally acceptable goals, these controversial goals imply things that are not comfortable for most Americans. They logically imply that not all life is worthwhile, and that the interests of society may be in conflict with those of the fetus … This encoded language also poses challenges to those who believe that the expressive character of prenatal diagnosis is hurtful, and even potentially dangerous, to those with disability: if the goals of prenatal testing are obscured and denied, it is difficult to demonstrate harm coming from those goals.[86]

This language also invokes Muller's concerns about the problem of expressed suppression. The social message disability rights critique should be understood as being based on fears about an institutional suppression of positive valuations of disability. Rather than a criticism of what any particular set of parents might be expressing with respect to any specific decision they make, the concern is about a social practice that is developing around these individual decisions that suppresses the possibility of introducing arguments that might "demonstrate harm" resulting from those unexpressed goals.

Arguments about the dangers of collective social messages of institutions, rather than individuals, are accepted in a number of contexts outside of selective abortion. For example, some scholars have suggested that the routine practice of sperm banks in assisting aspiring parents to choose sperm donors based on their race might be subject to some regulation, as a result of the social meaning and potential expressivist harm of such practices in light of our commitment to racial equality.[87] Expressivist arguments have been lodged against unjust legal schemes. Legal scholars over the past few decades have articulated various versions of legal expressivism, asserting that "laws and legal actions can express normative commitments and that laws may be evaluated according to whether their expressive content comports with constitutional or legal norms."[88] For example, scholars have asserted that:

---

85 *Id.* (citing G.C. Cunningham & K.W. Kizer, *Maternal Serum Alpha-Fetoprotein Screening Activities of State Health Agencies: A Survey*, 47 Am.J. of Human Genetics 899 (1990)).

86 *Id.* at 222–23.

87 Dov Fox, *Racial Classification in Assisted Reproduction,* 118 Yale L.J. 1844 (2009).

88 Matthew A. Edwards, Legal Expressivism, a Primer, at 8, available at http://ssrn.com/abstract=1361101 (generally referencing the contributions of scholars such as Elizabeth Anderson & Richard Pildes, *Expressive Theories of Law: A General Restatement,* 148 U. Pa. L. Rev. 1503 (2000); Matthew A. Adler, *Expressive Theories of Law: A Skeptical*

> Contemporary Equal Protection doctrine incorporates expressive concerns [by making] unconstitutional all laws that rest on certain impermissible purposes: those which express contempt, hostility, or inappropriate paternalism toward racial, ethnic, gender, and certain other groups, or that constitute them as social inferiors or as a stigmatized or pariah class.[89]

Another scholar recently has argued, "Granting patents on genes related to sexual orientation, and potentially other conditions such as deafness, high-functioning autism, or dwarfism, communicates government approval that these groups are pathological and should be cured. Such a communication expressively harms these groups."[90] These are all contexts in which arguments are made that some regulation of private practices might be justified, based not on what the individual actor intended to say about her specific action, but rather on the dangers stemming from the collective social message sent by some social practice or law.

Of course, opening up space in the debate for considering the social message disability rights critique does not determine the final outcome of the debate. Those asserting the social message disability rights critique have to accept that acknowledging a negative social message resulting from current practices does not provide an irrebuttable argument for ending the practice. Proponents of this critique must be equally open to honest engagement with the aspects of the practice of prenatal testing that suppress negative evaluation of a disability. For example, Press describes the anger expressed by a woman who chose abortion after a prenatal diagnosis of Down syndrome. Though prenatal testing and the abortion were presented to her and her husband as morally legitimate and legal choices, she describes a "punitive" feel to the way she was treated in undergoing the abortion: being placed in a ward in the maternity floor to recover, being treated rudely by the nursing staff, and not being given appropriate pain medication.[91] Scholars have raised concerns about the danger of prenatal testing becoming culturally or even legally mandatory, and the potential for totalitarian or social coercion in the use of reproductive technology.[92]

Another difficult issue that must be addressed by both sides debating the social message disability rights critique is the lack of congruence between the social

---

Overview, 148 U. PA. L. REV. 1363 (2000); Steven D. Smith, *Expressivist Jurisprudence and the Depletion of Meaning*, 60 MD. L. REV. 506 (2001); Cass R. Sunstein, *On the Expressive Function of the Law*, 144 U. PA. L. REV. 2012 (1996)).

89 Edwards, *supra* note 88, at 12 (referencing Anderson & Pildes, *supra* note 87, at 1533, and citing Andrew Koppelman, *On the Moral Foundations of Legal Expressivism*, 60 MD. L. REV. 777 (2001), for the proposition that "laws that denote inferior legal status constitute an intrinsic harm because they deny the human need for 'recognition'").

90 Edwards, *supra* note 88, at 13 (quoting Timothy R. Holbrook, *The Expressivist Impact of Patents*, 84 WASH. U. L. REV. 573, 581 (2006)).

91 Press, *supra* note 63, at 224.

92 Pergament, *supra* note 34, 74–75.

message of support for choosing not to abort based on a diagnosis of a disability, and the social message of support for actually raising a child with a disability. On the one hand, Nancy Mahowald argues:

> While individuals are unable to care adequately for a child in some instances, the same is hardly true for society as a whole, at least in the developed world. Collectively, society has all the resources necessary to care adequately for all of its people: healthy newborns, those with disabilities, or anyone who needs care that is not available through parents or other family members. Accordingly, society in general does not have the justification that some pregnant women may have for testing and abortion of fetuses whose subsequent care may be impossible for them to provide.[93]

On the other hand, Deborah Pergament laments "the paradox created when there is concerted effort to encourage women and their partners to choose to have a child with a prenatally diagnosed disability while government policies emphasize private responsibility for the care and education of children with disabilities and mandate restrictions on public expenditures for them."[94]

These broader questions about the wide panoply of collective social messages we send with respect to our brothers and sisters living with disabilities are, in the end, the crux of both versions of the expressivist critique of selective abortion addressed in this chapter, as well as the myriad versions of it that are beyond the scope of this work. Accepting as a shared common premise the ambiguity about disability that all participants in debate share will not be an easy step. However, it offers the possibility for a more honest conversation about the issues at stake, and perhaps a way forward in shaping social practices around selective abortion that are more satisfactory to both sides of the debate.

Opportunities for Finding Common Ground

Press makes clear that the conclusions from her research "are not intended as direct support for the expressivist argument." Rather, she hopes

> that this exploration of the silences, discomforts, multiple discourses, and structural tensions underlying the arena of prenatal testing will demonstrate the need to think in a broader way about what constitute the "messages" of prenatal testing, and who are the senders and receivers. This is important not primarily because of the putative negative effects of an offer of prenatal testing on those with disability. More crucial are the effects of our silences and evasions about

93 Nancy Mahowald, *Aren't We All Eugenicists? Commentary on Paul Lombardo's "Taking Eugenics Seriously"*, 30 Fla. St. U. L. Rev. 219, 232 (2003).

94 Pergament, *supra* note 34, at 115.

> our attitudes, desires, and intentions as regard the main driving forces of prenatal testing—selective abortion and attitudes toward disability. As we continue with increasing speed down an ever-widening path of prenatal testing, we need to ask: *What message are we sending to ourselves by being willing to do something which we cannot truly discuss?*[95]

Press has offered her explanations for the unwillingness of parents and the medical community to discuss selective abortion in the prenatal testing context: abortion is politically volatile and discussing it with prospective parents is difficult and uncomfortable. Bagenstos and Muller have offered their explanations for the unwillingness of the disability rights community to engage the selective abortion debate in the same forthright way in which they engaged the selective non-treatment debate: Bagenstos sees it as an inconsistency best resolved by choosing a side; Muller sees it largely as a consequence of our inability to acknowledge the ambivalent feelings about disability that all sides share. Lisa Blumberg, a frequent contributor to the disability rights journal *Disability Rag*, suggests some additional, pragmatic reasons:

> [T]he movement for quite legitimate reasons is unwilling to take a stand that could be seen as taking sides in the abortion controversy. The disability rights movement is for the most part a progressive movement and is increasingly cognizant of the need to forge alliances with other progressive movements. People with disabilities, like any other diverse group of people, have varying views on pregnancy termination. However, numerous people with disabilities are pro-choice, and indeed disabled women tend to perceive the same need to have access to abortion as nondisabled women.[96]

Muller expands: "The disability rights movement has traditionally aligned itself with the political left, including on the issue of abortion. It is at least plausible that restrictions on selective abortion could yield more costs in eroded political alliances and abortion rights than benefits for traditional notions of disability rights."[97]

But Blumberg, writing in 1994, makes a suggestion that is equally applicable today. She argues, "Now that we have an administration in Washington that is more receptive to reproductive choice than previous ones, the movement should not hesitate to speak out about eugenics." In other words, a political environment in which the disability rights community can feel more secure that its critique

---

95 Press, *supra* note 63, at 230–31 (emphasis added).

96 Lisa Blumberg, *Eugenics and Reproductive Choice*, in The Ragged Edge: The Disability Experience from the Pages of the First Fifteen Years of the Disability Rag 229, 232 (Barrett Shaw ed., 1994).

97 Muller, *supra* note 7, at 479. *But see* Pergament, *supra* note 34, at n.72 (taking issue with Muller's "presentation of the disability rights movement as somewhat monolithic in its alignment with the political left, particularly on the issue of abortion").

of selective abortion will not be misinterpreted as a general assault on women's reproductive rights might open up space for some more difficult, nuanced conversations. This position is supported by Muller's suggestion that a legal regime that consciously exposes and accentuates ambivalence about disability might allow for more forceful expressions of both poles of this ambivalence.[98] Blumberg suggests that

> the movement … carefully define the issues that should concern us as disability rights activists. As a movement, we should not take any position on the rights of a fetus versus the rights of a pregnant woman. However, what we can and must do is take a position against any medical, legal or social policy that is based on the attitude that people who have disabilities are categorically inferior to others and therefore would be better off if they did not exist and everyone else would benefit by their absence.[99]

Blumberg offers the following list of "concrete positions which disability rights groups along with other progressive groups should take to combat eugenics … which should in no way involve the movement in the debate over whether a woman should have a legal right to abortion":

- The decision whether to have prenatal tests must be solely that of the pregnant woman regardless of the woman's age, reproductive history, or disability status.
- All expectant couples should be informed as to the purpose of the different available prenatal tests as well as given information on the risks, limitations, and expense of the tests, the manner in which these tests will be performed, and when during the gestation period the results will be available. Consent and refusal forms must state that a woman's decision to forgo prenatal tests will not subject either her or her future child to loss of any medical care, insurance, legal benefits or community services that they would otherwise be entitled to. Legislation should be drafted as appropriate.
- The results of all prenatal tests must be strictly confidential and may only be released to a third party with the woman's consent.
- All women regardless of age, reproductive history, or disability status must be given the absolute right to continue a pregnancy after prenatal diagnosis. Legislation should be drafted as appropriate.
- Laws regulating abortion should be disability neutral.
- Disability groups should prepare packets of information to be offered to all couples who learn that their fetus has a disabling condition. These packets should contain (1) information that seeks to dispel common misconceptions about disability and to present disability from a disabled

98 *See supra* notes 56–59 and accompanying text.

99 Blumberg, *supra* note 96, at 233.

person's perspective, (2) information on community-based services for disabled children and their families as well as on financial assistance programs, (3) material on special needs adoption, and (4) a summary of major laws protecting the civil rights of persons with disabilities. People with disabilities and parents of people with disabilities should be available to talk with future parents.

- All medical students should be required to take at least one course in political and social issues of disability and all practicing physicians should be required to take such a course as part of their continuing education requirements. All genetic counselors as part of their specialized training must participate in an activity that will give them contact with disabled persons in nonmedical settings.
- Non-perjorative language must be used when describing persons with disabilities and potential persons with disabilities. The term "defective fetus" should be seen to be in the same category as "kike fetus" and "nigger fetus."
- Wrongful life suits are inherently discriminatory against persons with disabilities and should be prohibited. Wrongful birth suits should only be permitted with disabled children if they are permitted with nondisabled children.
- Family strengthening initiatives such as parental leave, part-time and flextime work, expanded childcare alternatives, comprehensive health care programs and programs assisting low-income families must be supported. Parenting a disabled child will become a more viable option for more people if society provides more support to parents in general.[100]

Some of these suggestions are similar to those offered by Muller to redress what he perceives as a current imbalance in the competing views of disability in the legal regime governing selective abortion. He suggests that the current background legal regime, with its sanction of selective abortion, offers a "quite meager" voice to the pole of ambiguity representing disability as a valued difference. He suggests that the emphasis on information expressed in the 2008 Kennedy-Brownback law could be made more robust "to encourage exchange between disability groups, prospective parents considering abortion, and the physicians and genetic counselors working with prospective parents. It could also do more to regulate how physicians and genetic counselors discuss diagnosis."[101] However, Muller also suggests that "it is not unforeseeable that more genuine restrictions on abortion could prove necessary to maintain a balance between expressions valuing and devaluing disability in this context," such as restrictions on government funding to selective abortion, heightened waiting periods on selective abortions, restrictions

100 *Id.* at 238–39.

101 Muller, *supra* note 7, at 507.

on testing, extension of the Child Abuse Amendments to cover viable fetuses, or limitations on wrongful birth or life tort claims.[102]

If friend and foe are to stand together in any place in the night battle of abortion, the most promising place to start might be in our shared common convictions about our brothers and sisters with disabilities—both the positive valuations shared in progressive legislation such as the ADA and IDEA, and the negative valuations that shape the silences that currently shroud the practice of selective abortion.

102 *Id.*

Chapter 6
Supporting Pregnant Women and Their Families to Reduce the Abortion Rate

Kristen Day

Americans are deeply divided over the issue of abortion. Since *Roe v. Wade*, there has been deep disagreement and debate over the legality of abortion: majorities regard it as morally wrong, or a tragic decision, in all or many circumstances. Substantial majorities oppose abortion in the second and third trimesters, 64 percent and 80 percent respectively. Fifty-two percent of Americans believe abortion should only be legal under certain circumstances.[1] A majority of pro-life and pro-choice people support parental consent for minors, waiting periods for abortion, informed consent for women seeking abortion and making abortion illegal in the third trimester.[2] This widespread consensus offers opportunities to take serious steps through Congress, state legislatures, and local governments to reduce the number of abortions in the United States.

However, politics is a game in which winning frequently trumps sound public policy. The needs and safety of the public are the victims in this game. A particular party or politician may enjoy a small short-term victory with a successful election or fundraising drive, but at the expense of the public—especially the poor, the weak, and the disenfranchised. For evidence, we need look no further than our current political situation, where we face a budget stalemate with no end in sight. House Republicans and Senate Democrats have differing views on future fiscal policy, and neither side will budge or compromise. They are strategizing for a political advantage in the next election cycle, eyeing the White House as the ultimate prize.

In the meantime, the sequestration, which triggered $1.2 trillion in automatic across-the-board spending cuts, has caused reductions to programs that help those who need assistance—including women facing unplanned pregnancies and families with young children. For instance, approximately 70,000 low-income children are being cut from Head Start. Likewise, an estimated 600,000 pregnant

1 Lydia Saad, *American's Abortion Views Steady Amid Gosnell Trial*, Gallup (May 10, 2013), http://www.gallup.com/poll/162374/americans-abortion-views-steady-amid-gosnell-trial.aspx.

2 Lydia Saad, *Plenty of Common Ground Found in Abortion Debate*, Gallup (August 8, 2011), http://www.gallup.com/poll/148880/plenty-common-ground-found-abortion-debate.aspx.

women or women with young children will be cut from the Women, Infants and Children (WIC) Program. Families who rely on childcare could lose services, affecting up to 30,000 children.[3] Approximately 125,000 low-income families will lose their rental housing vouchers. The Supplemental Nutrition Program (SNAP) has been cut, along with the Children's Health Insurance Program (CHIP), which provides healthcare to low-income children.

Economic and social factors put pressure on women to have abortions; often the decision to abort is a "choice" in name only. Most women who have abortions do so with great reluctance, and many would decide otherwise if they had greater support in bearing or raising the child and if alternatives were available to them. By far the two most common reasons for having abortions are that the woman's life would be dramatically changed (for example, losing educational or career opportunities) and that she cannot afford a child. These factors are each mentioned by up to three-fourths of women having abortions, and between them they constitute the most important reason women give in approximately half of abortions.[4]

Democrats have long recognized, since at least the New Deal, that economic insecurity can easily leave people without real choice, and that a strong safety net of social support can increase true freedom, promote the common good, and protect the most vulnerable among us. A strengthened safety net can also work, in the case of abortion, to protect the unborn child—the most vulnerable among us—as well as the woman who faces great economic and other difficulties in bearing and raising the child.

Republicans have taken up the mantle for the unborn and have managed to get a number of abortion restrictions passed. Several of these restrictions do, in fact, reduce abortion. Support for clinic regulations, required ultrasound, and informed-consent laws all have helped to reduce the number of abortions in the United States. Democrats, on the whole, support some of these measures. Conversely, some in the Republican Party support a stronger safety net to assist those women once they bring the child into the world.

Given these sharply divergent approaches to abortion, and a political climate that has generally become increasingly hostile, common ground on anything seems unattainable. Achieving common ground is possible, but only if enough politicians care more about solving problems than they do about winning an election or making money for their current fundraising appeal. That is easier said than done, however.

---

3 Letter from Kathleen Sebelius, Sec'y, U.S. Dep't of Health and Human Servs., to Barbara Mikulski, Chairwoman, Senate Comm. on Appropriations (February 1, 2013).

4 Lawrence B. Finer et al., *Reasons U.S. Women Have Abortions: Quantitative and Qualitative Perspectives*, 37 Persp. on Sexual & Reprod. Health 110, 113 (2005). In this study, 75 percent of respondents mentioned life changes from motherhood as a reason for having an abortion, and 73 percent mentioned inability to afford a child. The most important factors were unreadiness to have a child (25 percent of respondents) and inability to afford the child (23 percent).

For example, during the 2008 presidential race, a well-planned fundraising effort dominated attempts to defeat Obama. The "Stop FOCA" campaign referred to the Freedom of Choice Act. The bill was first introduced in 1989 and reintroduced in subsequent Congresses. However, even with a Democratic majority, no concrete actions were taken toward passing FOCA—not even a single committee hearing. The reality that there was just not enough support—even from Democrats—to move a bill that could potentially overturn reasonable restrictions, such as the partial-birth abortion ban,[5] and allow public financing of abortion, did not prevent conservative groups from using it to stir up support from their base. After President Obama was elected the drive continued, sending millions of postcards to Congressional offices. FOCA was never even introduced because pro-choice groups publically acknowledged that they simply did not have the votes to pass the bill.

The Left is equally culpable when it comes to manufacturing crises for political gain. When the Komen Foundation announced a policy change to discontinue grants to Planned Parenthood because it wanted the money to be used for mammograms, Planned Parenthood took full advantage of the situation. Even though Planned Parenthood does not perform mammograms and only issues referrals, it immediately launched a PR and fundraising campaign attacking Komen's decision. This campaign brought in approximately $3 million in three days.[6] The Komen Foundation, one of the most well-known breast cancer support groups, suffered from this smear campaign.[7] It recently announced the discontinuation of three-day walks in seven cities due to "economic uncertainty."[8]

Democrats For Life of America (DFLA) disagrees with both of these strategies. We have always sought common ground on abortion, particularly after the 2004 elections wrought devastating losses from Democrats.

Many polls showed that voters thought that the Democrats were out of touch on moral issues—including abortion. DFLA wanted to change the image that the party was a pro-abortion party that had little respect for unborn life. There were and are many pro-life people in the Democratic Party, yet the national leaders of the party did not reflect this diversity of views. Polls consistently show that about

---

5 *Executive Summary of the Freedom of Choice Act*, Memorandum from Am. Ctr. for Law and Justice to Interested Paries (May 1, 2007) (available at http://media.aclj.org/pdf/executive_summary_freedom_of_choice_act_05012007.pdf).

6 Megan McCarthy, *Planned Parenthood Raises $3 Million in Wake of Komen Funding Controversy*, Nat'l J. (February 3, 2010), http://www.nationaljournal.com/planned-parenthood-raises-3-million-in-wake-of-komen-funding-controversy-20120203.

7 Scott Hensley, *Planned Parenthood Controversy Hangs Over Komen's Fundraising Races*, NPR (June 1, 2012), http://www.npr.org/blogs/health/2012/06/01/154135526/planned-parenthood-controversy-hangs-over-komens-fundraising-races.

8 Lena H. Sun, *Komen Cancels 3-Day Walk in District, Six Other Cities in 2014*, Washington Post (June 4, 2013), http://www.washingtonpost.com/national/health-science/komen-cancels-3-day-walk-in-dc-six-other-cities-in-2014/2013/06/04/df9b50dc-cd4b-11e2-9f1a-1a7cdee20287_story.html.

one-third of Democrats consider themselves pro-life. Furthermore, a majority of Democrats support restrictions on abortion. Sixty-one percent of Democrats support parental consent; 60 percent support a 24-hour waiting period; and 84 percent support informed consent.[9] The Democratic leadership was, and still is, out of touch with these views, held by a majority of Democrats. DFLA's goal was to shift attitudes and bring acceptance for pro-life brothers and sisters within the party. We recognized that it would not be enough merely to change attitudes or messaging; we wanted substantive, effective policy proposals to commit our party to a genuine mission of reducing abortions.

Knowing that making abortion illegal was a non-starter for conversation, DFLA members sought to bring people on both sides of the issue together to support pregnant women and new mothers. We knew that unless a proposal aimed at reducing abortion had legitimate bipartisan support, it would not succeed and would not be taken seriously.

The biggest challenge proved to be moving our own party. The warrior call of "protecting a woman's right to choose" so dominated its consciousness that it was hard for any other message to be heard. President Clinton flirted with, and gained traction by embracing, the idea of making abortion safe, legal, and rare. But after his term ended, the party quickly returned to its comfort zone of protecting the right to abortion under the guise of women's health.

DFLA was undeterred by the challenges. We began by researching current law and identifying various proposals that had seemingly worked to reduce abortion. We eventually compiled a list of 30 to 40 different proposals. We whittled our list down to the measures around which we could build the most consensus, primarily programs to support pregnant mothers and new parents. We always kept in mind that to be taken seriously, any common-ground effort had to include people from both sides of the abortion divide. While we hoped to attract groups like NARAL and National Right to Life, we also understood that they both held partisan, uncompromising positions, and getting them on board would be difficult.

It was disappointing to us that support for Pregnancy Resource Centers (PRCs), which are based on Democratic principles of helping those who need assistance, have largely been opposed by the Democratic Party. The centers provide parenting classes, cribs, baby supplies, childcare, and job training to help families to care for their children. Sadly, any proposal to support these centers was a non-starter for the pro-choice community due to a misconception that the centers are first and foremost anti-choice organizations designed to trick women into not choosing abortion. For this reason, we decided not to include PRCs in the proposal. Likewise, we determined that abortion-restriction measures should not be included, even though they had majority support across the country.

9 2011 Gallup Poll.

***THE 95-10 INITIATIVE:** The 95-10 Initiative seeks to reduce the number of abortions in America through Federal, state and local efforts as well as support and encouragement to volunteers and dedicated people on the front line helping pregnant women. Much attention has been given to ending abortion or keeping it legal. We believe that we must do more to reduce the abortion rate by helping and supporting pregnant women.*

Figure 6.1 The 95-10 initiative

We dubbed our proposal the 95-10 Initiative.[10]

The 95-10 Initiative focused on helping and supporting children and their mothers from conception forward. We wanted to make sure that women continued to receive support once the babies were born.

We had a proposal, but we needed a legislative sponsor. A seasoned politician who had a clear position on abortion might trigger immediate skepticism from established interest groups and the sitting politicians they influence. A young, newly-elected, and eager pro-life Democratic Congressman from Ohio, Tim Ryan, caught our eye, and we set the meeting. We went through our ideas and our list of programs. After each point of the plan, he would respond, "That is great. What else do you have?" It was a thrilling moment and, we thought, a solid partnership.

On April 20, 2005, at a national press conference at the Democratic National Committee (DNC), we announced the 95-10 Initiative. Participants included Representatives Tim Ryan (D-OH), Lincoln Davis (D-TN), Marcy Kaptur (D-OH), and former Representative Tim Roemer (D-IN). In addition, Americans United for Life endorsed the proposal and spoke in support at the DNC.[11] It was a rare sight to see a pro-life group at the Democratic headquarters. Thankfully, our common-ground coalition was growing.

Over the next several months, we met and talked with various groups and prominent individuals including: the National Association of Evangelicals,

10 DFLA created the 95-10 Initiative to focus on reducing abortion by 95 percent over a 10-year period. Less than 5 percent of abortions can be attributed to rape, incest or life of the mother. DFLA wanted to address the other reasons women choose abortion.

11 Press Release, Congressman Tim Ryan, Congressman Tim Ryan and Pro-Life Democrats to Propose Abortion Reduction Plan — Proposal is Based on Democrats For Lief of America's 95-10 Initiative (April 20, 2005).

US Conference of Catholic Bishops, Americans United for Life, the Southern Baptist Convention, the National Council on Adoption, the Life Education and Resource Network, Redeem the Vote, CARENET, Tony Campolo (founder of the Evangelical Association for the Promotion of Education), Joe Turnham (Chair of the Alabama Democratic Party), Bob Casey, Jr. (who was a US Senate candidate at the time), actor Martin Sheen, Jim Wallis of Sojourners, and others to discuss the legislative language and how to build consensus around support for pregnant women. Everyone we met with endorsed this idea.

President Jimmy Carter also endorsed the concept. Martin Sheen wrote:

> This groundbreaking approach to reducing the number of abortions in America is a positive step in the right direction. I can only hope that the Congress will support this bi-partisan proposal, and that America will embrace the intent of the 95-10 Initiative. The legislation wisely calls attention to our collective responsibility to support women, children and families who find themselves in crisis pregnancies.[12]

In their book, *Take It Back: Our Party, Our Country, Our Future*, Paul Begala and James Carville write of the 95-10 Initiative:

> The pro-life democrats have concluded that the thirty-two-year fight to overturn Roe v. Wade hasn't stopped a single abortion. So they've decided to change tactics. Rather than trying to reduce the number of abortions by making an abortion more difficult to have, they want to reduce the number of abortions by making abortions less necessary to have. Instead of changing the Constitution, they want to change circumstances.[13]

All the pieces were coming into place for a historic shift in how we deal with abortion in this nation. But, consensus can be like a delicate card tower; one card falls and the tower crashes down.

In November of 2005, we met with Third Way to discuss the 95-10 Initiative. We were interested in finding a Senate sponsor and gaining bipartisan support from the upper chamber. At the time, Third Way described itself as a "Senate-focused progressive advocacy group," aimed at finding common ground solutions. Senator Mary Landrieu (D-LA) served on its Board of Directors and we saw her as the likely Senate sponsor. At first glance, Third Way looked like a well-funded ally in our effort.

However, this partnership turned into a tactical error that we could not foresee. Third Way caused long-term mistrust among pro-life supporters by insisting on additional language on pregnancy prevention and sex education. The content of sex

12 Public Statement provide to DFLA from Martin Sheen.

13 Paul Begala & James Carville, Take It Back: Our Party, Our Country, Our Future, 44–45 (2006).

education, and the promotion of widespread contraception access, especially for teenagers, sparks different reactions in different regions in the pro-life community; there is no single approach capable of generating the necessary consensus. That is why we decided not to include prevention in the common-ground proposal. We agreed that although prevention efforts were important to reducing abortion and that debate should occur on the issue, it would distract from what was unique about our platform.

Third Way, however, proposed adding seven additional titles to the legislation that would receive support from some Democratic law-makers, but would jeopardize any effort to achieve bipartisan support and would further alienate the coalition on which we were counting to push the bill forward. It would also detract from the main focus of our effort: inadequate support for pregnant women. In late May of 2006 we sent a letter to Congressman Ryan encouraging several changes to what became his version of DFLA's 95-10 Initiative and urged him to adhere to our initial agreement to focus on support for pregnant women:

> We did not review and do not have specific comments on Title II through Title VIII. We did not review those sections because we feel that a great deal of attention has been given to prevention by several organizations and we are trying to focus on pregnant women, a need that we believe has been ignored.

It became apparent that our goal of expanding the resources available to pregnant women would be overrun by tired arguments about sex education and contraception, which were quickly eroding any chance of consensus and bipartisanship. We decided to withdraw support from Congressman Ryan and sought out a new sponsor for a true common-ground proposal. We wanted to back a proposal that had real potential to become the law—not something to provide more fodder for abortion politics.

Lincoln Davis, a first term Member from Tennessee, who eagerly supported the 95-10 Initiative and had worked with us along the way, agreed with our assessment. He took up the cause and introduced the bill with bipartisan support from both pro-choice and pro-life Members. At our initial launch at a press conference on September 20, 2005, pro-choice Democrat Harold Ford (D-TN) and pro-life Republican Chris Smith (R-JN) joined with Congressman Davis to endorse the bill.[14] Other pro-choice Democrats, including James Clyburn (D-SC) and Alan Boyd (D-FL), supported the bill alongside a number of Republican Members.

The house of cards was salvaged. Legitimate bipartisan common ground survived.

Congressman Ryan joined forces with Congresswomen Rosa DeLauro (D-CT), to push their version of the 95-10 Initiative: the Reducing the Need for Abortions and Supporting Parents Act. But the legislative process can be painfully slow, and

14 Press Release, Democrats For Life, Abortion Reduction Bill to Be Introduced (September 20, 2005).

the Ryan/DeLauro team did not continue to actively pursue an abortion-reduction measure after its initial push in 2005. They eventually reintroduced their proposal but never pursued or found a Senate sponsor. Nevertheless, the long-term damage to our common-ground effort from the failed partnership continued to plague our subsequent efforts in Congress.

Thus, we were forced to focus on damage control rather than promoting the common-ground bill. Many of our supporters withdrew from the 95-10 Initiative because they opposed adding controversial language about contraception—including access to Plan B and potential abortion-inducing drugs that were included in the Ryan/DeLauro bill. Other coalition groups became confused about what they had agreed to support given that there were now two proposals. We gained some traction by explaining that we did not support many provisions in the Ryan/DeLauro bill and that the Davis bill was the genuine common-ground proposal. But the confusion among many individuals and groups was hard to overcome.

As a result, when Senator Casey (D-PA) introduced our proposal in the Senate, we could not generate any Republican support, as we had in the House.

During the following years, however, we did make progress developing support within our Party. The 2008 Democratic National Convention (DNC) showcased and included many pro-life voices, including Bishop Charles Blake, Pastor of the West Angeles Church of God in Christ, who proclaimed at a DNC Interfaith Gathering:

> May I observe as a pro-life democrat? May I observe that some of us have philosophic humanitarian and theological differences with those who put forth abortion as an appropriate, routine, and acceptable birth control procedure? There are millions of us who hold that such a position conflicts with our conviction regarding our sacred responsibility to our children and to human life itself. Surely we cannot be pleased with the routine administration of millions of surgically terminated pregnancies. Something within us must be calling for a better way. If we do not resist at this point, at what point will we resist? We know that our Party will understand and acknowledge the moral and spiritual pain that so many of us feel because of this disregard for the lives of the unborn. Those of us who support the Democratic Party despite our disagreement on this issue support it because the Democratic Party articulates and pursues more of the positions that are relevant to the lives and circumstances of our people, the people of America in general and the people of the world.[15]

Former Congressman and pro-life Democrat Tim Roemer spoke about the 95-10 Initiative on a DNC faith panel on "Common Ground and the Common

15 Bishop Charles Blake, Remarks to the 2008 Democratic National Convention, available at https://www.youtube.com/watch?v=de0VvX-mry0.

Good" saying, "There are all kinds of ways we can work together on a proposal called 95-10."

Our own Town Hall Meeting at the 2004 Democratic Convention in Denver on the 95-10 Initiative showcased the tremendous success in building support for the concept that aiding pregnant women is essential to reducing abortion. Pro-choice Senate candidate Bob Tuke (D-TN) and pro-life champions Lincoln Davis and Senator Bob Casey joined forces to promote the 95-10.

Senator Casey spoke at the convention, giving us great hope about the future of our 95-10 Initiative when he said:

> Barack Obama and I have an honest disagreement on the issue of abortion. But the fact that I'm speaking here tonight is testament to Barack's ability to show respect for the views of people who may disagree with him.[16]

We continued to argue that the 95-10 Initiative provided a sound strategy to reduce abortion through a wide-ranging set of proposals backed by proven research into why women have abortions and proven programs that will reduce the perceived need to abort. Other groups began to issue reports in support of our initiative.

The Center for American Progress published a study called "Parenting with Dignity" and highlighted the importance of home visits for new mothers.[17] They recommended more support for pregnant women in the workforce including "promoting flexible scheduling; improving family leave options; increasing breastfeeding accommodations in the workplace; establishing a system of quality, comprehensive childcare; and expanding access to Temporary Disability and Unemployment Insurance."

Candidate Obama began talking about abortion reduction:

> This is an issue that — look, it divides us. And in some ways, it may be difficult to — to reconcile the two views. But there surely is some common ground when both those who believe in choice and those who are opposed to abortion can come together and say, "We should try to prevent unintended pregnancies by providing appropriate education to our youth, communicating that sexuality is sacred and that they should not be engaged in cavalier activity, and providing options for adoption, and helping single mothers if they want to choose to keep the baby." Those are all things that we put in the Democratic platform for the first time this year, and I think that's where we can find some common ground,

16 Senator Robert Casey, Remarks to the 2008 Democratic National Convention (August 26, 2008), available at http://www.presidentialrhetoric.com/campaign2008/dnc2008/speeches/casey.html.

17 Jessica Arons, *Parenting with Dignity: A Series Exploring Real Supports for Pregnant Women*, American Progress (August 3, 2009), http://www.americanprogress.org/issues/women/news/2009/08/03/6601/parenting-with-dignity/.

> because nobody's pro-abortion. I think it's always a tragic situation. We should try to reduce these circumstances.[18]

And, once elected, he continued to talk about common ground. At a 2009 address at Notre Dame, the president outlined what we can do:

> Maybe we won't agree on abortion, but we can still agree that this heart-wrenching decision for any woman is not made casually, it has both moral and spiritual dimensions.
>
> So let us work together to reduce the number of women seeking abortions, let's reduce unintended pregnancies. Let's make adoption more available. Let's provide care and support for women who do carry their children to term. Let's honor the conscience of those who disagree with abortion, and draft a sensible conscience clause, and make sure that all of our health care policies are grounded not only in sound science, but also in clear ethics, as well as respect for the equality of women. Those are things we can do.[19]

The president instructed the White House Office of Faith-Based and Community Initiatives to develop a common-ground strategy to reduce abortion.[20] Per the president's instructions, the White House Faith-Based Office conducted a series of meetings with pro-life and pro-choice groups to develop a common-ground strategy to reduce abortion.

We submitted our abortion reduction package, but the issue of prevention continued to plague the effort for bipartisan cooperation. Just as certain groups believe that simply legally banning abortion or passing restrictions on abortion will solve the problem, there are others who believe prevention alone will adequately diminish abortion. Neither side was willing to concede to the other on the points that pregnancy prevention and restrictions do, in fact, both work to reduce abortion. The only common ground continues to coalesce around support for pregnant women.

At one White House meeting, one of the pro-choice participants insisted that we teach sex education and laid out specifics about what we should teach as early as kindergarten. I reasoned with her that, as the mother of a first grader, I am not sure he is ready for that type of education just yet. I pointed out that our consensus

---

18 William Saletan, *Safe, Legal, and Boring*, SLATE (October 16, 2008), http://www.slate.com/articles/health_and_science/human_nature/2008/10/safe_legal_and_boring.html.

19 President Barack Obama, Remarks by the President of the United States in Commencement Address at the University of Notre Dame (May 17, 2009), available at http://www.whitehouse.gov/the-press-office/remarks-president-notre-dame-commencement.

20 Thomas C. Fox, *Obama Reveals Task Force to Reduce Abortions*, NAT'L CATHOLIC REP. (Apr. 30, 2009), http://ncronline.org/news/politics/obama-reveals-task-force-reduce-abortions.

cannot be found with prevention proposals and that we should continue to bring the discussion back to how we can provide more support for pregnant women.

After months of meetings and discussion, the White House never issued a formal policy for common ground, apparently because it found that it would lose half of its common-ground allies when contraception and sex education were included.[21]

The debate over healthcare reform and abortion funding sidelined talk of abortion reduction, although abortion continued to dominate discussion. Talk of common ground was replaced with the most heated and partisan bickering I have seen in my over 20 years in politics, which caused a final blow to common ground on abortion in Congress—at least for the time being. Contentious debate between supporters and opponents of healthcare reform climaxed with a battle over abortion funding. Pro-choice Democrats and pro-life Republicans both felt betrayed by pro-life Democrats. The pro-choice groups claimed that the pro-life Democrats sought to restrict access to abortion, while the pro-life groups clamored that we allowed public funding of abortion. Both extreme sides of the abortion debate were furious, which may have been a sign that the negotiated language represented common ground. Regardless, pro-life Democrats were left with few friends and common-ground advocates were left with fewer champions.

We knew that support for pregnant women to reduce abortion was critical and never lost sight of the goal.

While fighting against abortion funding in the healthcare legislation, we also advocated for pregnant and parenting families. A majority of the 95-10 Initiative provisions were quietly included as part of the Affordable Care Act (ACA) due to the hard work and advocacy of Senator Casey.

The president made good on his promise to enact common-ground solutions to reduce abortion, although the outcome was not the fanfare we initially envisioned. We initially hoped for a Rose Garden ceremony with Republicans, Democrats, pro-choice groups, and pro-life groups praising this new law and new effort to greatly reduce abortion in this country. Still, the absence of fanfare is not as important as knowing that grants are being used to assist women in crisis pregnancy and to provide support and viable options for those women. We are proud of the work that is being doing around the country.

The 95-10 Initiative recommended that we end the practice of discriminating against pregnant women, because health insurance companies would regularly deny pregnant women coverage by treating pregnancy as a pre-existing condition. The ACA closed this loophole, so women and babies will now receive essential prenatal care and postnatal care.

---

21 Dan Gilgoff, *As White House Readies Abortion Plan, Packaging Emerges as Major Issue*, US News & World Report (June 29, 2009), http://www.usnews.com/news/blogs/god-and-country/2009/06/29/as-white-house-readies-abortion-plan-packaging-emerges-as-major-issue.

The 95-10 Initiative also recommended more support for adoption; the ACA included an increase in the adoption tax credit, making it more affordable for families to adopt children.

The bulk of the 95-10 Initiative was included as the Pregnancy Assistance Fund which is a $25 million grant program to support pregnant women. Seventeen states are now using the grant money to reduce abortion.

For example, college-age women are one of the most vulnerable groups when faced with unplanned pregnancies. Almost two-thirds of abortions are procured by women in their twenties[22] and one out of five abortions is procured by college-age women.[23] When women students are faced with an unplanned pregnancy, many see only two choices: drop out or have an abortion.

Available research suggests that the unaffordability of a child is a significant part of the problem for students. Childcare costs, potential loss of student housing (many students lose eligibility for student housing upon having a child), and other costs associated with raising a child can be daunting. Support on college campuses, including day care, counseling, and other innovative approaches, prevents abortion by providing a third option for pregnant students.

The state of Virginia is running a student–parent support program for eight Virginia institutions at 22 sites. The programs support new mothers with gas cards, transportation vouchers, and baby pantries stocked with necessities for infants. The program helps young parents find emergency housing, food, and childcare so they can stay in school instead of dropping out. Two sites provide private facilities for mothers to pump breast milk or breastfeed their infants.

The Virginia program established a PR campaign, another key point in the 95-10 Initiative, to alert pregnant women of the services available.

North Carolina is also utilizing the funds for outreach to 13- to 24-year-old expectant parents through social media. Their website recently won Grand Prize for non-profit websites in the Publications for Excellence (APEX) competition. Through text messages, they supply advice and support to pregnant girls and new mothers.

The 95-10 Initiative recognized the need to address pregnant and parenting teens, as many young girls who become pregnant drop out of high school, do not earn degrees, and live in poverty. A number of states have now developed programs to address teen pregnancy.

A Michigan grant program has enrolled and helped almost 2,000 pregnant and parenting teens with home visits to help new mothers learn to properly care for their infants. The Support Network for Anishinaabe Pregnant and Parenting Teens (SNAPPT) program targets American Indian teens who are more likely to live in poverty. A 2011 report indicated that 77 percent of Michigan American Indian teen

---

22 Rachel K. Jones, Lawrence B. Fisner, & Susheela Singh, *Characteristics of U.S. Abortion Patients, 2008*, Guttmacher Institute (May 2010).

23 Kate O'Beirne, *American's Earliest Feminists Opposed Abortion*, Chi. Sun-Times, January 8, 2006, at B3 (citing Serrin Foster, Feminists For Life of America).

mothers were covered by Medicaid,[24] and SNAPPT encourages and assists many of these mothers by providing a post-partum education completion plan.

Both Connecticut and the Washington, DC have developed programs aimed at helping pregnant and parenting teens. The Connecticut program offers flexible programs to complete high school, childcare, transportation, parenting classes, and programs to assist and education teen fathers. The program has proven successful with 80 percent of teen mothers graduating or staying in school and 98 percent of new babies receiving well-child visits, including immunizations.

Washington, DC established a school-based coordinator to help pregnant and parenting teens continue their education. One 18-year-old mother of twins credits the program with helping her stay in school, earn good grades, and gain acceptance to four different college programs.

The 95-10 Initiative also recommended greater efforts to counteract violence against pregnant women. Pregnant women are often forced by a boyfriend or husband to undergo an abortion because the men want to avoid the financial or parental responsibility. Threats of death or violence are often carried out. According to the CDC, 324,000 pregnant women are victims of violence from a partner. Called Intimate Partner Violence (IPC), the CDC said this number is probably underestimated due to lack of reporting. The number one cause of death for pregnant women is homicide—higher than birth-related mortality. The ACA included programs to protect pregnant women and new mothers experiencing domestic violence. Furthermore, the Violence Against Women Act Reauthorization was recently signed into law and will provide further protections for pregnant women and new mothers.

We learned over these many years pursuing common ground on abortion reduction that achieving the goal is difficult but attainable. Establishing cooperative relationships with people who seek abortion reduction—not for partisan gain, presidential aspirations or successful fundraising appeals, but to protect unborn life and help the mothers and fathers facing the unplanned or crisis pregnancies both during the pregnancy and beyond—is the answer.

Unfortunately, there will always be some who prefer to pursue a political advantage by perpetuating the stale argument over who is right and wrong on the issue of abortion's legality. They criticize, question, and attack those who support an opposing view and prevent good legislation.

This familiar pattern is playing out even today in New York. Governor Andrew Cuomo (D-NY) is currently pushing a 10-point "Women's Equality Bill" that includes nine points to support women, including addressing domestic violence, human trafficking, equal pay for equal work, and other good proposals to empower women. The first nine points enjoy bipartisan support and consensus. But, as he is considering a presidential bid, he will need support from the abortion lobby. For that reason, he has included a provision to expand abortion in New York,

24 Michigan Department of Community Health, 2011 Vital Statistics, MI Live Birth Records.

which already holds the unfortunate title of the state with the highest abortion rate in the nation—almost twice national average. In his proposed budget, he zeroed out funding for the only program in the state that supports pregnant women and proposed unlimited funding for abortion. It is highly likely that he will sink the entire package if he does not achieve a victory for the abortion lobby.

On the other side, we have Arkansas and several other states pursuing outright bans on abortion as early as six weeks, without providing any additional support to the support mother and child.

The continued divisiveness will not help women nor reduce abortion. That is not what our country wants or deserves.

Public opinion in the United States continues to move in a more pro-life direction. The advent of the ultrasound and the reality of the life in the womb touches us at the very core of our humanity. Recent polling reinforces this assertion. A majority of Americans desire fewer abortions and most American support common-sense restrictions. We can no longer allow the extremists to stop progress.

DFLA is committed to standing up to those who are intransigent and those who are all too ready to impede any attempts at cooperation. We offer the next steps and urge those who agree to work together and join us.

The 95-10 Initiative was the first successful effort at bringing people on all sides together. Its successes, however, need to be expanded and replicated. Abortion politics will continue to plague any consensus-building effort to help women. Both the pro-life and the pro-choice lobbies are heavily financed and influential. Confronted with these challenges, we should continue to look for cooperative efforts to solve the remaining problems and help the women and families who are faced with difficult and sometimes terrifying situations. To that end, I propose the following.

First, Senator Casey introduced new legislation to add additional funding to the Pregnancy Assistance Fund. The programs currently in place are helping women and their families. We must continue to support innovative programs and approve additional funding for the PAF.

Second, we must support an expanded social safety net for pregnant women. The 95-10 Initiative offered increased support for the Women, Infants and Children Program. Only one in 10 people eligible for the program participate, in part due to difficulty in signing up or in accessing stores that accept the program's benefits. Stores in mostly rural and inner-city areas are unable to process WIC benefits because they don't have the necessary equipment. Furthermore, some women are kicked out of the program for making minor mistakes in the application process. Despite the importance of this type of assistance for making pregnancy and birth a viable choice for women, many conservative pro-life groups have registered their opposition.

Third, we must be more supportive of pregnant women facing unplanned pregnancies, those who are considering abortion and those who have experienced abortion. Some women do regret the abortion or have side effects such as eating disorders, depression, or even suicidal thoughts.[25] Many feel immediate relief, but many do, in fact, experience negative emotions—sometimes years later. Groups, like Rachel's Vineyard, provide post-abortive healing. Bringing more awareness to support groups, and also to perinatal hospices that help those families faced with the possibility that their unborn child may not survive, will bring more compassion to families facing difficult decisions.

Fourth, a majority of Americans support reasonable restrictions on abortion. Whether you agree with abortion or not, the safety of women should come first. Abortion clinics should not receive an exemption from oversight under the pretext that it interferes with women's right to choose. The failure to demand consistent oversight harms women, as the recent case involving abortion doctor Kermit Gosnell tragically illustrates. He was convicted of killing babies born alive and for the preventable death of one woman. He risked the lives and health of women for over a decade with no oversight or inspections. There are other clinics that are engaging in similar practices. Requiring an ultrasound prior to abortion is also another reasonable restriction. In fact, Planned Parenthood already requires an ultrasound prior to abortion.[26] It is the only way to determine the accurate age of the fetus. Yet, they consistently oppose the requirement. We must put women first.

Fifth, we need to continued expanding prevention efforts, while respecting regional differences and religious conscience. The current debate over the contraception mandate could have been avoided if the reasonable accommodation crafted for businesses and individuals who oppose certain types of contraception that can cause abortion. Instead, the ACA has ushered in partisan and costly litigation over the right of conscience.

The fourth and fifth points challenge the notion of common ground, but are nonetheless important to achieve abortion reduction. Both points hold majority opinion in the United States, but neither has been able to achieve bipartisan consensus in the political arena.

While small groups of vocal well-financed advocates cling to purist positions on their sides of the abortion debate and continue to accomplish little, we will push forward. We still believe that we can and should continue to work to reduce the abortion rate in this nation.

As a nation, we must put the needs and safety of pregnant women and their unborn children first and work cooperatively to pass legislative solutions and support private efforts. That is the only way to reduce abortion. For now, we celebrate the innovative programs that are currently in place, the people who are

25 Susanne Babbel, Ph.D., MFT, *Post Abortion Stress Syndrome (PASS) – Does it Exist?* Psychology Today (October 25, 2010), http://www.psychologytoday.com/blog/somatic-psychology/201010/post-abortion-stress-syndrome-pass-does-it-exist.

26 Alana Goodman, *Planned Parenthood Says it Won't Do Abortions Without Ultrasounds*, Commentary Magazine (February 22, 2012), http://www.commentarymagazine.com/2012/02/22/planned-parenthood-abortions-ultrasounds/.

on the front lines supporting women and will continue on our journey to truly make abortion rare.

Chapter 7
Can a Catholic Realist Approach Aid in the Effort to Find Common Ground in Debates About Abortion?

Susan J. Stabile

Introduction

In "An Effort to Articulate a Catholic Realist Approach to Abortion," I examined whether it is possible to outline a Catholic realist way of thinking about abortion that might help advance reasoned public debate on this contentious issue.[1] That article was premised on the view that, despite the difficulty of the task, the goal of finding common ground on abortion is important and worthy enough to justify exploring what a Catholic realist position might add to the debate. The article identified the key elements required to call a position on abortion a Catholic realist position—a basis in actual facts, viability, and consistency with Catholic moral teaching. It then raised five questions as a way of determining whether it is possible to articulate a Catholic realist position on abortion that might help us move toward the achievement of common ground.

This chapter revisits four of the questions I raised in that article in light of some specific recent events and developments related to the abortion question: selective reduction of multiple pregnancies, the increased prevalence of aborting fetuses with Down syndrome, and the question of mandating coverage of artificial contraception as part of required preventive health services. I consider here both how several of the questions I posed in the earlier article help us to think about these three issues, as well as how those issues might help in formulating a response to those questions. I begin by briefly setting out the three current issues, after which I return to them in the context of questions identified in my earlier article.

1 Susan J. Stabile, *An Effort to Articulate a Catholic Realist Approach to Abortion*, 7 St. Thomas L.J. 340 (2010).

Recent Events and Developments

Selective Pregnancy Reduction to a Singleton

Selective pregnancy reduction is a medical procedure used to reduce a multiple pregnancy to either maximize the chances of survival of the remaining fetuses or to allow the pregnant mother to choose how many fetuses she wishes to bring to term. Selective pregnancy reduction is similar to an abortion, in that "both are surgical procedures performed on a pregnant woman for the purpose of terminating one or more fetuses." It is medically different from an abortion, however, in that the procedure "does not involve the expulsion or extraction of the terminated fetuses from the womb; instead the terminated fetuses remain in the uterus until resorption and ultimate delivery with the placenta."[2]

Selective pregnancy reduction is typically associated with in vitro fertilization or some other infertility treatment undertaken by women who have difficulty conceiving. The wide use of fertility drugs and artificial reproduction technology has led to a dramatic increase—more than 30 percent by some estimates—in the number of multi-fetal pregnancies.[3] In fact, "[t]he majority of all multiples are conceived after infertility treatment."[4] Correspondingly, the result of improvements in techniques of infertility treatment and more multi-fetal pregnancies has been an increase in the frequency with which multi-fetal pregnancy reduction is performed.[5] There is every reason to think that selective pregnancy reductions will continue to be performed with even greater frequency, given that the demand for infertility treatment and artificial reproduction technology will grow "as more and more women postpone childbearing to have careers and increasing numbers of individuals defy traditional norms of child-rearing by opting to have children alone or with same-sex partners."[6]

Selective pregnancy reduction initially emerged as a solution to the dangers of multiple pregnancies. As such, the intent behind the procedure was very different from the intent behind an abortion (other than abortions undertaken to protect the health of the mother). That is, whereas the intent behind abortion is the termination of pregnancy, the intent behind terminating one or more fetuses in a multiple pregnancy (usually triplets or more) was to "create a better environment for her

---

2 Stacey Pinchuk, *A Difficult Choice in a Different Voice: Multiple Births, Selective Reduction and Abortion*, 7 Duke J. Gender L. & Pol'y 29, 34 (2000).

3 Debora Spar & Anna M. Harrington, *Building a Better Baby Business*, 10 Minn. J.L. Sci. & Tech. 41, 58 (2009).

4 Mark I. Evans, *The Truth About Multiples*, 35 The Female Patient 1, 1 (2010).

5 Marian A. Ormont & Peter A. Shapiro, *Multifetal Pregnancy Reduction: A Review of an Evolving Technology and its Psychosocial Implications*, 36 Psychosomatics 522, 522 (1995).

6 Spar & Harrington, *supra* note 3, at 45.

[remaining] fetus(es) to develop."[7] It was the dangers to the life and health of the mother and to the remaining fetuses that motivated the reduction.

The ethical view of selective pregnancy reduction mirrored that intent. The view of medical ethicists was that selective pregnancy reduction "seemed warranted only in life and death situations—where the mother was of small stature and carrying four or more embryos, for example."[8] Although such justification would not be accepted as a matter of Catholic Church doctrine—which is opposed to all forms of artificial reproductive technology and to abortions under any circumstances—there is support by at least some Jewish rabbis for pregnancy reduction where the life of the mother or the continuation of the pregnancy is threatened.

More recently, selective pregnancy reduction has been used to reduce twins to a single pregnancy: "What began as an intervention for extreme medical circumstances has quietly become an option for women carrying twins," and "the demand for reduction to a singleton, while still fairly rare, is rising."[9] The issue gained wide attention when the *New York Times Magazine* published an article in August 2011 titled "Unnatural Selection."[10] The article began by recounting the experience of a woman who chose, 14 weeks into her pregnancy, to terminate one of two healthy fetuses. She explained:

> If I had conceived these twins naturally, I wouldn't have reduced this pregnancy, because you feel like there's a natural order, then you don't want to disturb it. But we created this child in such an artificial manner—in a test tube, choosing an egg donor, having the embryo placed in me—and somehow, making a decision about how many to carry seemed to be just another choice. The pregnancy was all so consumerish to begin with, and this became yet another thing we could control.[11]

The article raised the question "what is it about terminating half a twin pregnancy that seems more controversial than reducing triplets to twins or aborting a single fetus?"[12] That is the issue I wish to focus on here. That is, I don't want to address the ethics of in vitro fertilization, which the Catholic Church views to be morally unacceptable, or selective reduction to save the life of the mother or other fetuses. Nor am I speaking here about sex selection abortions, which merits its own discussion. My focus here is the limited issue of the use of selective pregnancy reduction to reduce from twins [or triplets] to a singleton.

7 Judith F. Daar, *Selective Reduction of Multiple Pregnancy: Lifeboat Ethics in the Womb*, 25 U.C. Davis L. Rev. 773, 783 (1992).

8 Mark I. Evans & David W. Britt, *Multifetal Pregnancy Reduction: Evolution of the Ethical Arguments*, 28 Seminars in Reproductive Medicine 295, 297 (2010).

9 Ruth Padawar, *Unnatural Selection*, N.Y. Times Magazine, August 14, 2011, at 22.

10 *Id.*

11 *Id.* at 24.

12 *Id.*

Abortion of Down Syndrome Fetuses

The combination of greater access to prenatal testing, access to abortion, and a culture increasingly intolerant of imperfection, has led to increasing abortions of fetuses identified as having Down syndrome and, indeed, reports of pressure being placed on women who decide to bear such children rather than abort them. According to some estimates, in North America, 80–90 percent of those who discover that they are carrying a child that would have Down syndrome now elect to terminate their pregnancies.[13] Other studies report physicians and others in the healthcare community actively encouraging those carrying a Down syndrome fetus to terminate, as well as biases following the birth of such a child.

We live in a world of new techniques for noninvasive prenatal testing, meaning that women have much more information than they ever had before about their pregnancies and the child they are carrying. Many fear that the increased availability and reliability of noninvasive forms of screening will result in an increase in abortions of fetuses with Down syndrome. Indeed, the American College of Obstetricians and Gynecologists now recommends that all pregnant women, regardless of age, be screened. One of the lead authors of the recommendation makes clear the purpose of the recommendation: "There are many couples who do not want to have a baby with Down syndrome. They don't have the resources, don't have the emotional stamina, don't have the family support. We are recommending this testing be offered so that parents have a choice."[14]

Disability rights advocates have expressed concern that the effect of a screening that reveals an abnormality is that "a single trait stands in for the whole, the trait obliterates the whole."[15] Specifically:

> detection of a genetic disability often leads to selective abortion because the parents view the fetus only in terms of the disability, paying no regard to the many other qualities of the potential child. The parent sees the prospective child only as the disability, and this single trait enables the parents to justify their action. The abortion is ridding society of the disability—not of a child who, despite or possibly because of the disability, could lead a productive and happy life.[16]

---

13 Margaret Somerville, *"Deselecting" Our Children*, The Globe and Mail (August 22, 2011), http://www.theglobeandmail.com/commentary/deselecting-our-children/article626406/.

14 Amy Harmon, *Prenatal Test Puts Down Syndrome in Hard Focus*, N.Y. Times (May 9, 2007), http://www.nytimes.com/2007/05/09/us/09down.html?_r=0.

15 Judith F. Daar, *One Small Step for Genetics, One Great Leap for Genocide?*, 42 Rutgers L.J. 705, 714 (2011); Mary A. Crossley, *Choice, Conscience, and Context*, 47 Hastings L.J. 1223, 1231–32 (1996).

16 Daar, *supra* note 15, at 714.

That parents take such a view is not surprising; doctors and genetic counselors "overly focus on the medical complications of a child with the genetic condition," adopting a "medical model" that "envisions disability itself as the problem rather than the discrimination that persons with disabilities face."[17]

One writer commented on the irony of the fact that people in the West decry the abortion of unwanted girls in Asia—terming such practices gendercide—while practicing "its own form of selective abortion when it comes to fetuses diagnosed in utero with Down syndrome and other chromosomal conditions."[18] As one commentator observed, "[a] societal-level message is: 'We don't want you in our society unless you measure up to a certain standard.'"[19]

That may be a harsh judgment. Doubtless many women who abort fetuses identified with Down Syndrome are more concerned with a lack of ability to care for a special needs child or the challenges such a child will face in life. Nonetheless, it is hard to ignore the societal message (and the message of the medical community) that there is something wrong with deciding to bring to term a child that does not conform to the norm.

Contraception as Preventive Medical Services

For years prescription contraceptives were excluded from coverage under most employer health plans, an exclusion that received little attention until relatively recently. The decision by a significant number of plans in the mid-1990s to cover Viagra made the failure of plans to cover prescription contraceptives a cause célèbre of women's groups, who began to fight for such coverage. As a result, states began to pass laws of various types requiring mandatory coverage of prescription contraceptives.

State statutes requiring that employers provide contraceptive coverage created no serious problem for most private employers. For religious employers with moral objections to the use of artificial contraception, however, the statutes created an issue of conscience. Recognizing the conscience concern, many of the mandatory contraception coverage statutes were enacted with some carve-out for religious employers, although some of those were defined quite narrowly. In addition, because the effect of pre-emption of state law by the Employer Retirement Income Security Act (ERISA), state laws in this area took the form of insurance laws (which are exempted from ERISA's pre-emptive effect). As a result, religious employers could avoid being subject to state law by self-insuring, which some

17 Rachel Rebouché & Karen H. Rothenberg, *Mixed Messages: The Intersection of Prenatal Genetic Testing and Abortion*, 55 Howard L.J. 983, 1010–11 (2012).

18 Amy Julia Becker, *The Social Construction of Selective Abortion*, The Atlantic (January 22, 2013), http://www.theatlantic.com/sexes/archive/2013/01/the-social-construction-of-selective-abortion/267386/.

19 Somerville, *supra* note 13.

Catholic entities, such as some Catholic hospital systems and Catholic universities, have done.

In 2010, Congress passed the Patient Protection and Affordable Care Act, requiring employers to either provide a specified minimum level of health coverage or pay a monthly tax. To satisfy the statutory requirements, such plans must provide preventive care without any cost sharing.

An interpretive regulation issued by the Department of Health and Human Services (HHS) providing that the preventive services that must be provided without cost-sharing include coverage of all FDA-approved contraceptives (including Plan B and ella), as well as sterilization generated significant controversy among Catholics and some other Christians. Although the interim final rules promulgated by the HHS contained an exemption for "religious employers," the Catholic Church and other religious entities objected to the narrowness of the definition, which was drafted in a manner that excludes not only private employers with strong religious beliefs, but also Catholic hospitals, universities, and charities. In response to outcries by religious groups, HHS announced a temporary enforcement safe harbor and, subsequently, President Obama announced that HHS would propose further accommodation to religious employers. Despite further revisions by the HHS to its proposed rules, a number of lawsuits have been filed, including on behalf of for-profit businesses claiming violation of their religious freedom in being forced to provide contraceptives to their employees.

My concern here is not primarily with the religious freedom claim of religious employers, a claim I've explored in the past[20]—as important as that issue is. Rather, my interest, particularly with respect to the last of the five questions I raised in my prior article (the question whether a Catholic realist position on abortion could support the use of artificial contraception if doing so would reduce abortion) is with the mandate itself.

Questions Posed by a Catholic Realist Perspective[21]

Can a Catholic Realist Position Accept That There is a Dignity Interest in Women Not Being Forced to Carry a Pregnancy to Term?

One of the consequences of the polarization of the abortion debate is that each side finds it almost impossible to grant any quarter to the position of the other side. Thus, both pro-choice and pro-life advocates find themselves taking extreme positions out of fear that any movement away from the extreme will give

20 Susan J. Stabile, *State Attempts to Define Religion: The Ramifications of Applying Mandatory Prescription Contraceptive Coverage Statutes to Religious Employers*, 28 Harv. J.L. & Pub. Pol'y 741 (2005); Susan J. Stabile, *When Conscience Clashes With State Law & Policy: Catholic Institutions*, 46 St. John's J. Catholic Legal Stud. 137 (2007).

21 Portions of this section are excerpted from Stabile, *supra* note 1.

ammunition to the other that will weaken their position. As one writer criticized, each of the pro-choice and the pro-life forces "deliberately erases the merits of the other side's arguments and suggests that any nuanced consideration of reality at the margin is tantamount to betrayal of the cause."[22] This makes it very difficult to forge common ground.

Central to the Catholic position on abortion is human dignity—the notion that a human life is at issue and must be protected. That every human person, regardless of stage of life, has dignity and is worthy of respect is a fundamental principle of Catholic social thought. From this principle there flows directly a respect of human life from the moment of conception to natural death. That raises for me the question whether it is possible from a Catholic realist position to acknowledge that there is another dignity interest involved—that is, a dignity interest of the woman in not being forced to carry an unwanted pregnancy to term.

Let me be very clear about what I am not doing in raising this question. I'm not here making any argument or judgment about the strength of that dignity interest in relation to the dignity interest of the fetus or saying that such an interest ought to lead us to speak about a "right" to abortion. Indeed, my goal is to get away from "rights" talk. Nor am I making an argument about the morality of a woman choosing not to continue a pregnancy. I am also not addressing or evaluating claims that the current abortion industry is not itself protective of the dignity interests of women. "The shoddy treatment of women in abortion clinics is well-documented by women who have gone through the procedure."[23] Here, I am merely raising the question whether a Catholic realist could recognize that there exists an interest that has to do with a women's self-determination—an interest on the part of the woman in not being forced by the law to use her body in a particular way.

There is value in asking this question because perhaps a willingness of pro-life advocates to acknowledge such a dignity interest—that is, to acknowledge that there is an interest on the part of the woman—might encourage pro-choice advocates to acknowledge that there is a life involved on the other side of the equation. It may be that increased dialogue about the personal experiences of women, post-abortion, might help advance understanding of the woman's dignity interest. If both sides could see that the woman and the fetus have co-existing legitimate interests, it might lead to less heat in the public abortion debate.

A fundamental question is what is the nature or meaning of this dignity interest. The Supreme Court's decisions in *Roe v. Wade*[24] and *Planned Parenthood v. Casey*[25] both speak of a dignity interest of women in terms of autonomy, privacy, and self-

22 Sherry F. Colb, *Sending Out Partial Birth Announcements: Symbolism and Deception by Pro-Life Legislators*, FindLaw's Writ (June 18, 2003), http://writ.news.findlaw.com/colb/20030618.html.

23 Janet Morana, Recall Abortion: Ending the Abortion Industry's Exploitation of Women (2013).

24 410 U.S. 113 (1973).

25 505 U.S. 833 (1992).

determination. Their focus is on a woman's bodily integrity, something that has been recognized, for example, in the criminal context. Autonomy is understood differently in different feminist circles, with some emphasizing the freedom of women "to shape our own lives, to define who we (each) are, rather than accepting the definition given to us by others,"[26] and others speaking in terms of a "relational autonomy" that "acknowledges the many social and contextual constraints and pressures that may be placed on choices while simultaneously recognizing that there is value in self-determination."[27] Other times "dignity interest" is spoken of in terms of equality: that is, the "dignity interest of the person to be treated as a rational human being, equal with all others."[28] Human dignity thus becomes equated with respecting the fundamental equality of women and men.

The Catholic notion of human dignity is not coextensive with these secular notions. From a Catholic perspective, human dignity is grounded in the creation of all human beings in the image and likeness of God, and the corresponding sacredness of the human person. Thus, a Catholic articulation of the dignity interest belonging to women would focus less on autonomy and self-determination and more on the ability to flourish as a human person.

My own view is that the Catholic conception of human dignity could support recognizing a dignity interest in a woman not being forced to carry a pregnancy to term, at least where the circumstances of the pregnancy are such that it would be difficult for a woman to lovingly welcome a child into her life. This could allow for a dignity interest in a woman not being forced to carry to term a pregnancy that results from an act in which she did not willingly participate, such as rape, and perhaps in other circumstances in which the woman feels an inability to cope with an unintended pregnancy because of economic circumstances or where the pregnancy is the result of incest.[29] However the interest is formulated, simply acknowledging that an interest exists does not compel one to take any particularly position regarding the law and, thus, involves no cooperation with evil. It merely acknowledges that there is something important at play in addition to the life of the fetus. Such an acknowledgment is not without complications; making choices among competing dignity interests will not be easy and inevitably one dignity interest will end up being subordinated to the other. Nonetheless, the

26 Jennifer Nedelsky, *Reconceiving Autonomy: Sources, Thoughts and Possibilities*, 1 YALE J.L. & FEMINISM 7, 8 (1989).

27 Pamela Laufer-Ukeles, *Reproductive Choices and Informed Consent: Fetal Interests, Women's Identity and Relational Autonomy*, 37 AM. J.L. & MED. 567, 610 (2011).

28 J.L. Hill, *The Five Faces of Freedom in American Political and Constitutional Thought*, 45 B.C. L. REV. 499, 564 (2004).

29 The articulation in more narrow terms, like the examples in the text, helps define a limit on the interest which prevents drawing unreasonable conclusions from the existence of the interest. Framed too broadly, one might argue that a women's dignity interest is relevant not only when the question is a fetus *in utero*, but with, e.g., a six-month-old being carried in a backpack, or perhaps beyond.

acknowledgment could be a useful step in the effort to seek common ground and might lead to fruitful discussion about what dignity requires.

How does the idea of a woman's dignity interest play out with respect to the issue of selective pregnancy reduction to a singleton?

There is an enormous difference between suggesting a woman has a dignity interest in not being forced to go through an unwanted pregnancy—regardless of whether one thinks that dignity interest ought to overcome the dignity interest of the fetus—and suggesting a woman has a dignity interest in selectively reducing a pregnancy. In the former case, what the woman doesn't want is precisely the pregnancy.

In the case of selective reduction, however, the woman is going to carry one fetus to term. The woman wants the pregnancy; indeed, in most cases she has gone through time and significant expense in order to get pregnant. What she doesn't want is not the pregnancy, but one of the babies. It seems much less of an intrusion on a woman's dignity interest, absent some real medical threat, to ask her to carry a second fetus to term and give it up for adoption than to suggest someone ought to be forced to go through pregnancy.

What complicates the question is that there may be some, albeit minimal, health benefit from reducing from twins to a singleton, reflected in the divergent views of some obstetricians. While some want no part in the procedures, others believe that "evidence now suggests that reducing twins to a singleton leads, on average, to better outcomes."[30]

Even in the face of some potential health benefit, it seems harder to frame a dignity interest when a woman has deliberately and knowingly chosen a course of conduct she knows will produce multiple fetuses and then wishes to engage in abortion to terminate the unwanted babies. Here, a woman (and her partner) "deliberately seeks to create, and is potentially willing to deliberately destroy, fetal life" in order to produce a child, using "human life, albeit unborn human life, instrumentally for no purpose other than to advance their own ends."[31] Again, it is one thing to be sympathetic to the dignity interest of a woman who finds herself unexpectedly pregnant, who never desired to have a child, than to one who simply doesn't want the burden of the birth of a child she knew would be the result of her efforts to get pregnant.

Clearly, in some respects, selective reduction is no different from any other abortion; from a moral perspective each involves the taking of human life. Nonetheless, even many pro-choice people are nervous about the use of abortion to reduce twins to a single birth, "because it requires recognition of the humanity of one child while rejecting the humanity of his or her sibling."[32] Although some

---

30 Tom Blackwell, *When is Twins Too Many?*, National Post (December 10, 2010), http://www.nationalpost.com/news/When+twins+many/3960709/story.html.

31 Crossley, *supra* note 15, at 1228.

32 Mary McClusky, *Which Child to Abort?*, United States Conference of Catholic Bishops: Life Issues Forum (September 14, 2012), http://www.usccb.org/about/pro-life-

pro-life advocates believe that nervousness is feigned, seeing it as no more than a desire to appear moderate to those with more conflicted views toward abortion,[33] selective reduction to a single fetus would seem to be at least a potential area upon which to build common ground. While a woman's dignity interest might ground an argument for freedom to choose abortion in certain circumstances, it seems to me difficult for anyone to claim a woman has a dignity interest in abortion under these circumstances.

To What Extent Does the Level of Societal Agreement on Claims About the Morality of Abortion Affect the Need for Law to Restrict Abortions?

In its 1973 landmark decision *Roe v. Wade*,[34] the Supreme Court ruled that women have a constitutionally protected right to have an abortion in the early stages of pregnancy—that is, before viability—free from government interference.[35] In 1992, the Court reaffirmed the right to abortion, albeit not an unlimited one, in *Planned Parenthood v. Casey*.[36] *Casey* made clear that states may enact restrictions that do not create an "undue burden" for women seeking abortion. Based on the right created by *Roe* and reaffirmed in *Casey*, pro-choice forces have argued for federal funding of abortions and for various measures that would force those opposed to abortion to facilitate the ability of a woman to obtain an abortion, arguing, for example, that Catholic hospitals should be forced to provide abortions.

The question that needs to be explored here is how much mileage we would get from public consensus on the anthropological claims of Catholicism with respect to abortion—that is, that abortion presents a grave moral issue because it involves the taking of a life.

It is clear that it is problematic from a Catholic perspective to treat abortion as simply an aspect of reproductive health that presents no moral issue. Thus, it is difficult to achieve common ground acceptable to Catholics if one's strategy is to agree to take steps to reduce the need for abortion, but still argue that abortion is a viable choice if made freely—a choice that involves no bad or immoral act.

Instead, what I'm asking here is what would be the effect of consensus, reflected in the language used by political leaders and other public commentators, that abortion is a morally wrong act—that it is always a tragic choice when it occurs, that we frown on people using abortion to, for example, select sex. Would such a consensus make it possible from a Catholic perspective to stop short of

---

activities/life-issues-forum/life-issues-forum-which-child-to-abort.cfm.

33 Michael J. New, *The New York Times Gives Pro-Lifers Food for Thought*, Nat'l Review Online (August 26, 2011), http://www.nationalreview.com/content/new-york-times-gives-pro-lifers-food-thought.

34 410 U.S. 113, 163 (1973).

35 The companion case to *Roe*, *Doe v. Bolton*, 410 U.S. 179 (1973), made clear that a woman could obtain an abortion after viability if necessary for her health.

36 505 U.S. 833 (1992).

demanding government action that prohibits people from having abortions or overturns decisions like *Roe* and *Casey*? Or, is agreement on the anthropological question insufficient, such that there must be some legal change, at a minimum overturning *Roe* and *Casey*, to achieve common ground?

It may be that this is largely a hypothetical question at this point. While a significant percentage of the American public believes that abortion is morally wrong, and while many political figures (e.g. Bill Clinton) have expressed personal opposition to abortion and spoken in terms that suggested that abortion should be safe, legal, and rare, President Obama has not expressed personal opposition to abortion and some of his language suggests that he does not view abortion as a tragic choice. Obama has been accused of admitting "at the University of Notre Dame that his views and the views of those who consider abortion an intrinsic evil are irreconcilable. This makes it nearly impossible to find common ground since he views as good what pro-life citizens view as evil."[37] On other occasions, he has expressed a commitment to adopting policies that would reduce the actual number of abortions.

The language Obama sometimes employs is very different from that of, for example, Rep. Rosa DeLauro of Connecticut, one of the principal pro-choice sponsors of the proposed Preventing Unintended Pregnancies, Reducing the Need for Abortion, and Supporting Parents Act.[38] DeLauro suggests, "we all want to see fewer unintended pregnancies and abortions" and "we must also foster an environment that encourages pregnancies to be carried to term."[39]

Let's assume for the purposes of this discussion that the language used by politicians and other commentators consistently sounded more like DeLauro's language rather than the language often used by pro-choice advocates. What difference would it make to have public acknowledgement "that abortion is not a triumph for anyone" and of "a commitment to work toward a society in which abortion is rare"?[40] In thinking about whether a Catholic realist position could accept the continued existence of *Roe* and *Casey* under these circumstances, it is useful to consider several things.

As a starting point, there is a robust debate about the proper role of law in addressing various social ills. While some Catholic commentators have expressed

---

37 Denise Hunnell, *Robert George vs. Doug Kmiec: How Should a Pro-life Citizen Respond to Obama?*, EXAMINER.COM (May 28, 2009), http://www.examiner.com/article/robert-george-vs-douglas-kmiec-how-should-a-pro-life-citizen-respond-to-obama.

38 Reducing the Need for Abortion and Supporting Parents Act, H.R. 1074, 110th Cong. (1st Sess. 2007).

39 William Saletan, *Culture of Death: The Right-Wing Assault on Abortion Reduction*, SLATE (July 27, 2009), http://www.slate.com/articles/health_and_science/human_nature/2009/07/culture_of_death.html.

40 Amelia J. Uelmen, *Dear Mr. President*, 200 AMERICA: THE NATIONAL CATHOLIC WEEKLY 12, 16 (2009).

disagreement with arguments for "legal modesty" in the context of abortion,[41] even John Paul II acknowledged that law cannot be the primary vehicle for truly profound social change.[42] That makes it legitimate to question whether it is necessary that law be part of the strategy for reducing abortions under circumstances where we have broad societal agreement that abortion is a moral issue and a moral wrong.

My own inclination is to tend toward a notion of "legal modesty." Nonetheless, law has an important signaling effect that helps both create and strengthen social norms. As Amy Uelmen has observed, laws "play a very important and sometimes decisive role in influencing patterns of thought and behavior."[43] The signaling effect is of potential value even if there were already societal agreement on the moral issue presented by abortion: "the law can reaffirm the values already present in a given culture and so reinforce the non-legal norms operating within it."[44]

Just as the presence of laws restricting abortion can strengthen a societal norm that recognizes the moral issues presented by abortion, increasingly permissive laws can reinforce the opposite signal. The reality is that "[m]any will take as authorization what is perhaps only the abstention from punishment."[45]

This is a particular danger since the society in which we live moves so easily from negative rights (that is, a right to be free from interference) to positive rights (that is, entitlements). We so easily blur the line between the law merely permitting something and interpreting that permission to mean that what is permitted is an affirmative good that should be promoted. The reality is that the fact that the law permits something does not mean it is right or moral and therefore does not mean that the law must or should facilitate it. Yet, we don't do a good job of distinguishing a zone of noninterference from positive good and legal entitlement.

This movement is evident in the abortion context. *Roe* established simply that the law should not (in most cases) prevent someone from choosing abortion. Yet from that starting point—a zone of noninterference—many people quickly concluded that every person must accommodate and even support another person's "right" to have an abortion, and claimed that the government should pay for those who cannot afford to have one.

Having said that, does a Catholic realist need to ask what the value of the signaling effect in terms of abortion rates is? One might answer no, arguing that

41 John M. Breen, *John Paul II, the Structures of Sin and the Limits of the Law*, 52 St. Louis U. L.J. 317, 348–51 (2008).

42 Pope John Paul II, *Centesimus Annus*, Encyclical Letter, ¶ 36 (May 1, 1991), http://www.vatican.va/holy_father/john_paul_ii/encyclicals/documents/hf_jp-ii_enc_01051991_centesimus-annus_en.html.

43 Amelia J. Uelmen, *The Spirituality of Communion: A Resource for Dialogue with Catholics in Public Life*, 43 Cath. Law. 289, 301 (2004).

44 Breen, *supra* note 41, at 323.

45 Congregation for the Doctrine of the Faith, *Declaration on Procured Abortion*, ¶ 20, available at http://www.vatican.va/roman_curia/congregations/cfaith/documents/rc_con_cfaith_doc_19741118_declaration-abortion_en.html.

the law should make a positive statement regardless of its effect and that, in the case of abortion, a strong pro-life witness is important regardless of the impact on abortion rates. However, if one believes the educative function of the law is meant to change behavior, the effect of a legal statement arguably matters.

Lamentably, this is one of those areas where it is very difficult to assess the evidence. Although there is tremendous disagreement about the effectiveness of the law prior to *Roe* in reducing abortions, it is hard to argue with the conclusion that there has been an increase in the number of the abortions in the years since the Supreme Court's decision in *Roe*. The Center for Disease Control reports that the abortion rate in the United States from 1970 to 1973 was 10.75 abortions per 1,000 women aged 15–44 and that from 1973 to 1976, the abortion rate for that group increased to 17.5. The total number of abortions from 1970 to 1973 was 1.9 million and increased to 3.2 million from 1973 to 1976.[46] The rate has declined since 1990. Equally relevant in terms of the signaling effect is the question whether *Roe* promoted a promiscuous atmosphere that contributes to high unwanted pregnancy rates, which then contributes to an increased use of abortion. One commentator lamented that "[e]asy access to abortion has increased the expectation and frequency of sexual intercourse (including unprotected intercourse) among young people, making it more difficult for a young woman to deny herself to a man without losing him, thus increasing pregnancies and sexually transmitted infections."[47]

Nonetheless, the Catholic realist concerned with whether the signaling effect of the law will bear results must also consider whether the effect created by *Roe* is reversible. It may very well be that the genie cannot be put back in the bottle and that it is not possible to reverse the "culture of death" we have created.

However, it may also be that more restrictive abortion laws and a legal setting that did not treat abortion as a right might have some positive effect. The existence of the *Roe* and *Casey* decisions clearly tilts the scale toward broad acceptance of abortion; the mere overturning of those decisions, without any further legislation addressing abortion, could affect the tenor of discussions as well as the analysis of what legal measures to reduce abortions would be viewed as permissible and desirable.

Where does that leave the Catholic realist? The United States Conference of Catholic Bishops (USCCB) has taken the clear position that it is not enough to seek to reduce abortion where the law allows an intrinsic evil to exist. It argues that "[t]o make intrinsically evil actions legal is itself wrong … The legal system as such can be said to cooperate with evil when it fails to protect the lives of those

---

46 Lilo T. Strauss, et al., *Abortion Surveillance—United States, 2004*, CDC Morbidity & Mortality Weekly Report (Nov. 23, 2007), http://www.cdc.gov/mmwr/preview/mmwrhtml/ss5609a1.htm.

47 Richard Stith, *How the Abortion Option Can Make Women More Vulnerable to Exploitation and Abandonment*, Mirror of Justice, available at http://mirrorofjustice.blogs.com/mirrorofjustice/stith/abortionwomenvulnerable.pdf.

who have no protection except the law."[48] In a similar vein, Archbishop Burke suggests that anything less than the whole must be an interim approach and that Catholic politicians must always seek opportunities to overturn "unjust laws" (the category into which he puts *Roe*). In a 2003 Pastoral Letter, Burke wrote:

> When Catholic politicians cannot immediately overturn an unjust law, they must never cease to work toward that end. At the very least, they must limit, as much as possible, the evil caused by the unjust law … Catholic politicians are obliged to restrict the scope of the gravest of injustices whenever the opportunity presents itself.[49]

The conclusion I drew from such language in my 2010 article was that it does not seem to permit a conclusion that law need not be part of the scheme for addressing abortion, but that a Catholic realist position had to at least consider the possibility. How do the issues of selective reduction abortions and abortions of fetuses with Down syndrome affect our views of this discussion?

The practice of selective reduction to a single fetus to satisfy the preferences of the pregnant woman runs strongly counter to the effort to achieve a consensus that abortion is a morally wrong act. Abortion is now simply one acceptable option to deal with the effects of artificial reproductive technology, a byproduct of such technology. Making a decision about how many embryos to carry to term (versus how many to kill) becomes a decision fraught with no more moral consequence than whether to purchase one dozen eggs or two.

Neither does there seem to be any strong move to counter this way of thinking. As noted earlier, the practice of selective pregnancy reduction to a singleton is rising and doctors are becoming increasingly comfortable with it.

The increased practice of abortion based on Down syndrome has the same effect of undermining an effort to achieve consensus that abortion is a morally wrong act. The move to screen all women for genetic abnormalities, and treating abortion as the expected result of a determination that the fetus suffers from some abnormality, pushes in quite the opposite direction. Treating "testing and abortion as interconnected health care choices"[50] encourages and justifies abortion as the preferred response based on an evaluation that a fetus with a genetic abnormality is "unworthy" of life; that it would be a "mistake" to allow such an "inferior

48 United States Conference of Catholic Bishops, *Catholics in Political Life*, http://old.usccb.org/bishops/catholicsinpoliticallife.shtml.

49 Raymond L. Burke, *Bishop Burke on the Dignity of Human Life and Civic Responsibility: Pastoral Letter Accompanies Recent Decree on Pro-Abortion Politicians*, Zenit (January 10, 2004), http://www.zenit.org/en/articles/bishop-burke-on-the-dignity-of-human-life-and-civic-responsibility.

50 Rachel Rebouché & Karen H. Rothenberg, *Mixed Messages: The Intersection of Prenatal Genetic Testing and Abortion*, 55 Howard L.J. 983, 1023 (2012).

human being" to be born.[51] It is completely inconsistent with an effort to achieve consensus that abortion is a morally wrong act when there are physicians speaking of abortion as a "cure" for Down syndrome.[52]

The effect of both of these practices is to render the question I consider here little more than hypothetical. It may in fact be that a high level of societal agreement on claims about the morality of abortion might affect the need for laws restricting abortions. However, these practices move us away from a societal agreement on the morality of abortion and are based on a way of thinking that is completely antithetical to Catholic thought, which recognizes the inherent dignity of every human person. They lead me to the conclusion that the question I raised is no longer a helpful one for moving forward the abortion debate.

Can a Catholic Realist Position Accept Reducing Abortions by Means Other Than Making Them Illegal as a Primary Aim?

This question and the next focus on whether it is possible to substantially reduce abortions without making them illegal. My focus here is on reducing abortions by addressing the economic pressures that impact a woman's decision to abort. In the next section, I will separately address efforts to reduce abortions by reducing unwanted pregnancies—that is, the issue of access to contraception.

The economic issue is one that cannot be ignored. Fifty-seven percent of women who have abortions have incomes 200 percent below the poverty level.[53] Whereas women earning more than three times the poverty level have 25 percent of all abortions, women living at less than two times the poverty level (30 percent of all women) have 57 percent of abortions.[54] Such statistics prompt us to consider the viability of socioeconomic policies to reduce abortion.

There are a variety of possible strategies that attempt to alter the decision to abort on economic grounds, such as providing economic support for pregnant women (prenatal care) and new mothers (healthcare, childcare, nurses for new mothers with infants, etc.), providing economic incentives and greater support for adoptions, as well as policies that increase male employment rates and reduce poverty.

---

51 Leon R. Kass, *Triumph or Tragedy? The Moral Meaning of Genetic Technology*, 45 Am. J. Juris. 1, 9 (2000).

52 Teresa Santin, *Is Down Syndrome Doomed?: How State Statutes Can Help Expectant Parents Make Informed Decisions about Prenatal Down Syndrome Diagnoses*, 6 Pitt. J. Envtl. Pub. Health L. 239, 251–52 (2012).

53 Rachel K. Jones, Jacqueline E. Darroch & Stanley K. Henshaw, *Patterns in Socioeconomic Characteristics of Women Obtaining Abortions in 2000–2001*, 34 Perspectives on Sexual and Reproductive Health 226, 231 (2002), *available at* http://www.guttmacher.org/pubs/journals/3422602.pdf.

54 Helen M. Alvaré, *The Consistent Ethic of Life: A Proposal for Improving Its Legislative Grasp*, 2 U. St. Thomas L.J. 326, 336 (2005).

Federal legislation proposed in 2007—the Ryan/DeLauro Reducing the Need for Abortion and Supporting Parents Act—is illustrative of a coordinated effort to address the economic causes of abortion. The proposed legislation, *inter alia*, (1) provides for expanded Medicaid and State Children's Health Insurance Program coverage of pregnant women; (2) prohibits health insurers from treating pregnancy as a pre-existing condition; (3) provides for supportive services for women who learn through ultrasound that they are carrying a fetus with Down syndrome and other prenatally diagnosed conditions; (4) provides support for students who become pregnant so that they can continue their education; (5) funds group housing for pregnant and parenting women and, as a requirement for funding of such homes, requires the provision of both adoption counseling and counseling on parenting skills; (6) expands adoption assistance; and (7) provides support for new parents under supplemental nutrition programs.[55]

It is hard to argue against measures such as the foregoing, each of which has benefits above and beyond whatever effect they might have on the abortion rate. Nonetheless, notwithstanding its intuitive appeal, a number of interrelated factors at least raise the question about how effective this strategy will be in reducing abortions.

The first relates to a point I made earlier. One has to factor in the evidence suggesting that legalization of abortion contributes to a promiscuous atmosphere that contributes to high unwanted pregnancy rates resulting in an increased use of abortion.

As one commentator noted: "Easy access to abortion has increased the expectation and frequency of sexual intercourse (including unprotected intercourse) among young people, making it more difficult for a young woman to deny herself to a man without losing him, thus increasing pregnancies and sexually transmitted infections."[56]

Related to this is evidence suggesting that states that adopted pro-life legislation during the 1990s experienced a larger reduction in abortion rates than those states

---

55 Reducing the Need for Abortion and Supporting Parents Act, H.R. 1074, 110th Cong. (1st Sess. 2007). The proposed legislation also contains a number of provisions designed to addresses non-economic factors contributing to abortions, such as increased funding for after-school programs (based on a finding that the likelihood of unintended teen pregnancy increases with the number of unsupervised hours teens have during the week); grants to provide support for innovative and creative ways to prevent teenage pregnancy; resources to promote and strengthen communication between parents and teens based on findings that teens with strong emotional attachments to their parents are more likely to delay becoming sexually active; educational programs; and funding for training of health care and other professionals to identify, treat and refer women who are victims of rape and domestic violence.

56 Richard Stith, *How the Abortion Option Can Make Women More Vulnerable to Exploitation and Abandonment*, Mirror of Justice, *available at* http://mirrorofjustice.blogs.com/mirrorofjustice/stith/abortionwomenvulnerable.pdf.

that did not adopt such legislation. This suggests that there is much more at play than economic pressures.

Finally, assessing the potential effectiveness of economic strategies also requires assessing evidence that many abortions are the result of outside pressure. One study found that 64 percent of American woman who have abortions feel pressured to do so by others.[57] How much of that pressure would continue to operate if we addressed economic concerns is open to question.

There is no question that from a Catholic perspective, economic strategies are clearly permissible, even desirable, as part of a comprehensive strategy to address abortion. The CDF *Declaration on Procured Abortion* speaks of the importance of putting "positive policy" into force "so that there will always be a concrete, honorable and possible alternative to abortion."[58] And, the USCCB has advocated a comprehensive strategy to reduce abortions.[59]

However, the question is whether a focus on economic solutions alone represents a viable Catholic realist position. There has been consistent criticism of Catholics who focus on poverty and other economic issues without being consistently pro-life. Even focusing on economic issues as a strategy for promoting pro-life goals probably will not quell criticism from those who believe that the economic solution does not do enough to reduce or eliminate abortions.

On the other hand, what if trying to do more is counterproductive? What if attempts to reduce abortion through legal means create more polarization, making it actually more difficult to enact policies likely to reduce abortions? I'm not suggesting it necessarily is. It may be that pro-life and pro-choice advocates can both agree that reducing abortions is morally justifiable and find common ground regarding some level of restrictions. The point is that a Catholic realist position must take into account what is possible and what is counterproductive; it must also take into account what will be most effective in decreasing the number of abortions.

How does the economic concern play out with respect to the issues I began with? The short answer is: not at all with respect to selective pregnancy reduction. As already noted, selective pregnancy reduction is typically the result of in vitro fertilization or some other infertility treatment undertaken by women who have difficulty conceiving. Almost by definition, this is an issue faced by well-to-do women. The average price of an in vitro fertilization cycle in the United States is about 12,000 dollars; these are not procedures being utilized by low-income women. While it is true that some couples might prefer to only undergo the costs

57 Vincent M. Rue et al., *Induced Abortion and Traumatic Stress: A Preliminary Comparison of American and Russian Women*, 10 Med. Sci. Monitor SR5 (2004).

58 Congregation for the Doctrine of the Faith, *Declaration on Procured Abortion* ¶ 23, *available at* http://www.vatican.va/roman_curia/congregations/cfaith/documents/rc_con_cfaith_doc_19741118_declaration-abortion_en.html.

59 United States Conference of Catholic Bishops, *Living the Gospel of Life: A Challenge to American Catholics* ¶¶ 34–39, http://old.usccb.org/prolife/gospel.shtml.

of raising one child versus multiple children, it is difficult to be concerned about economic factors in these cases. These are not abortions motivated by economic concerns. A focus on addressing economic pressures impacting a woman's decision to abort is beside the point when it comes to this issue.

The Down syndrome issue is different because raising a special-needs child carries a heavy economic cost. Down syndrome is often associated with heart problems, hearing loss and increased risk of skin and lung infections, among other medical challenges, giving rise to medical costs higher than for those with a child without such a condition. In addition to health costs, parents of a child with Down syndrome need to be concerned with financially supporting their child for a lifetime. They need to factor in that their child may outlive them, but never be able to economically support himself or herself. Government assistance programs provide some help with basic medical care and other benefits, but often far less help than is necessary for couples of low and moderate means. Even for people not in poverty, the costs can be frightening.

For some couples who find they are carrying a fetus with Down syndrome, economic concerns may be part of the driving force behind a decision to abort. A Catholic realist position should support efforts to provide economic and other forms of assistance that would help such couples come to an alternative decision—that would allow them to feel supported in their decision to bring their child to term. It may be that in this situation, a focus on economic and other forms of support could have a real impact on the decisions of at least some women carrying Down syndrome fetuses whether to abort.

Assuming Access to Contraception is Effective at Reducing Abortions, Can a Catholic Realist Position Support Access to Contraception?

One of the more contentious issues surrounding the abortion debates has to do with the question of contraception. Even many Catholics do not accept the Catholic Church's position on artificial contraception, and non-Catholics have difficulty understanding how the Church can oppose something that seems to them self-evidently an important part of an anti-abortion strategy.

There are two parts to this question. First, can we deal with reducing abortions as a realistic matter without addressing contraception? Second, if the answer to that is no (as many believe), then the relevant question is whether a Catholic, without materially cooperating with evil, can accept the use of contraception for the purpose of reducing abortions.

First, does access to contraception reduce abortion? This is an issue as to which there is strong divergence of view, creating tremendous difficulty from a Catholic realist perspective. If, on the one hand, one accepts "unplanned pregnancy" as the leading cause or reason for obtaining an abortion, then it seems intuitive—and many believe it to be so—that providing robust access to, and education about, contraception would be one of the best ways to reduce abortions.[60] On the other hand, somewhat paradoxically, there is some evidence that once contraception became an accepted means of regulating births, the unintended birth rate actually increased, suggesting that access to contraception is not likely to reduce abortion.[61] The empirical evidence is mixed.[62] Added to this, there is evidence suggesting that only a small percentage of abortions involve women lacking access to contraception.[63]

Pope John Paul II addressed this issue quite clearly in *Evangelium Vitae*, rejecting the assertion "that contraception, if made safe and available to all, is the most effective remedy against abortion," and arguing that the "contraceptive mentality" promotes an unwillingness to accept responsibility.[64] He wrote:

> It may be that many people use contraception with a view to excluding the subsequent temptation of abortion. But the negative values inherent in the "contraceptive mentality"—which is very different from responsible parenthood, lived in respect for the full truth of the conjugal act—are such that they in fact strengthen this temptation when an unwanted life is conceived.[65]

Although accepting the fact that abortion and contraception are "specifically different evils," he argues that they are

> often closely connected, as fruits of the same tree. It is true that in many cases contraception and even abortion are practiced under the pressure of real-life difficulties, which nonetheless can never exonerate from striving to observe God's law fully. Still, in very many other instances such practices are rooted in a hedonistic mentality unwilling to accept responsibility in matters of sexuality, and they imply a self-centered concept of freedom, which regards procreation as an obstacle to personal fulfillment. The life which could result from a sexual

60 Jennifer Shaw, *The Prevention First Act Examined: An Overview of the State of Contraception Law as Viewed Through the Lens of Federal Legislation*, 30 Women's Rights L. Rep. 700, 704–05 (2009).

61 G.E.M. Anscombe, *Contraception and Chastity*, *in* Why Humanae Vitae Was Right: A Reader 119, 124 (Janet E. Smith ed., 1993).

62 *See* Cicely Marston & John Cleland, *Relationships Between Contraception and Abortion: A Review of the Evidence*, 29 Int'l Family Planning Perspectives 6, 6 (2003), *available at* http://www.guttmacher.org/pubs/journals/2900603.pdf; *Contraception Counts: Ranking State Effort*, Guttmacher Institute: In Brief, no. 1 (2006), http://www.guttmacher.org/pubs/2006/2/23/IB2006n1.pdf.

63 Jones et al., *supra* note 53, at 298.

64 Pope John Paul II, *Evangelium Vitae*, Encyclical Letter, ¶ 13 (March 25, 1995), http://www.vatican.va/holy_father/john_paul_ii/encyclicals/documents/hf_jp-ii_enc_25031995_evangelium-vitae_en.html.

65 *Id.*

> encounter thus becomes an enemy to be avoided at all costs, and abortion becomes the only possible decisive response to failed contraception.[66]

Whatever one thinks of the validity of Pope John Paul's statements, there is a reality that Catholic realism has to face: a norm of smaller family size and a culture in which control over not only the size of the family but the timing and spacing of children is important. That norm may be inconsistent with Catholic thought.[67] Nonetheless, that is the culture in which we live, a culture to some extent the product of women being more educated and working outside of the home in large numbers. A Catholic realist can't ignore or simply wish away this reality. Absent the ability to change the norm, the Catholic realist needs to work to obtain what can be obtained within the framework of the existing norm, consistent with Catholic teaching.

Whatever one ultimately thinks about the first question, the more interesting question is: assuming that access to contraception will in fact reduce the number of abortions, can a Catholic realist position support access to contraception?

The position of the Catholic Church on contraception is unambiguous. The Catechism of the Catholic Church labels as "intrinsically evil" any action which, "whether in anticipation of the conjugal act, or in its accomplishment, or in the development of its natural consequences, proposes, whether as an end or as a means, to render procreation impossible."[68] In his 1930 encyclical, *Casti Connubii*, Pope Pius XI reaffirmed earlier Church statements that procreation was the primary end of human sexuality and that the use of means to deprive the sexual act of its power of procreating life "is an offense against the law of God and nature, and those who indulge in such are branded with the guilt of a grave sin."[69] Twenty years later, Pope Pius XII claimed that the condemnation of artificial contraception "is as valid today as it was yesterday; and it will be the same tomorrow and always, because it does not imply a precept of the human law but is the expression of a law which is natural and divine."[70]

66 *Id.*

67 I say "may be" because the Catholic Church accepts the use of natural family planning as a means to control the spacing and number of births. Pope Paul VI, *Humanae Vitae* ¶ 11 (July 25, 1968), *available at* http://www.vatican.va/holy_father/paul_vi/encyclicals/documents/hf_p-vi_enc_25071968_humanae-vitae_en.html.

68 Catechism of the Catholic Church, Part Three, Section Two, Ch. Two, Art. 6, III:2370, *available at* http://www.vatican.va/archive/ENG0015/_P86.HTM. I discuss the historical development of the Church's position on artificial contraception in Stabile, *supra* note 20, at 750 n.37.

69 Pope Pius XI, *Casti Connubii*, Encyclical Letter, ¶ 56 (December 31, 1930), http://www.vatican.va/holy_father/pius_xi/encyclicals/documents/hf_p-xi_enc_31121930_casti-connubii_en.html.

70 Pope Pius XII, *Address to the Midwives on the Nature of Their Profession* (October 29, 1951), http://www.papalencyclicals.net/Pius12/P12midwives.htm.

Despite recognizing the substantial opposition to the Church's teachings on artificial contraception, Pope Paul VI reiterated the position in 1969 in *Humanae Vitae*, stating that "there are certain limits, beyond which it is wrong to go, to the power of man over his own body and its natural functions," limits which "are expressly imposed because of the reverence due to the whole human organism and its natural functions."[71] In his 1995 encyclical, *Evangelium Vitae*, Pope John Paul II expressed the Church's continued moral opposition to artificial means of birth control, based on the "sacredness" and "inviolability" of life.[72]

Notwithstanding the clarity of the Church's position on contraception, the question I am raising is this: if abortion is worse than contraception, can one "support" the latter to avoid the former? It is clear that the Church makes a distinction between abortion and artificial contraception. Although the Church has been consistent in recent years in its efforts to secure a change in the law regarding abortion, it has not felt the need to actively oppose legal access to contraception. Whether based on a notion that the former involves a matter of public morality whereas the latter involves a matter of private morality, and thus a matter not appropriate for the law to address, or on the ground that the former involves the actual ending of life whereas the latter prevents life from coming into being, contraception appears to be a "lesser evil" from the Catholic perspective.

Thus, as phrased earlier, the question is whether "it would be licit, based on the theory of the lesser evil, to be responsible for the passage of a law or the application of a strategy which, while being unjust in the abstract, would effectively reduce evil and thus be considered *hic et nunc* as morally acceptable or defensible."[73]

The first question that has to be asked, harkening back to an earlier point, is to consider whether context makes a difference. If we say, for example, that abstinence is better, that young girls should not be having sex, that sex does matter, etc., does that make it easier for Catholics to accept contraception as part of the equation for reducing the number of abortions? Illustrative is the Ryan/DeLauro approach. It requires that applicants for grants for programs preventing teen pregnancies agree that the project will "encourag[e] teens to delay sexual activity and provid[e] educational services and interventions, including information about contraception for sexually active teens or teens at risk of becoming sexually active." It also requires that all information provided "will be age-appropriate,

71 Pope Paul VI, *Humanae Vitae*, Encyclical Letter, ¶ 17 (July 25, 1968), http://www.vatican.va/holy_father/paul_vi/encyclicals/documents/hf_p-vi_enc_25071968_humanae-vitae_en.html.

72 Pope John Paul II, *Evangelium Vitae*, Encyclical Letter, ¶¶ 13, 40 (March 25, 1995), http://www.vatican.va/holy_father/john_paul_ii/encyclicals/documents/hf_jp-ii_enc_25031995_evangelium-vitae_en.html.

73 Angel Rodríguez Luño, *Evangelium Vitae 73: The Catholic Lawmaker and the Problem of a Seriously Unjust Law*, L'Osservatore, November 4, 2008, at 3–8.

factually and medically accurate and complete, and scientifically based."[74] Further, the statute provides for "educating both young men and women about the responsibilities and pressures that come along with parenting" and "helping parents communicate with teens about sexuality," as well as "teaching young people responsible decision-making."[75]

However, even put in the best positive context, the language of *Humanae Vitae* makes it difficult to think the Church could be persuaded of this approach. Although recognizing that it is at times "lawful to tolerate a lesser moral evil in order to avoid a greater evil or in order to promote a greater good," *Humanae Vitae* suggests that it is never permissible to support something that is intrinsically evil. In the 1968 encyclical Paul VI wrote, "it is never lawful, even for the gravest reasons, to do evil that good may come of it—in other words, to have as the object of a positive act of the will something which intrinsically contradicts the moral order … even though the intention is to protect or promote the welfare of an individual, or a family or of society in general,"[76] a statement that was reaffirmed by Pope John Paul II in *Veritatis Splendor*.[77] In the words of one professor of moral theology, "a moral evil may not be the direct object of the will, even when it is a lesser evil … What is intrinsically evil cannot be the direct object of the will, no matter what the cost."[78]

The Church believes artificial contraception to be an intrinsic evil. It is convinced that the "port of entry for the culture of death in our society has been the abandonment of the respect for the procreative meaning of the conjugal act. It is the contraceptive way of thinking, the fear of the life-giving dimension of conjugal love, which very much sustains that culture."[79]

Given that, there doesn't seem to be any play in the joints here. While the Church may not feel it necessary to insist on legal measures to prevent access to contraception, I think it impossible from a Catholic realist perspective to include

---

74 Reducing the Need for Abortion and Supporting Parents Act, H.R. 1074, 110th Cong, § 102(c) (1st Sess. 2007).

75 *Id.* The legislation would also provide coverage for family planning services. A separate question relevant to the Catholic realist is whether any of these steps will have any effect. It is not entirely clear that educating teens about the responsibilities of parenting has any effect on their sexual activity.

76 Pope Paul VI, *Humanae Vitae*, Encyclical Letter, ¶ 14 (July 25, 1968), http://www.vatican.va/holy_father/paul_vi/encyclicals/documents/hf_p-vi_enc_25071968_humanae-vitae_en.html.

77 Pope John Paul II, *Veritatis Splendor*, Encyclical Letter, ¶ 80 (August 6, 1993), http://www.vatican.va/holy_father/john_paul_ii/encyclicals/documents/hf_jp-ii_enc_06081993_veritatis-splendor_en.html.

78 Luño, *supra* note 73, at 3–5.

79 Raymond L. Burke, *Bishop Burke on the Dignity of Human Life and Civic Responsibility: Pastoral Letter Accompanies Recent Decree on Pro-Abortion Politicians*, ZENIT 12 (January 10, 2004), http://www.zenit.org/en/articles/bishop-burke-on-the-dignity-of-human-life-and-civic-responsibility.

active support for the use of artificial contraception, even if doing so would reduce the actual number of abortions. In contrast to the economic strategies discussed earlier, which involve no intrinsic evil, it does not seem that contraception can be part of a Catholic realist approach to abortion. This will be a difficult conclusion for many people to accept, including those Catholics who do not accept the Church's position on artificial contraception. Nonetheless, a Catholic realist position must accord with Catholic teaching on intrinsic evil.

Where there is substantial room for common ground, however, is in what I labeled before as "context"—that is, the culture surrounding sex, particularly among young people. Rather than focusing on arguments over access to contraception versus abstinence-only education, Catholic realists could profitably join forces with feminists and other pro-choice advocates to try to affect a shift in the cultural expectation of sexual activity among the young. There is clearly no formal or material cooperation in evil for a Catholic realist to work with secular forces to try to change what might be referred to as either a culture of promiscuity or a culture of sexual inevitability, to help women (young and old) understand they have both a right and an obligation to themselves to not engage in unwanted sex. This is an approach to reducing abortion on which we all ought to be able to agree.

The current controversy over the HHS mandate that contraception coverage be included as part of preventive healthcare services casts more light on why a Catholic realist position could not accept contraception as part of the common ground for reducing abortions.

First, treating contraception as preventive healthcare affects the context, to go back to a point I made earlier, highlighting Pope Paul VI's concerns about a "contraceptive mentality." The effect of the mandate is to cement a sense that contraception is no longer something for couples to consider as part of a decision about family, but is an ordinary aspect of healthcare, which in turn contributes to a view of sex as routine and not part of a long-term committed relationship.

Even some who are critical of the Church's position on sexuality admit that "the cultural dissociation of sex from responsibility for procreation has contributed to widespread [acceptance of abortion] and to the destabilization of families in industrialized nations."[80] I think there is little question that the attitudes of young people (and society) toward contraception are likely to influence their attitudes toward abortion. In the words of one woman:

> As long as I accepted the premise that engaging in sex with a contraceptive mentality was morally acceptable, I could not bring myself to consider that abortion might not be acceptable. It seemed inhumane to make a woman deal with life-altering consequences for an act that was not supposed to have life-altering consequences.[81]

80 Lisa Sowle Cahill, Sex, Gender, and Christian Ethics 206 (1996).

81 Jennifer Fulwiler, *A Sexual Revolution*, 199 America: The National Catholic Review, no. 1, 2008, at 13.

Recalling that a Catholic realist position requires a correspondence between belief and reality prompts the question whether a Catholic realist position requires conceding, in effect, that that train has already left the station. That is, must we accept a view of sexual relations that disassociates sex from procreation as a given? I'm not convinced we must. There may be value in the continued witness to the position that sexual activity ought to be viewed as part of a loving and complete self-gift, a value to some force pushing against the "contraceptive mentality."

Second, the line between abortion and contraception is becoming increasingly blurred and the HHS mandate contributes mightily to that blurring. Part of that blurring is inherent in the pill, the most common form of artificial contraception. The pill operates in several ways, working both to prevent conception and to ensure that if an egg is fertilized, it does not implant itself onto the uterine wall. It is for that reason that in the view of some Catholics, taking birth control pills itself risks aborting a fetus.[82]

The blurring is aggravated by legal mandates that employers provide contraception coverage to their employees. As was the case in some of the state laws mandating contraception coverage, the HHS regulations under the ACA make no distinction between contraceptives that operate to prevent contraception and those that are abortifacients; the mandate is for coverage of all FDA-approved methods of contraception. It is not an illegitimate fear on the part of the Catholic Church to believe that compromise on contraception is not far removed from compromise on abortion.

There is a particular fear about blurring the lines with respect to how a mandate might evolve. Several years ago, a bill was introduced in the New York State legislature requiring that any insurance policies that offer maternity coverage must also cover abortions, leading to the fear that it is only a small step from requiring that an employer cover contraceptives and requiring that it cover abortions. Similarly, there is fear that that the logic being used to support requiring religious organizations to provide contraceptive coverage to its employees could be extended to compel Catholic hospitals to perform sterilization or abortion procedures. The blurrier the line between contraception and abortion, the more realistic such fears become.

All of this strengthens the conclusion I came to in my 2010 article—that it is impossible from a Catholic realist position to include active support for the use of artificial contraception, even if doing so would reduce the actual number of abortions.

82 Janet Morana, Recall Abortion: Ending the Abortion Industry's Exploitation of Women 10–11 (2013).

Conclusion

As I concluded in my 2010 article, there are difficulties in trying to articulate a Catholic realist approach to abortion, and the questions I posed in that article do not admit of easy answers. Nonetheless, I continue to believe that Catholic thought has something meaningful to add to the abortion debate and that finding common ground is a laudable goal. My modest hope in this chapter is to have shown that the questions I set forth in my 2010 article can provide a useful vehicle for thinking about particular questions that may arise as part of the abortion debate.

Index

The figure is in italic and notes as 1n2 (page 1 note 2).